The
Great Chattanooga
BICYCLE RACE

The Great Chattanooga

BICYCLE RACE

Mike H. Mizrahi

REDEMPTION
PRESS

Published by Redemption Press, PO Box 427, Enumclaw, WA 98022

Toll Free (844) 2REDEEM (273-3336)

Redemption Press is honored to present this title in partnership with the author. The views expressed or implied in this work are those of the author. Redemption Press provides our imprint seal representing design excellence, creative content, and high quality production.

All Scripture quotations, unless otherwise indicated, are taken from the Holy Bible, King James Version, © 1979, 1980, 1982 by Thomas Nelson, Inc., Publishers. Used by permission.

ISBN 13: 978-1-68314-180-8 (Print)
978-1-68314-181-5 (ePub)
978-1-68314-182-2 (Mobi)

Library of Congress Catalog Card Number: 2017933358

"A close study of the southern newspapers fails to show that the bloomer craze has gained any decided hold south of the Mason and Dixon line. Indeed, the bicycle is a new thing, and the women who ride are as fearful of criticism as a woman in tight knickerbockers would be in some Northern places. . . . South of Virginia the real southern women do not ride the bicycle much. The climate is against the exercise. . . . A Tennessee paper so late as last week was wondering if any woman would have the temerity to introduce bloomers in that region. If any did it said, they would surely bring on themselves such notoriety as must be exceedingly unpleasant to modest, womanly women. . . . Some few women in New Orleans wear bloomers, but in almost every southern newspaper the appearance of a pair of bloomers is treated almost as would be the coming ashore of the sea serpent."

—*Los Angeles Herald*, Sept. 15, 1895

Chapter One

Brooklyn, New York
June 1895

SHE IMAGINED THE inscription on her tombstone: Here lies Anna Gaines, age nineteen. She died while riding a bicycle.

Her hands gripped the handlebars so tight that her knuckles turned white and began to tingle. The initial excitement at mastering the nation's new favorite pastime gave way to deep anxiety. An unrelenting panic threw her back in time, when instead of handlebars, her fists gripped the reins of her beloved Appaloosa, Longstreet. She couldn't stop the memory of the terror that had surged up within her just before he bucked her to the ground. Five years of training, gone in an instant . . . and a whole life of dreams. The tumble had reset the trajectory of her life. The broken leg eventually healed, but the limp remained.

Nothing would be the same.

Outgoing by nature, she turned inward. Months in bed caused her to miss out on the fun of her youth. Later, the thought of men being interested in her seemed unimaginable. The obvious disability didn't help.

Beads of sweat coalesced and found pathways to trickle down her cheeks, despite mild temperatures that created the perfect day for a ride in the city. Wiping the droplets on the back of her hand, she pictured her life back in Chattanooga, where she was captive behind block walls.

With an ache in her chest, she thought of her overprotective mama. Ever since the accident, Mama had hovered like a fearful nurse. And then, there was the town she lived in, with all its rules, scrutiny, and expectations. To make matters worse, some of her prison time was self-imposed. A lack of confidence had long held her back from expanding her borders. She inhaled and slowly released. Could she break away by cycling with this slew of bloomer-clad ladies?

She glanced around at the determined riders, many of them women, ready for this challenge. Then she realized that she wasn't like them. She couldn't do this. At least not now. Maybe never. What if she crashed into another unsuspecting cyclist, and both of them fell headlong onto the hard, crushed limestone surface of the new Coney Island cycle path? Death might be an overreaction, but the possibility of a collision existed nonetheless, and the prospect frightened her.

"Auntie Harriet?" Her voice trembled with the rest of her body, causing her words to crack. "I can't do this. I'm not a practiced enough cyclist after one week."

Harriet cast an all too familiar glance. "You overcame a terrible injury, so you can tackle this challenge. Either shrink away or overcome." A predictable response. She'd been called to account by Aunt Harriet so many times before. Tackle this challenge. Easy to say, hard to do . . . at least for her.

"Perhaps we should turn around," Anna said.

"Don't worry, dear. All will be fine." Harriet turned to the cyclist on her left and asked about the woman's bicycle.

Under normal circumstances, Anna admired her aunt's single-minded focus on the person with whom she conversed, especially when

Anna was the object of Harriet's rapt attention. Everyone around them would freeze in time, like an old ambrotype of people whose voices had long since been stilled. But these were not normal circumstances, and she needed Aunt Harriet's assistance. Rather than appear rude, she muttered her concerns below her breath.

Not a minute later, Anna's moment with destiny arrived.

The last speaker concluded his remarks, and the marching band launched into a rousing John Philip Sousa tune. The music stirred the multitudes, but the blaring trumpets drowned out her mental review of the rules of riding. Like Anna and her aunt, excited riders from all walks of life gathered to make history by cycling the nation's first dedicated bicycle pathway. The lane started in Brooklyn's Prospect Park and ran parallel to Ocean Parkway for almost six miles.

The path whispered to her, *Come ride me.* Anna whispered back. "Please. Not today."

The cyclists around her champed at the bit like Longstreet had on that fateful day. One scorcher in a hurry to reach Coney Island or a meek rider who jerked his or her handlebar the wrong way, and down she would go, like the day she had turned thirteen. The country's Independence Day, and her birthday, came and went that year without incident for most people in Chattanooga. For Anna, many days of dependence followed.

What did Aunt Harriet talk her into, and what about her aunt's scandalous outfit?

Discreditable—by Chattanooga's standards anyway. Many females in the crowd donned the same risqué costume. Bloomers, according to what she had read over the last few days, opened up the world of cycling to women. Her new hero, Annie Londonderry, wore them on her cycling trip around the world. Still, to see women dressed this way in public would take some getting used to.

She tried to picture herself on the corner of Market and Ninth Streets in Chattanooga, wearing this garb that her aunt said represented the new woman emerging all across America. The lens shattered, and the image dissolved. Someone else, but not her. Sometime in the future, maybe . . . but not yet.

Chattanooga and New York existed on different planets. The winds of social change may be blowing across America, but a dissimilar breeze swished through Chattanooga, one bound to turn into a gale with the mere mention of women in bloomers. Unable to attract Aunt Harriet's attention, Anna caught the notice of an adolescent girl on her right side.

Anna asked, "What does your mama make of your bloomer outfit? I mean, showing all that . . ."

"Much of my body?" The girl, amused by the question, brought her hand to her mouth in a gracious attempt to hide her giggle. "You're not from around here, are you?"

"That obvious?"

The young girl pointed to a middle-aged female rider wearing bloomers, one bicycle up and over to the right from her.

"Don't tell me—that's your mama?"

Anna shook her head in disbelief. The picture of her own mama on a wheel, by her side and half naked, came and vanished in almost the same instant. Inconceivable. The twinkle from the young lady's eyes caused Anna to focus on her rather than the riding garb and what Mama's reaction would be. As she opened her mouth to ask about the proper way to mount the wheel, the young cyclist beat her to the punch.

"What you're wearing today is lovely. Earlier I admired your skirt. Very fashionable, falling to the top of your boots, and so complemented by the cutaway jacket. I love your straw hat. Very new woman-ish."

"Why, thank you."

"Someday you should try riding in bloomers. So much easier and freeing. Enjoy your ride." The girl walked her bike forward to get closer to her mother.

Anna wiped her sweaty hands on her skirt, part of the spicy new outfit Aunt Harriet had bought her for their memorable ride. A distant cry from the minimal covering of bloomers on a lady, even this alternative gave her pause. After all, as the girl pointed out, the skirt stopped above her ankles, revealing more of her legs than ever before. The looming eyes of her mama somehow reached from Chattanooga to Brooklyn, demanding she change into the hooped dress of a proper Southern woman.

"Aunt Harriet, are you ignoring me?"

Her aunt faced her. "Trust yourself."

"I'm scared out of my wits. I can't remember how to mount."

"You and your wheel will become as one person. Mounting is straightforward and simple."

"Perhaps for you, but . . ."

The riders ahead of her climbed aboard their wheels. The moment of truth had arrived. Her heart thumped. The familiar odd tingling from head to toe told her danger lay ahead, and she experienced an overwhelming instinct to flee. Escape no longer an option, Anna began to pedal, her balance wobbly for a few seconds. She fought through her discomfort until the recent lessons kicked in and then shot out like a bullet from a gun.

Ten yards turned into fifty, and a hundred. By some miracle, she still sat upright, the uncertainty about launching moments ago fading like a distant memory. As she pedaled harder, the wheels rotated faster, advancing her speed. The thrill set her senses ablaze. The marching band grew faint in the distance, the rhythmical oompahs from the tubas being the last brass sound hanging onto the wind.

She leaned into the bars, invigorated by a mild breeze. A newfound freedom washed over her—mobility unleashed by the pedals and chain that turned the back wheel with every revolution of her legs. As she breathed in the bouquet of late spring, tinged with the grit of New York's city streets in summer, she burst into peals of laughter. The riders on both sides caught her giddiness, smiling as she passed through.

The shady trees lining the lane almost hypnotized her. She gazed over at the pleasure carriages, horse-drawn wagons, and electric rail cars that filled the adjacent street. Citizens walked on sidewalks to their destinations. As she experienced big city life from a bicycle seat, she concluded that the wheel had rightfully taken its place among these varied forms of transportation.

Authorities had set a speed limit of twelve miles per hour on the path. One policeman along the way reminded the riders to avoid speeding. "You will regret the penalty if you're caught scorching down the path."

The cyclists rode on, Anna imagining her wheel lifting off the ground, climbing up into a blue sky, the backdrop for some silky clouds, thin and wispy. Rays of sunlight warmed her face. She pictured the aerial view of thousands of cyclists stretching for miles down the new cycling path below. Coney Island waited beyond. Birds of varying species, sizes, and colors winged their way home for the summer, sharing her airspace, unperturbed by her presence.

Something outside herself warned of danger, causing the dreamy vision to blow away like smoke, much to her disappointment. A flash beside Anna made her jerk the handlebar to the left, narrowly averting a collision with a racer on wheels. She shifted the bar back to the right to compensate and stabilize, avoiding a nasty tumble into Aunt Harriet's bicycle.

Her aunt didn't flinch. "Perfect recovery."

She cried out, "Oh, Aunt Harriet, I'm in love."

She searched for the perfect one-word description of their day at Coney. Enchanting. A time that left an indelible impression and a motto she pledged to never forget: People are never too old to enjoy life in a childlike manner. The ride on the new path back to Prospect Park capped an extraordinary time with her aunt.

As they neared Prospect Park, Anna's joyous mood turned somber. "Oh, Auntie . . . will I ever ride a wheel again?"

"If that's what you truly want, then yes."

"What about the shunning sure to befall a woman cyclist on the streets of Chattanooga? I'm not sure I have the courage to endure the community outrage . . . or Mama's disdain."

Southern ladies didn't engage in activities meant for men.

Chapter Two

Chattanooga, Tennessee

PETER SAWYER ARRIVED early, around seven o'clock, and his new protégé, Frederick Douglas Crawford, a colored man who lived in a Negro tenement in Hill City across the Walnut Street Bridge, entered the store soon thereafter.

"Mornin', Mr. Sawyer."

Young Frederick took pride in being named after the famed abolitionist, who had died earlier in the year, and sought to make something of himself like his namesake. Peter became a boss and a mentor and enjoyed teaching the lad the grocery business.

"And to you, Frederick. But when will you call me Peter, like I asked?" He sealed the question with a smile.

The oldest at fifteen, Frederick came looking for employment several weeks back, and being a soft heart, Peter put the gangly lad to the task of tidying up. Times were hard for the Crawford family, and Peter's father, Chester Sawyer, taught him that a man willing to work deserves a job. The customer flow at Sawyer's Grocery & Sundries had increased steadily over the past year as the city continued to recover from the recent depression. The timing was perfect; he needed the help to keep up.

At twenty-two, Peter's own work ethic and natural instincts pleased his father. He never took his loyal shoppers for granted and called most of them by name. The future had been plotted for Peter in Sawyer Enterprises. The grocery, the lumberyard, and the Texas ranch needed managing. All that Peter could ever desire was in his grasp. Except for one thing.

Like his brothers, he wanted to make his own way in the world. He loved his father, a wise mentor, and didn't want to hurt him. So, he locked away his selfish need and stored the key for the right day when he would announce his intentions. For now, there he stood, inside Sawyer's Grocery & Sundries, prepared for a busy Monday morning. He wanted to do right and to please his parents.

His Achilles' heel: the bicycle.

He gazed over at his wheel, standing against the wall at the back of the market, and walked in that direction. As he stared, the difficult questions his father had asked two nights ago echoed in his mind.

"Do you think you're spending too much time wheeling and not enough on the grocery? Is being president of the Cycle Club causing a lack of focus on your work?"

"Come by the grocery so you can see for yourself," he had said. "Everything's in proper order."

The unpleasant scene dissolved as he stood before his primary source of transportation. To appease his father, he had decided to refocus efforts on the grocery . . . for the sake of their relationship.

"Say, Mr. Sawyer . . . I mean Peter. Ain't it time?" The boy's voice snapped him out of his musings.

The morning setup had remained the same since he and his brothers helped their father to open on Saturdays. Frederick fetched the broom and dustpan and began sweeping, first in front of the building. As Peter scanned the store, he took a visual inventory of what needed restocking. The candy containers, nearly empty by the end of each day, always came first. He popped his favorite mint into his mouth as he replenished that jar.

After Frederick cleaned the front walkway, he came inside and whipped up a cloud of dirt and dust with his broad sweeping motions against the wood-planked floor. Peter sneezed, then again, followed by two more. Frederick continued to sweep. "Bless you, Mr. Sawyer. Catching a cold, sir?"

"Thank you. Naw, I'm healthy as a racehorse."

"Well, sir, you just let me know if you're needing a break."

The youth began to sing softly, as he often did during the morning preparations. The words, like the spirituals he'd sung before, spoke of being rescued from the hard and cruel life, but this one sounded different. New. "Beautiful song," Peter said. "Where did you pick that up?"

"Done been passed down in my family. My great-granddaddy wrote it a long time ago, and I play the tune on my daddy's guitar."

"Wonderful. Bring the instrument in one day and play the song for me. For now, begin retrieving stock from the back as I call out what I need. I'll finish the sweeping before we open."

"Okay, sir. But tell me if you start to feeling sickly. I can handle the whole opening. Been ready for more responsibility."

The six bins in the long wooden container needed refilling. Peter called out to his assistant: "Dry foods. Flour, oats, beans." One at a time they stocked the bins and moved on to other items, like canned goods on the shelves and individual baskets with corn, fruits, and vegetables in the fresh produce section. Smoking pipes of all varieties sat on the front counter, along with a container filled with tobacco. He asked Frederick to tidy up and replenish the display, while he polished the huge hand-cranked commercial-grade coffee grinder, which made the whole store smell delightful, and the proper two-sided scale to ensure customers were charged the correct amount. The latest fabrics stood against a wall.

Frederick took his place at the cash register behind the counter, while Peter did the last bit of indoor sweeping. A quick check of his pocket watch showed the time at 8:59, one minute before opening. A line began to form outside the door. With his hand on the doorknob, he peered through the glass.

"Ready?"

The young apprentice nodded. "Here they come."

Like a herd of cattle, the faithful shoppers of Sawyer's grocery filed through the gate and into the pen.

⚜

The morning flew by like a flock of migrating sand hill cranes. At noontime, when business slowed, Peter and Frederick stood behind the counter and talked baseball and about their local star, a centerfield acrobat named Strang Nicklin. The eighteen-year-old amateur outfielder, the pride and joy of all sports-minded Chattanoogans, had recently played against the Cincinnati Reds when the team stopped in town for an exhibition game. The young man and his daddy attended the contest, courtesy of Peter's father.

"Gosh, Mr. Sawyer, you should have seen how Buck Ewing swatted one to deep center field. With a second set of eyes in the back of his head, Strang turns at the crack of the bat, starts chasing the baseball down, and makes a leaping catch. The stands roared. Gotta say, I cheered mighty loud along with 'em."

Frederick's eyes shifted over Peter's shoulder. As a customer came through the front door, Peter turned and there she stood, like one of the heavenly hosts sent on a rescue assignment to earth. Her dark auburn hair, bundled back on her head, and the perfect pale skin and soft features of her face, took him aback. He fought the temptation to stare lest his mind wander into dangerous territory. She had hardly noticed him whenever she came to shop.

He approached her, racking his brain for the perfect salutation that would endear him to her. Most ladies enjoyed a man who held his own in a conversation. An articulate speaker in public and in dialogue with men, sometimes he stumbled before women. He needed to grow in the art of wooing the ladies.

"Welcome to Sawyer's." Original. He rubbed the nape of his neck.

"Morning." She stopped. Her feet pointed away, in the same direction as her eyes. Was she about to walk away? He couldn't tell which of them seemed more uncomfortable.

After an eternity, which lasted several seconds, she proceeded straight to the tobacco container. Did she smoke a pipe? Impossible. Hesitant, he wandered over in her direction, careful not to look like a stalker. He fumbled through the candle bin nearby, his attention fixed on rearranging the stock, which had already been readied for the opening. She finished bagging and moved toward the register.

He needed to say something before her angel wings whisked her away. "I see you've bought some tobacco. Do you . . .?"

She turned to face him, her hand cupping her mouth. "Smoke a . . . Why, heavens no." She cast her eyes down and away, her face and neck turning a light shade of red. As he took one step forward, she retreated the same distance. "This is for my papa. I'll be seeing him on the weekend. Today seemed like a good time to come. Anyway . . ."

"Oh . . ."

The longest awkward moment of his short adult life followed, until she stepped to the cash register. Determined to open a dialogue, he sauntered toward the door as Frederick counted out her change. When she turned to exit, Peter stood in her path. After a quick glance into his eyes, she again turned her gaze to the floor.

"You're Peter Sawyer, the Cycling Club President."

"Yes." An opening. He crawled through, determined to widen the crack. "And you're Anna Gaines, one of my old classmates. We've crossed paths, but never talked."

"Yes. Well . . ." Several more awkward seconds followed.

Was there something they might share in common? Baseball and cycling were out. He didn't know if she enjoyed sporting events, and of course she didn't ride the wheel. A female cyclist in these southern parts would create a scandal that clubs and church groups would feed on like hungry sharks. Would the day come when he found enough gumption to come right out and tell her that he had admired her from afar for more than two years?

She broke the ice. "You're a wheelman."

A breakthrough he could run with. "Oh, yes, I love the freedom. Such a shame women can't ride, don't you think? Maybe the community should . . ."

For some reason unbeknownst to him, the comment triggered her hasty retreat. "Yes . . . a pleasure to speak with you, but I must return to work. Thank you and . . ." Without her looking at him again, his chance left the premises. What did he do or say to offend her? The comment about riding? He had long anticipated and supported women cyclists wheeling through the roads and byways of Chattanooga like they did in other major northern cities. During a lull in the checkout process, Peter wandered over to the counter, baffled by the mysteries of the female species.

"A word to the wise. Never ask me for advice concerning women."

Frederick shook his head. "I done seen something different, boss. When you started fiddling with them candles, the missy stared at you like you're some kind of stage star."

Chapter Three

THE NEXT DAY, Anna returned to work at Loveman's Department Store.

It had been a dry goods establishment in her youth, and one day she asked her papa about the soon-to-be opened emporium of the future, the first to be built in Chattanooga. His answer echoed through the winds of her youth: "A place with separate sections where you can buy clothes, appliances, furniture, women's perfume, and so much more. Even children's toys."

Now Anna was a seamstress at Loveman's thanks to her best friend, Emma Kelly, and a childhood dream had turned into a daily dose of monotony.

She held out hope of attending a university to become a professor like Aunt Harriet. The prospects were still daunting in 1895. For now, the employment financed her move into the city, away from the farm. The buffer between her and Mama had done them good over the last six months, and she enjoyed the time back in the nearby Chickamauga Valley on weekends.

At mid-morning, having produced well beyond half of her daily quota, she stopped and glanced over at Emma's empty chair. She pined for her friend, who had left unexpectedly to care for her sick grandma in Virginia. Before Anna left for Brooklyn, they had talked about whether her job would be waiting after so much time away. Now Emma, gone for almost two weeks, faced the same uncertainty.

In fairness, Loveman's was not the problem. Her disfavor rested with one cruel taskmaster, Mr. Helms. At his pleasure this morning, she labored over the machine more than usual, shoulders hunched and eyes focused for hours, and with minimal rest times. At close to noon, the supervisor made his way past the many seamstresses at work, stopped at Emma's empty machine, and inched toward Anna.

"With Miss Kelly gone, I expect you to pick up the slack. Perhaps if you looked people in the eyes, you'd do better in life. I predict Loveman's will be the peak of your working life. Best maintain our standards and production quotas . . . *if* you want to keep this job."

"Of course, Mr. Helms." His mere presence daunted her, but standing this close, she began to tremble.

He left the floor, and none too soon. Should she quit? Pain shot through her tensed shoulders all the way down to her fingers. She flexed them before resuming her work. The constant rhythm of the thirty machines in the large concrete room usually faded to the background, but now it was magnified by her pounding heartbeat. The fusty smell irritated her more than usual, as the odor of scorched fibers caused by needles moving rapidly up and down invaded her nostrils. Would she ever be free of this grind? She felt stuck. She was stuck. A flash memory of a feeling—the freedom she'd exulted in when she rode that trail in New York—waved over her. She forced it away. It only made the sadness grow, and she refused to allow the negative to overtake her. After all, things could be worse. She reminded herself that sweatshops abounded around town with more dingy workspaces, crueler taskmasters, and much lower pay, which aged the seamstresses before their time.

The rest of the week dragged as Anna mindlessly sat at her sewing machine, watching the simple hypnotic motion of the bobbing needle, like a hen pecking at the ground. She stitched the seams of an endless stream of cloaks, dresses with new styles of pleats and collars, and new undergarments that complemented the designs.

The lack of adequate light on the factory floor strained her eyes, and the stuffiness caused by the early summer heat and humidity made her feel faint at times. But she didn't dare cease working or Mr. Helms might fire her—which would destroy her newfound deliverance on the wheel.

On Saturday, Anna caught the Harrison Avenue and Highland Park electric trolleys to East Lake, where her papa, Joseph Gaines, waited with the buggy. Climbing down, he greeted her with a kiss on each cheek. "To keep you balanced," his traditional greeting since the terrible fall from Longstreet had left her with unbalanced legs, one longer than other.

"Missed you, Papa. Glad to be visiting home and working the harvest with my brothers and cousins." As they pulled away, the mid-morning sun cast the vehicle's long shadow in a southwesterly direction. The silhouette of the single horse pranced against the ground, reminding Anna of a strutting peacock.

"So how's your free-spirited Aunt Harriet?"

Anna smiled sheepishly. Should she tell him?

"What's behind that grin?"

He never missed a beat with her, so she threw caution to the wind.

"Oh, Papa, she taught me to ride the bicycle. The release I experienced for the first time in a long time—to let go and be myself. I can't describe the sensation with words."

His eyebrows shifted apart, one high and one low, as he stroked his chin. "Sounds like my sister. Go on."

"Cycling is like a slice of heaven." She told almost all—the lessons at the cycling school, the special shortened, two-piece outfit Harriet bought for her, and the ride to Coney Island. She skipped any mention of the women in bloomers. Despite his open mind, Papa would be hard-pressed to accept such a radical departure in acceptable women's clothing. Or would he?

His encouragements always lifted her to flights of fancy, like the way Aunt Harriet's belief had catapulted her into the clouds, above the throngs of cyclists on the path to Coney Island. Mama, on the other hand, would sooner lock her away and toss the key into East Lake so nothing could ever hurt her again. This kind of protection smothered her, but she would never appreciate the heart of a mother until she became one, so she gave her mama an extra measure of understanding.

How could she explain the majesty of what had happened to her?

"The world seems bigger in just a week," she said.

"You've been to Brooklyn before and to Atlanta to visit Cousin Oscar. But on this trip, the planet expands, and you come home a changed person?"

All of a sudden, the buggy wheel dipped into a deep pothole, lifting them both from their seats and throwing Anna to the right. Surprised, they laughed as she moved back into her seat. Her papa pulled the buggy to a stop.

"Yes. Changed forever, Papa." As he began to lift the reins, she stopped him. "Wait, Papa. Listen. And look at this peaceful place."

The breath of heaven gently moved its way across the late-spring meadow ahead. The murmuring wind shook the tall, green field grass, and for a moment, the sun's rays created schools of moving lights that scampered across the ground, intent on reaching new destinations, but soon disappearing. The green treetops gave way to a crystal blue sky, a shroud that concealed the depths of the universe from the human eye. The clouds that had dropped enough water to create the hole in the roadway hours before had passed through. The valley awakened her soul.

Drawing near, she kissed his cheek and spoke of touring the city and of the many children peddling goods like newspapers, fruit, and flowers on busy street corners when they should be in school. She described men and women cycling everywhere, with several groups of men competing in one hundred-mile races. And Madison Square Garden, which had recently held the Sportsmen's Exhibition. She told him about the Lantern Club, where writers like Mark Twain, Stephen Crane, and Theodore Roosevelt held court and shared their work.

"Papa, there are even milk stations throughout the city that sell pasteurized milk and give some away to poor people who can't pay."

His eyes glistened in the sunlight. Reaching across the seat, he took her small hand into his big paw. "Tell me more."

There was so much more, but parts would remain as confidences between two women. New York had opened up her dreams of attending a university and becoming a teacher like her aunt. "An amazing young mother is now my new hero—after you, of course. Her name is Annie Londonderry. Well, her real last name is Kopchovsky, but the other is much easier to pronounce."

"And?"

"Listen to this, Papa. She's finishing up a bicycle ride around the world. I mean, all across America and Europe and to faraway places like French Indochina. When I arrived at Aunt Harriet's last week, she shared newspaper clippings, so I read about Annie's ride."

Without responding, her papa turned straight forward, called out to Winnie, their horse, and the buggy lurched ahead into a patch of forest. Strange. No apparent reaction. Moments later, he began whistling "Dixie," his favorite tune, and happened to catch her goggling at him.

Papa's joyful song faded, and they rode for a while in the stillness of the morning. She loved this part of the road, abounding with trees that emitted an outdoor, woodsy fragrance that tickled her nose. She breathed in deeply. In a slow trot, Winnie stooped her head down low, took a quick sniff of some droppings, and then straightened. Before long, the buggy emerged from the forest into another meadow, revealing the sky's fiery ball and more of the earth's lush green carpet.

Winged performers in flight, and some perched in the trees, chirped out their original melodies, penetrating the silence. They sang in perfect tune, not a note out of place. An eagle launched from the top of a nearby tree; its majesty spoke to Anna about the freedom to fly, to let the power of your own wings and the winds at your back carry you to new heights and distant places. That's the kind of life she wanted. Well, maybe.

The goal of breaking free of all restraints, particularly those that were self-imposed but also the chains others wrapped her with, both drove her toward independence and caused her at times to cower in fear. An amazing life waited somewhere for her, maybe in a place like New York or perhaps right here in her own backyard.

Either way, to discover the pathway, something had to change. She needed a lantern to light the way and the courage to follow the path. As of now, she had neither.

Still, she asked him the critical question that had occupied her thoughts since boarding the train for home.

Chapter Four

"PAPA, DO YOU suppose Chattanooga is ready for female cyclists?"

"Whoa!" Winnie slowed to a stop as commanded.

The loud clanging of the horse's metal shoes and the iron-tired buggy wheels against the hard road faded into quietude. With eyes focused ahead, he uttered a contemplative response. "Hmm." They always chattered during the five-plus miles on the McFarland Gap Road to the Gaines family farm. But the question drew her papa inward. He gently slapped the reins on Winnie's hind end. "Let's go, girl." They started off again.

The traditional woman inside centered her on someday nurturing children and caring for a husband—running a household like her mama. In the South, such women offered little encouragement to their sisters who dared to step into the realms of men. And Chattanooga, the front door to the Deep South, oozed tradition.

She had guessed Papa would be more accepting of a daughter choosing to be a new woman. Now she wasn't so sure, given his lack of response. No guesswork when it came to her mama. Steeped in Southern ideas about appropriate behavior for women, Mama would view the activities of emancipators like a swarm of bees. If you allow dangerous precedents to shake the hive—like ladies who cycle clad in bloomers, pursue professional careers, and seek the right to vote—you're likely to get stung.

Would it be possible to plant one's feet in both worlds?

⚜

Papa turned onto the long winding road that led to the farmhouse surrounded by one hundred and fifty acres of wheat, corn, fruit orchards, and open fields for horses and cows.

He pulled the rig to a slow stop and turned toward her.

"Acceptance of women on wheels."

"Huh?"

"A while back you asked me if Chattanooga would accept female cyclists. Right?"

"Ten minutes ago . . . yes." Braced for a thoughtful but unfavorable response, Anna breathed deep and grabbed the dried and cracked leather seat, warm from the exposure to direct sunlight. She trusted his wise counsel and would abide by his opinion on the matter.

"Been thinking on the point. Bicycle riding and women make for an unlikely combination in our neck of the woods. As you know, our ways are rooted in old-fashioned ideas about the proper places for men and women."

Done. Case closed. "So, your answer is no."

"An uphill, bruising battle. At the same time, progress is never made without change, and I figure new ideas bring advancement. Look at Aunt Harriet . . . a pioneer."

Becoming a trailblazer was serious business. That's why she so admired her aunt. Papa gave her a glimmer of hope about cycling, maybe even going to college.

Winnie neighed and stomped her right hoof on the ground three times, as if she wanted to say something about giving equal rights to women. Perfect timing and amusing. Papa chuckled.

"Easy, girl," he said, as he took a sturdier grip on the leather controls. Winnie stretched her neck back in disapproval but settled down as commanded. "Some things around here need changing, but lasting change takes sacrifice. It requires that we give up some things we'd like to have now, so the real advancement can happen later."

Like anonymity? She weighed her father's response. The probable challenges sobered her, like being labeled a pariah by Chattanooga's haughty belles and pious church leaders. The bigger, more immediate hill to climb would be her mother's reaction.

"Do you think Mama is ready? She's overprotective and coddling—and so mindful of what others are thinking. I love her so, but she's one reason I moved to town."

If her mama allowed for a compromise, Anna would be satisfied to cycle around the farm. Why talk in hypotheticals, tossing out silly propositions when she didn't even own a wheel. Still, she pondered the question. What if?

"Well, I can predict your mama's first reaction. No surprise, but she's more Old South than me. On the other hand, who can deny the new sparkle in your beautiful blue eyes? So, I'm thinking Mama, facing such a situation, would come around in time."

She sighed. Sheer foolishness. She needed to leave bicycle riding to the big-city women. Most wheels cost around a hundred dollars, an amount that far exceeded her bank account balance.

"Let's go, Winnie," Papa said.

The slackened reins and the familiar sounding voice gave Winnie permission to continue on.

❖

When they arrived, Anna greeted her mama and walked upstairs to her old room where she changed into tattered work clothes that she covered from the waist down with a white apron. She wrapped an intricate headdress over her hair for protection against the sun's grueling post-morning rays.

Stepping outside, she scanned the acres of golden-yellow wheat stocks all around her and prepared to pitch in with the harvest. She loved this season. The rustling sound as the stocks swayed in the breeze; the dry, earthy smells reminding her of harvests gone by. As she always did, Anna picked the grain-bearing tip of one stalk, broke off a kernel, and rubbed it between her fingers. She popped a grain in her mouth and savored the nutty taste. Ripe and ready for harvest.

At home in the Chickamauga Valley, she almost forgot about her pronounced limp and the loss of one inch in her left leg when the bones failed to heal correctly. She had blamed Longstreet for throwing her, even though Papa had suggested that some ground critter might have spooked him. Nevertheless, she refused to climb upon his back again and wouldn't even look at him. Eventually, she insisted that Papa sell her treasured horse, a decision that haunted her to this day.

The year she spent in bed and hobbling on crutches, led her to pull inward. After several months of limping along, refusing to venture back out into the world, her father had enlisted a boot maker in Chattanooga to adjust the sole on Anna's left shoe, adding one-half inch. The adjustments replaced the pronounced uneven step with a slight one, but the damage to her self-confidence would not be so easily corrected.

She greeted her siblings and cousins and took her traditional spot. Up ahead in the process, her brothers grabbed fistfuls of wheat, carefully cut the bottoms, and dropped the stalks in a pile. Using four pieces of wheat, Anna tied the bundles into sheaves, and her cousin behind her stacked the sheaves into stooks, and they were left to dry. As she scanned the field, the piles of grain turned into American Indian tepees, filled with natives sitting around small fires, smoking their long pipes.

Strange the way she saw her surroundings. The voice of the wheat spoke about the past bounties that sprang forth from nature and clods of earth; she shrugged off the increasing pain from her leg to hear the field tell its stories of old. The harvest became a spiritual experience for her.

As she toiled away, her thoughts shifted to Grover. Many of her friends had married, and she too longed for companionship; someone who would love her and whom she could love and serve. No prospects had appeared on the horizon, save but one bright star. A newcomer to Chattanooga, Grover Biggs, had helped her to overcome her awkwardness around men. A real looker, and the first man ever to indicate interest in her, Grover had asked her papa's permission to call, and he had agreed.

When Mama rang the bell for the midday dinner, everyone ran to take their places at the row of outside tables. They sat beneath the two tall elm trees that spread their wings a few yards from the kitchen, dropping shade over the feast of eggs, ham, and fruit that lay before them. The magical, well-worn loaf pans, filled with Mama's warm, award-winning bread, released a tantalizingly sweet aroma that wafted up and around the table. Any feast in the life to come would surely include Mama's contributions.

Some of the boys grabbed a piece and began slopping it with butter and Mama's homemade preserves. Anna knew better. Papa put a stop to the premature feeding frenzy. "Let us not forget to praise the One who bestowed this bounty upon us."

Anna, sitting next to him, drew comfort from holding his dry, work-worn hand. A sense of safety, the same security she had experienced with his touch as a little girl, filled her now. She offered her own silent prayer of thanks. With a resounding "Amen!" the army of harvesters snatched up the bowls filled with Mama's lavish meal. Everyone jabbered about the latest goings-on in their lives and did their parts to advance the Chattanooga-Chickamauga gossip mill.

As they ate, Anna spotted someone approaching from afar, a swiftly moving dot on the long, winding, tree-lined road leading to the farm. A moment later, she jumped up from her seat. The table hushed as the others turned, wondering what had caught her attention. The person of interest came toward them faster than normal because he rode a bicycle. She ran out to greet her favorite cousin—Aunt Harriet's son Oscar who lived in Atlanta.

She hugged him. "What are you doing here? Why are you on a woman's wheel?"

An accomplished cyclist, he had long thrilled her with his trick riding and ability to cycle sure and true at fast speeds. Short in stature and two years her senior, he stood the same height as she did, a physical equality she had often mentioned in their younger years. Almost overnight, the teenage Oscar became strong as an ox, belying his small frame.

"Received a telegram from mother," he said. "Sounds like you two had a unique visit."

This time had indeed been different. In the past, the separation between adult and child had remained clear. Aunt Harriet always treated her special, but this time they went deep, woman to woman. They spoke of men and Anna's lack of composure around them. The talks extended long into the night. Perhaps she had crossed the threshold from adolescence to adulthood, and Aunt Harriet welcomed her to the other side.

"I adore Harriet Dennison and want to hitch my star to hers," Anna said. "Tell me about this communication."

"Here, you can read the note for yourself." The date: June 17, 1895, two days after they had cycled to Coney Island.

Oscar dear, asking big favor this weekend. Board train for Chattanooga. Go straight to bicycle shop and purchase a wheel. A woman's drop-down if you can find one. A present for Cousin Anna. Ride new wheel out to the farm. Will send money to reimburse. Our next visit? Your loving mother.

"So here I am," he said. "Came into town yesterday and stayed with a friend. An ad in the Times caught my eye, so I wandered over to Graham Cycle Company, the bike store on East Eighth."

"I don't know what to say." Anna had read the same advertisement for women's bikes, diamond-shaped with the lowered middle bar. The shop forged new ground with its pitch for female riders, but she dismissed the possibility that she would ever own one. Might this be the shop's first sale of a drop-down bicycle? She was overwrought with gratitude and thankfulness.

"Don't need to say, cousin. Just ride . . . safely."

The black color gleamed in the bright sunlight. "This wheel is beautiful," Anna said.

"Rides nicely too. A Columbia brand safety bicycle, Fleetwing-style. I enjoyed the ten-mile jaunt out here."

She leaned forward and whispered in his ear. "Not so sure Mama will thank Auntie or you for the gesture."

He mumbled back. "Make the purchase, ask permission later. I'm half-starved and ready to claim some of the food over yonder before the vultures pick all the bones clean."

As they walked back to the table arm-in-arm, she stopped out of earshot of the others. "How did your family work with a mother who taught at a university, raised three kids, tended to her husband, and kept a home?"

He gave the question some consideration. "Not always easy, to be honest. But Ma always insisted women are capable of doing it all."

Anna was beginning to agree. "How did she do?"

"Fair to middling—most of the time."

Uncertain whether such a dual citizenship could survive in Chattanooga, Anna still dared to contemplate juggling both life endeavors.

The dreaded talk started as Anna and Mama carried the kitchenware inside to the sink, and Anna mentioned that the bike now belonged to her, a gift from Aunt Harriet. She tried to share little bits of her visit, but Mama reacted worse than expected. No daughter of hers would make a spectacle of herself on a bicycle, she proclaimed, before men craning their necks for a better view and friends who would question her judgment. And probably her chastity.

Anna made little headway, even with Papa's occasional supportive comments. Mule-headed, Mama would not budge.

"The idea is preposterous," she said. "No daughter in her right mind would ever subject her parents to such ridicule from the citizenry."

The self-centered proclamation wounded Anna. A wild dream had just come true, and all Mama could think about was herself and how other people would view her. Tears threatened to fall, but she held them back, wanting to prove that this girl had grown into a woman who could control her emotions, the pains and disappointments of life. While she loved and respected Mama, the attempt to master her feelings waned, and she began to let loose her own angry tirade.

"It's time, Mama, for you to . . ." She caught Papa's frown and hesitated. Did she dare continue? Disharmony threatened to take up residence with the family. The moistness in Mama's eyes disarmed her. "But Mama, I'm not meaning to . . ."

Mama held her hand up and spoke sternly. "I won't allow you to thumb your nose at Southern propriety. My final word."

A salty tear found its way to Anna's mouth.

Despite her proclamation, Mama had more to say. Oscar steered clear of the explosive discussion.

The rest of the clan had already returned to the fields to continue the harvest.

Disagreements between Anna and her mother always followed the same pattern. Why not sit on the couch, where they could face each other and talk things through calmly? But no. She walked behind Mama from the sink, the dishes now washed and stacked neatly for the next meal, as Mama continued to rail against the idea, working herself into a tizzy. The dressing down exasperated Anna; apparently she lacked everything from common sense to Southern culture to understanding the rules that real ladies follow.

Outside, both of them disengaged, thankfully, as they each carried two buckets filled with leftover slop to the pigsty. The animals snooted, several rolling in the mud, until they saw their meal being dumped into the trough. Anna smiled as they head-butted and snorted with delight, the chomping and squealing one of her favorite farm choruses. The respite helped to calm her.

The deep ravine that separated her from Mama seemed almost as insurmountable as Pickett Gulf from top to bottom. That place held her most cherished memories of past family travels, even though the spots she wanted to climb down to were unreachable. Much like her mama at this moment. The loud white water fell from the river above, where she used to stand and daydream, and gathered into a small lake below. How she longed as a child to venture down. Rugged rock formations and trees surrounded the water, making passage impossible.

As Mama poured the contents of her bucket into the pen, Anna pictured her mother standing high above the gulf, calling out warnings about the dangerous waters, but the younger Anna in this imaginary visit swam to her delight, enjoying the panoply of sights and sounds. Desperate to be set free, in a flash, she swam beyond the lake, riding a rapid toward new discoveries, her mama's voice fading away.

There at the pigpen, the chasm widened as Mama sidestepped her, collected some gardening tools in the shed, and walked toward the front of the house. Anna followed her, silent, as Mama continued her gardening project. Small in stature, she hunched as she hoed, her deep hazel eyes still misty, the furrowed lines etched in her forehead and her cheeks appearing more pronounced. Perhaps this was due to Mama's anxiety or concentration over the disagreement. Or maybe for the first time, Anna had become aware of the years taking their toll on a hardworking farm wife who had begun to tire.

As Anna gazed at her mother, she wondered how many wrinkles she had chiseled into her face. The accident and long convalescence had carved their share. And now the worry she would face from a community shunning, her daughter being branded a woman of ill repute. Should she say anything more about the bicycle or let the subject slip away for now? Mama began to sow the flower bed.

Unable to help herself, she jumped back into a contest of wills. "Give me a chance to explain, Mama." No sooner than the words had left her lips, she wanted to catch them in the air and shove them back into her mouth. With a scowl, Mama shot back.

"These progressive ideas about women and their changing place in the family and community may be fine in New York City, but not here."

"Mama . . ."

"Mark my words—never in Chattanooga, let alone the Deep South." She poked a long finger toward Anna's face for emphasis. Mama's flushed cheeks and neck told Anna that she had reached a heightened state of agitation. A smoking and flaming volcano was now about to spew streams of lava.

At the risk of being consumed by Mama's magma, Anna tried one last time to make her understand. She chose her words carefully, clothing them with respect. "Riding a wheel is clean fun and wonderful exercise, Mama. Can a simple bicycle turn me into a reckless girl? You taught me a woman's proper place, and the bicycle won't change me."

How she longed for understanding between them.

"I'll not allow Harriet to influence my only daughter with her harebrained schemes about cycling. Women on wheels. Honestly, things are getting out of hand."

"I . . ."

"No. The matter is finished. Please tell Oscar to thank his mother for her thoughtful gesture, but he can return the bike and get a refund."

This time, the argument did end—at least between Anna and her mother.

The next morning before church, as Oscar said his goodbyes and climbed aboard the wheel to return it to the bicycle shop, Anna stopped him. She learned that the conversation had continued behind closed doors, late into the night. Her mama and papa, who never came to verbal blows in front of their children, settled on a compromise. They agreed to let Anna cycle around the farm on the weekends, but not in the city. This would allow Mama to monitor her riding and the clothes she wore.

Oscar decided he would stay a bit longer and later give her a riding lesson.

Pure excitement burned a wide hole through her patience as they entered the small country church where the family attended. Visions filled her head of scorching across fields and on hidden paths within the forest; of greeting her neighbors and watching their children play in front yards as she rode through Chattanooga's many tree-lined, macadamized residential streets. Maybe not now, but someday.

Upon returning home, she streaked to the barn, gathered up the wheel, and gave everyone a cycling exhibition. Oscar, an amateur racer who delivered medicines for a prominent Atlanta druggist, gave Anna safety pointers. Mama chose to tidy up the kitchen and prepare the Sunday meal.

After her lesson, Anna rode beyond the farmhouse into the partially cleared wheat fields and through the fifteen-acre orchard. She pedaled hard between the rows of trees, careful to dodge the rotting fruit on the ground, spoiled by the pecking of hungry birds or cast aside by the mother tree as unworthy of attachment. A small hill lay ahead, perfect for coasting down. As she glided, she bathed in the breeze against her face.

She owned this ride. No joy-robbing thief would steal it from her, and no well-meaning judge could render an order to cease and desist. Not even her mama. Anna and the wheel became as one: She steered the vehicle, making her the controlling partner. Free once again, she emerged from a wall of trees into an open, grassy field, the blue sky dotted with white and grey cloud puffs that flirted with the mountain ridges. With a burst of energy, she pushed hard to rejoin her family.

From a distance, she noticed a buggy headed up the McFarland Gap Road toward eastern Chattanooga. A woman looking intently toward her appeared to be monitoring her movements.

Chapter Five

THE CARRIAGE HEADING back to the Fort Wood district carried Bertha Millwood and her quiet husband.

The idea had fallen flat from the outset. Hopeful that a casual Sunday ride into the countryside would help thaw the deep freeze that separated her from Edward, Bertha found the discourse as sparse as ever. The bountiful picnic lunch lay untouched in the basket. Nothing worked—her questions about his accounting practice, the business trends in town, and why he no longer played his violin. They all received one- or two-word responses. If that.

When would his withdrawal from their marriage end? She craved companionship again. To be touched, held on the occasions when a broken heart caused her to falter. After all, it had been two years since their world collapsed, when their daughter Constance had been found murdered in a hotel room, and she practically lived alone. Over time, she had found a way to move past the inconsolable grief that engulfed them at first, choking off their ability to draw near.

The lunches and teas and discussions in social and philanthropic organizations, like the Kosmos Club and the Women's Club, helped the weeks to pass. She recently had doubled her church involvements.

The love that had caused her to cleave to Edward in the beginning still burned. Or did it simply smolder? Loneliness and emptiness had darkened her outlook and turned her cold, like a clouded sky refusing to allow life-giving sunbeams to break through. She could not help herself, and it didn't help that Edward also withdrew, clinging to his business practice and separate routines at home. The work that she had interpreted as a special calling made him crawl deeper into his safe havens. What would it take to be reunited?

Now, seeing a woman cyclist caused her to wring her hands.

"There . . . you see, Edward? A woman on a wheel. How appalling. With all this talk about new women, I've been expecting something like this."

No response. The long-predicted danger she had warned against for months had arrived at their front doorstep. Emancipators—the misguided invaders seeking to conquer a man's world—had sent a lone female soldier to the road, sitting astride the most effective tool used to date to advance their agenda. The wheel. Now that they had boldly drawn the lines of battle, the Kosmos ladies must be warned. But first, she would take matters into her own hands with help from other like-minded allies.

For now, Edward would be her sounding board. She would make him listen. "The women who ride the wheel are exchanging gentility and breeding for unrestricted, immoral behavior."

"Oh, Bertha. Please." He flinched and turned away.

So, he lived and breathed. She would rather a response of disgust than none at all.

"They risk ruining their own health, not to mention their femininity and shapeliness," she said. "Do you realize recent medical reports show women cyclists are developing unsightly lumps in their arms and legs? They begin to take on the physique of a man."

Edward continued to avert his gaze, irritating her.

"Are you listening?"

Her husband nodded.

She rolled her eyes. "Believe me, this is only the beginning. Women will be taking to the streets in bloomers, violating all standards of decency and morality. Commanding the attention of our men. This is not New York or San Francisco. We must maintain our decorum here, don't you agree?"

He nodded again but with no interest. Maybe he disagreed. Either way, this did not bode well for her efforts to bind them back together. The buggy driver made a sweeping turn onto Oak Street, which was filled with exclusive Victorian houses on setbacks with raised yards. The wide sidewalk and paved, tree-shaded street made for pleasant strolls around the neighborhood.

The driver pulled around their home and onto the long driveway leading to the carriage house. Edward's tepid reaction began to gnaw at her resolve.

"Well, I will be pursuing an appropriate response from the community, despite the fact that I can't obtain one from my own husband. I will expect your public support."

He looked into her eyes and exited the buggy without a word. Already plotting her next moves, she decided to keep the idea of a petition drive under her best Sunday hat.

Chapter Six

PETER PUSHED AWAY from the Sunday dinner table and followed his father, Chester, to the porch for a smoke and brandy. Meanwhile, his mother cleared and washed the dishes.

The setting sun, veiled somewhat by the hills around the Sawyer property, resisted the planet's vain attempts to blot it from the sky. Streams of light filtered through the trees, as father and son sipped their drinks and lit up, sending pungent clouds billowing into the twilight. Not an avid smoker, Peter enjoyed a fine cigar now and again, but his father preferred a nightly ritual with his pipe. He puffed away, gripping the letter in his left hand.

"Must be an important note, Father. Been toting it around since before we ate."

"Huh? Oh, this . . ." He passed the handwritten message to Peter and took another sip of his liquid refreshment. "Take a peek."

Peter recognized the writing after reading the salutation. "My dear friend (and boss), Chester . . ." Correspondence from Walter Mendelson always began with those words. Finding trustworthy people like Walter had contributed to his father's success early in life. The foreman of their thirty-acre Texas ranch had reported trouble with a commercial cattle contract and sought advice from his friend and employer.

"Father, how will you handle the pricing discrepancy?"

The wise businessman took a pull on his pipe, the smoke wafting out and up, dissipating into the night. "Well, son, let me turn your question on its heels. Pray tell, how would you solve the impasse?"

Peter responded without missing a beat. "Intervene directly. Take a visit down there. Travel is the downside of running a business so far from home. But sometimes we must be onsite to help solve difficult problems." His father had groomed him well.

"Let's not talk of cows and horses tonight. How are things at the store?"

"Fine, sir. The new hire, Frederick, is making significant progress. I'm increasing his responsibilities each week, and soon he should be ready to open on his own."

"Pleased to hear this, son." His father nodded and then stared at him. "What else is on your mind?"

The harmonizing click beetles and field crickets filled the night air with their own conversations, the sounds reverberating around the house.

"How do you do that, sir? I mean, read my thoughts."

Peter appreciated his father's valuable insights. In this case, he might have some ideas about how to talk with a woman who acted uninterested in a man's overtures. After all, the Sawyer marriage had flourished for almost thirty years. They still got along well, so his father must understand a thing or two about the art of courtship. Peter spoke about Anna Gaines, and upon mentioning the name, his father shared that he knew Joseph Gaines, also a member in the local Chamber of Commerce.

"Her father is a good man." Chester asked the obvious question. "Have you spoken to her about your affections?"

"Well . . . not exactly. Been thinking of that."

"Step number one, son. Tell her your feelings, and don't take forever or someone else will snatch her away. To your moment of truth. Hope the time comes soon." Raising their glasses, they clinked, emptied their last bit of brandy, and rose to join his mother in the parlor.

"Seems someone may have done so already. Late on the draw, as usual when it comes to women."

"A load of bosh, Peter. Many a young woman in town would welcome being swept off her feet by you. Who is this . . . someone?"

"Ironically, our hire at the lumberyard a few months ago. A man named Grover Biggs."

Several lines creased his father's forehead. "Oh . . . that muddies the circumstances. In more ways than one."

"Like the Tennessee River flood waters, sir. The man's a shady character, far as I can tell. A member of the Cycle Club, so we come into frequent contact with each other. Don't trust him or his intentions."

"Be careful, son. Never know what vermin has burrowed under a suspicious rock. Turn the stone over, and you're likely to find some deadly insects." He pulled on his pipe, casting a sidelong glance at Peter. "So . . . I intended to tell you before tonight, but now the opportunity is upon us. I've hired a private investigator out of Atlanta."

A silvery voice emerged from behind the screen door. "Some pie, anyone?" The smell of Peter's favorite dessert, his mother's award-winning apple pie, had already created a swirling flood in his mouth.

"Be right in, Abigail," Chester said. She turned back to the kitchen. "Best not to dawdle. No doubt, your mother makes the best apple pie in Hamilton County."

The revelation piqued Peter's curiosity. "For what purpose?" His father's face went blank. "The investigator, I mean."

"Ah, yes. Sorry, son. Distracted by that homemade pie in the kitchen. Mr. Seymour Leland, the proprietor of Seymour's Private Detective Agency. Best private detective in the business down in Atlanta." He relit his pipe and took several strong puffs. "Some strange financial dealings at the lumberyard and around town have caught my attention. Way too early to tell, but it may involve this Biggs fellow. For the next few weeks, I'll be spending time in Knoxville on business. While I'm gone, I would like you to manage progress of the investigation with Seymour."

Peter agreed out of duty, but he had some misgivings about running such an inquiry. For one, he had never done this before. He had confessed to his father that he didn't trust the man, even saw him as a troublemaker, but the idea of snooping behind Grover's back seemed disingenuous, plotting. That's the very behavior he abhorred in Grover. As he mulled his father's request further, he wondered if the task might yield some serendipitous opportunities for increased contact with Anna Gaines. The prospect piqued his interest, until a dangerous possibility jolted him from his reverie.

Panicked, he thought, *What if Leland's sleuthing does uncover a link to Grover Biggs? Such a connection might put Anna in harm's way.*

Chapter Seven

PAPA DROVE ANNA and Oscar to East Lake, where they boarded the trolley back to the city. At Irish Hill, they departed, Oscar to spend the night with a mutual friend in town, and Anna to walk the short distance on East Ninth Street to Mrs. Byrne's boarding house. Oscar would catch his train at Union Depot the next morning.

As she entered the house, the other boarders began gathering in the dining area for the Sunday night meal. "Good evening, Mrs. Byrne. Looks like my timing is perfect. May I say that you look splendid in your gown?"

The kind landlord, a regular among Chattanooga's social circles before her lifetime mate had passed away, always wore her best when serving the boarders. Mrs. Byrne good-naturedly called herself an "old throwback to an earlier time" when she and her husband attended balls, receptions, and private parties in the homes of Chattanooga's most prestigious families. These gatherings defined a social life for the well-connected upper-class citizens in the 1880s.

"Thank you, my dear," Mrs. Byrne said. "The seamstress who stitched together this lovely gown is gifted."

Custom-made Crépon skirts and full-length gowns, and other pre-made items on the rack, ready to buy in different sizes, were all the rage during the spring. The dress was of an elegant style for an older lady with gray hair and life's natural markings on her face, and Mrs. Byrne wore the garment with grace.

Acquainted with the unbreakable rules of high society, this daughter of Ireland carried not a pretentious bone in her body. Her spunky but humble way appealed to Anna the first time they met. And the day at Loveman's, when Mrs. Byrne stood by Anna's machine, directing as she finished the custom gown, stood out as a worthy memory.

Anna acknowledged the compliment. "Soon as I freshen up, I'll be down. Is Emma in?"

"Should still be upstairs in her room. Arrived home earlier today."

"Thank you." She climbed the staircase, tracing her fingers along the heavy, red oak bannister and the newel posts so prominent in Tennessee's Victorian-era homes. Anna appreciated the beautiful appointments adorning the interior of Mrs. Byrne's house, even if the décor had seemed a tad overwhelming at first.

"Say, Anna . . ." She stopped halfway up the stairs and turned her face toward the proprietress.

"Yes, Mrs. Byrne?"

"Did something happen to you?"

"Whatever do you mean?"

The woman smiled, her wise eyes squinting as she spoke. "For one of the first times since you came here, your eyes looked into mine the whole time we spoke. A lovely shade of blue, they are. Try not to hide them, dear."

Touched by Mrs. Byrne's kindness, Anna smiled gratefully. "I promise to try. Thank you."

"Good enough. If you do, I expect a gentleman caller or two will be coming around here soon."

Anna giggled nervously as Mrs. Byrne hurried back to the kitchen to oversee final preparations for the meal. A gentleman caller or two. She sighed, and hoped. There was the possibility of Grover, but who else?

She clambered up the remaining stairs to Emma's room, knocked, and opened the door. Beads in hand, Emma prayed the Rosary as Anna barged into the narrow quarters. "Oops . . . sorry, Emma."

She hushed until Emma finished, and when she had, she popped up from her bed and gave Anna a squeeze. "Let me look at ya. Beautiful from top to bottom, the curves in all the right places."

Interesting how some women viewed another woman's physical appearance in higher regard than her own. Anna would trade her plain face and shapeless body for Emma's uniquely attractive looks any day, starting with her green eyes and fair skin with pink undertones. At twenty-two and of medium stature, Emma was a fun-loving bundle of unending energy. As an orator, Emma was captivating, a commanding presence who spoke with insight. How Anna wished that she, too, could capture people's attention in large crowds or private conversations.

"How are you, Em? I've missed you so."

"Grand. Gráim thú."

"I love you, too." Emma had taught her several Irish endearments and leaned heavily on the natural lilt when Anna requested to hear it. She loved the smoky, folksy tone.

Emma's spontaneous outlook on life always kept Anna on her toes. In her company, Anna laughed often, medicine for her soul, and she almost always learned something new. They had met two years ago at Saint Peter and Paul Catholic Church where Emma attended, but they had grown close in the last six months when they both moved into the boarding house.

"Now come sit and tell me all about your time with Harriet." Anna carefully placed a stool beneath her hooped skirt and sat by Emma's bed.

Anna shared the week's events, capped by Oscar's surprise visit with the new wheel, and her parents' final decision to allow her to ride at the farm on weekends. "Aunt Harriet shocked and surprised me with such a generous gift."

"What a wonderful turn of events. That reminds me." Emma jumped from the bed and went to the closet, where she pulled out a bulky package. "Before Oscar cycled to the farmhouse, he stopped here to drop this off. Another present from your aunt."

Anna opened the attached envelope and read the short note: *Better for you to open this in your room at Mrs. Byrne's house.*

Fingers shaking with excitement, Anna removed the strings circling the parcel and tore the paper away to discover its contents. Amused, she lifted the lid and peered inside. First, she withdrew an unusual item—trousers made of rich dark velvet, cut full with elastic hems at the bottoms of the short pant legs.

"Pants? An odd gift. Leave it to Aunt Harriet." Next she withdrew some leggings from the box.

Emma brought one hand to her mouth, gasping with surprise. Next came the matching double-breasted coat, and a new pair of leather riding boots—all sized to fit Anna's frame. Late on the take, the obvious finally struck Anna like a swipe from a lion's heavy paw. The shock left her speechless at first.

"Oh . . . oh . . . oh my goodness."

"You know what those are, right?"

"Women's bloomers! Harriet would cause me to be tarred and feathered if I ever wore this in public. The first bucket of tar would be dumped by my own mama."

Emma blurted out her response. "Ha!" Her trademark funny snort and deep laugh followed. "Put the outfit on, right this minute."

"I can't . . ."

"Yes, you can." Emma sprang to her feet to help Anna undress.

"Do I dare to—?"

"Yes, you dare." Off came the bodice and her bell-shaped skirt.

First she tugged the leggings up. With a mischievous snigger, she slipped her left leg through the baggy trousers and then the right. The moment of truth: She hesitated, and in one motion pulled up the bloomers. A perfect fit. What a strange sensation to wear clothing that covered only half of her legs. Emma searched the closet and found a matching blouse for the outfit. The tailored double-breasted jacket of brown wool with black braid trim at the collar and hem tied everything together.

The first female cyclist from Chattanooga was crowned with the final touch—a straw hat, the perfect finish for a progressive yet stylish ensemble. A shudder of excitement vibrated through Anna's body like years ago when she had flirted on the edges of naughtiness with her brothers.

"Ha!"

Anna put her finger to her lips. "Quiet. We're making a racket. How do I look?" Dressed like a new woman, she turned full circle.

"Modern. Smashing!"

A light knock on the door shook them from their glee. Mrs. Byrne called out. "May I enter?"

Anna panicked. "Quick. Help me take this off."

❧❖☙

On his way to the clubhouse, Peter thought about how he would handle tonight's agenda. Upon considerable reflection, he had decided to ask Quincy Goodenough to deliver the club's official response to the first reading of the Chattanooga City Council's proposed bicycle ordinance, just a few days away. An ally, Quincy spoke well in public and could be trusted to advance the club's best interests.

The wheelmen would deliver their position in simple terms: The riders opposed speed limits on city streets. Otherwise, the mayor and nine aldermen might be emboldened to pass other restrictions without public input.

The second piece of business would take more time and require greater skill in meeting management: form committees to plan the club's first annual Labor Day Bicycle Races to be held on September 2 at the Chattanooga Driving Club on McCallie Avenue.

Peter pulled his wheel up to the building on Seventh Street, where the Young Men's Business League also met, and went into the offices for the meeting. First, he brought the regular Tuesday night meeting to order and then requested approval of the minutes from last month's meeting. Approved and seconded. Any chance the rest of this session might proceed as smoothly? Not likely.

He had expected storm clouds to gather, waiting to rain chaos on the proceedings. Grover Biggs sat front and center, looking smug and frightfully superior. But looks were deceiving, as Peter found him to be insecure, even though he projected confidence.

On both sides of him, in chairs forming a loose circle, sat his closest allies. All of them had barely passed twenty years of age and had proved themselves to be excellent cyclists. There was a smattering of older club members, eager to move the meeting along so they could get home after a long workday. By unanimous decision, they had elected him club president in the fall because they respected his leadership qualities.

The clock on the wall indicated the time: 7 p.m.

Peter took up the ordinance, suggesting that a common-sense argument might appease both sides. The club would offer a new service designed to lessen the number of collisions between cyclists and pedestrians. The restrictions and fines would be unnecessary.

"Those of us who ride a wheel in Chattanooga are aware of the real problem: pedestrian confusion when confronted with an oncoming wheelman," he said.

"Right," Grover said. "This organization needs to stand united and dig our heels in. We need to come out swinging next week, or next thing we'll see are rules on where we can ride. Maybe even support for women riding in unacceptable garments."

A warning shot across the bow. Grover Biggs from Atlanta held his cards close to the vest, but perhaps now he intended to tip his hand. Peter proceeded warily. Nothing good came from Grover's proposals.

"May I continue?" Peter asked.

Everyone nodded, so Peter returned to the discussion at hand. "The pedestrians freeze, accounting for most collisions. Perhaps we can propose seminars, taught by club members, on how to safely share the city streets. Also, a pledge to avoid speeding might go a long way to appease the lawmakers."

The concept gained approval. Now a wheelman must be selected to speak at the council meeting. He surveyed the room, but before he could voice a suggestion, Jackson McHenry rose to address the group. "Best one to speak on our behalf is you, Peter."

The other men clamored for him to accept. "Hear, hear! Peter Sawyer."

Several others shouted out. "Agreed."

"Sawyer speaks."

Peter viewed himself as a peacekeeper, an attribute he inherited from his father. He sought agreeable middle ground between people or groups at odds with each other. Such a temperament would be necessary to win votes, but he would rather that someone else make the case.

McHenry carried on. "Peter, you're well-spoken when you need to be. The club members, many with at least some gray hair like me, elected a young whippersnapper like you for many reasons, not the least of which are your oratory skills."

Another man jumped up. "Look at you. A living advertisement for the modern-day cyclist. Young, lean, and muscular, and . . ."

McHenry chimed in. "Aw, sit down, Jackson McSwain, ya carrot top. Sounds like you're getting sweet on Mr. Sawyer here." The men guffawed.

No bowing out now. For the sake of the club, and against his better judgment, he accepted. A fierce competitor and an accomplished amateur racer, Peter would promote the sport he loved. But the quick and insistent clamor for him to speak seemed orchestrated, insincere. Something didn't ring true about their endorsements. Maybe because they came from Grover's cronies. Even though he didn't much like the man, a tinge of guilt surfaced when he glanced at Grover, knowing that now, at his father's request, he must oversee an investigation into the man's doings. It made him feel ungentlemanly . . . until he considered Anna's involvement.

He prided himself on running an efficient meeting. "Let's move on. Time to begin planning our role in the Labor Day festivities."

An influential association managed all aspects of the celebration—the grand procession of floats, bands, marching groups, and a picnic at East Lake. The bike races scheduled for the afternoon required the club's careful coordination, as riders from several nearby cities, and even the states that shared a border with Tennessee, would be invited to participate. The committee chairs needed to be appointed to organize the contests and plan the wheelmen's parade.

"All due respect."

He expected the interruption. Peter scanned the attendees, his eyes stopping at Grover. *Here we go.*

"Mr. Biggs?"

Grover stood to address the members. A forceful speaker, he had gathered a following soon after joining the group. The men found him gregarious and fun. Peter thought him deceitful—a double-dealer who took both sides of an issue to achieve his own designs.

"Before we begin with our Labor Day business, an important topic related to the council meeting on July 2 must be discussed."

"Please, Mr. Biggs—enlighten us," Peter said.

Rather, quit your sneaky, backstabbing ways.

Many of them had quietly signed a petition asking the aldermen to outlaw women from riding within the city limits. Peter had prepared for the other shoe to drop at this meeting, thanks to a warning from a confidante. Nobody had asked him to put his name to paper, nor did he believe such a sweeping measure would pass. As a fallback, the appeal demanded stiff penalties for women wearing bloomers in public.

No surprise to find Grover pushing the effort behind the scenes. The two men stood at odds with each other on most matters. Grover cleared his throat and scanned the cluster of wheelmen seated around him, men taken in by his charisma.

"Thank you. In my hand is a petition signed by many of our members. Let the record show that I move we submit these names to the City Council on Tuesday night. Most of us are supporting the movement to block females from taking to the wheel."

One of Grover's cronies jumped up. "Seconded."

Wary of dragging the club into a community controversy, Peter nonetheless followed meeting protocol. "Any discussion?"

The men bantered about the downside of allowing scantily clad women on bicycles.

Patrick Johnston, twenty-four, married and expecting his first child at any time, rose to make a point. "Wheeling, a man's sport, threatens to spawn this . . . this new breed of woman, what the papers are calling . . ."

"The new woman," someone blurted out. "Like that limper, what's her name . . .?"

"Anna Gaines," Patrick said. "Been riding out near Chickamauga, I hear."

The news hit Peter like a blow to the stomach. The furor about women wheelers seemed so out of context for Chattanooga. Now, to hear that Anna played some role in all this sounded almost preposterous. It didn't square with the shy individual he admired from afar. The mystery intrigued him, made him want to spend time with her even more. Too bad Grover Biggs complicated things.

"Right you are," Grover said. "Anna Gaines—Chattanooga's own new woman. Beware that cycling doesn't bring this new kind into our beds, with their wild ideas about taking different roles outside our homes. Believe me, the Northern men know of what I speak."

Another shouted out. "What about just being a wife and mother? Honorable duties, but I guess not important enough for them."

Peter allowed the interchange to continue, but Grover's conniving expression annoyed him. Whenever any discord surfaced in the club, this outsider seemed to relish stirring the pot. Grover fueled the discussion further.

"This so-called new woman believes herself to be the equal of a man, and she's using the wheel to make her point. Stop this movement or our city will soon become a hotbed for suffrage and a breeding ground for social decay. When that happens, you truly won't recognize the lady in your bed."

The hair on the back of Peter's neck bristled when the Atlanta man called Chattanooga "our city." The noise in the room became disruptive, so Peter called the meeting back to order. The idea for putting Grover in his rightful place came to him out of thin air.

"Am I to take from your comments that you suspect Miss Gaines' motivation for wheeling is to become like a man?"

Laughs bubbled up from several men. Unruffled, Grover stepped up to take the challenge. "Let me say this: I believe she is misguided about her role."

Filled with growing anger, Peter delivered an unexpected blow to his adversary. "Are you not pursuing a relationship with Miss Gaines? To court a woman who is confused about her femininity would be unlike you, Mr. Biggs."

A momentary hush fell over the room. The liaison between Anna and Grover had distressed Peter the moment he learned of Grover's interest. This ravening wolf in sheep's clothing would devour Anna in all her innocence. Even if nothing came of Peter's hoped-for friendship with her, he would dig to the bottom of Grover Biggs' machinations. He struck again, a right hook to follow his jab.

"Appears you are working against her interests at the same time you're cozying up to her."

The challenger stumbled. "Well, I want to help her see the folly . . . that is to say, the . . ."

Peter delivered a knockout punch. "I'm not sure what you're trying to accomplish here, Mr. Biggs. Perhaps Miss Gaines simply seeks the same pleasures from the wheel that you and I, and dare I say, everyone in this room, are free to enjoy."

After several more minutes of continued debate, the majority of members voted to submit their signatures at the council meeting and stand in favor of the restrictions. The more vocal attendees, again led by Grover Biggs, made an additional proposal—that the Cycle Club join a company of young men in Edmeston, Connecticut who had formed an anti-bloomer association. The secretary read their vow into the record:

I hereby agree to refrain from associating with all ladies who adopt the bloomer cycling costume and pledge myself to the use of all honorable means to render such costumes unpopular in the community where I reside.

Although Grover won the battle, Peter adeptly tabled that skirmish for another meeting. The momentum against women cyclists gained steam, and Anna would be the center of interest.

Chapter Eight

MIDWAY INTO THE morning, Anna gazed over at Cora Rosenfeld, an old acquaintance from the Jewish community and a new seamstress hired at the end of the previous week. What had thrown the woman so far behind in her production?

The seamstresses worked all morning on stitching together cloaks for multiple occasions, of all styles and materials, in an effort to build Loveman's ready-to-buy stock for the fall. Called away for a management gathering, Mr. Helms left them with instructions on meeting their quotas. Cora appeared frustrated and worried, floundering at her machine, so Anna rose from her station and moved three spots down to help.

Emma cautioned her. "Be careful. Our Mr. Helms is a disagreeable sort. You don't want him catching you away from your station."

Anna tutored Cora, whose skills at finishing had never been tested in a high-end shop like Loveman's. She spent more than an hour helping the frightened woman to recover before returning to her own station. Now her output lagged. As she worked feverishly to catch up, Mr. Helms returned to the floor. It took him only a moment to realize that Anna had not kept pace with the production schedule.

More than a job stood between her and the domineering supervisor. Her newfound independence hung in the balance, along with her growing self-assurance. Failure, and having to tell her parents she had been fired, scared her. Her heart hammered against her ribs like a sledge pounding away at a pile of rocks. Resigned to being dismissed, Anna waited for his recrimination.

"Miss Gaines, you are behind in your work. I cannot allow such a lapse in our operation. Please explain yourself."

Flushed, she tried to speak, averting her eyes from the bully. "Mr. Helms, I . . . I . . ."

"Yes, Miss Gaines? Speak up."

She attempted again to center herself. "No excuses, but—"

"But you can't articulate a legitimate reason for your unacceptable performance. Therefore, I must let you go. Please make your way to the front office with me, and I will arrange for any wages due to you."

All of Anna's internal thumping stopped.

Emma rose from her seat. "Beg your pardon, Mr. Helms. If you're about firin' someone today, it surely will be me."

The man eyes flared as he walked over. A tall, lumbering man, he towered over her smaller frame by several inches, intent on using his size and proximity to intimidate her. The Emma that Anna admired, no shrinking violet in defending herself, stood her ground against the autocrat. Still, Mr. Helms held all the power.

"You are a rabble-rouser with crazy ideas. Between you and Miss Gaines being absent over the last couple of weeks, the output in this shop suffered. But go ahead, Miss Kelly. I'm listening."

"I'm the one failing to meet quota. Family troubles are robbing my concentration, so I left my station. Anna tried to keep my production up, and that caused her output to fall."

Emma winked at Anna, who shook at the encounter. She turned toward Cora. Would she say something to make this right? The woman appeared speechless like her, unwilling to correct the record. For the first time in her life, Anna faced circumstances where one man held total power over whether another person ate or went hungry. Mr. Helms scrutinized Emma.

"I'm skeptical, Miss Kelly, and suspect a ruse. I'll accept your resignation. Follow me to the administrative offices."

Emma gathered her personal effects and waited for the supervisor. Anna stood and moved toward him, trying to formulate a response, but the appropriate words wouldn't come, only feeble utterances. "Please, Mr. Helms . . . don't fire your best seamstress. She . . ."

He moved to within inches of her face, causing her to look slightly away. That was enough to silence her. The man's imposing figure, his heavy exhales tainted with the disturbing combination of cigarette smoke and mouthwash, invaded her nose, nauseating her. He reminded her of an enraged bull preparing to charge. This kind of suppression, men discounting women because . . . well, they could . . . vexed her, yet she still could not face him, eye to eye, and that made her angry. About to slither away back to her station like a frightened snake, Anna opened her mouth, and the words ringing in her own ears shocked and amazed her.

"Do not think your cowardly actions will remain unnoticed forever, Mr. Helms."

He took a step back, his face turning two shades of pale. Then he stiffened and seemed to regain his resolve.

"Perhaps you underestimate my willingness to fire you, like your friend. I let her stay this long because of her work ethic, but today that slipped, and we cannot afford delays. Don't test me again. Do you understand?"

"Ye-es, Mr. Helms."

"Take your station, Miss Gaines. I will be monitoring production, and you may be the next to go. Other fine seamstresses would jump at the opportunity to be employed in a prestigious store like this one. So, I suggest you keep a quiet profile befitting a Southern lady and finish your work in a timely fashion."

The whirring of her machine joined the mechanical chatter all around her. The slave driver had cracked his whip, but the sting of his lash was not as strong.

Chapter Nine

THURSDAY NIGHT, JUNE 27, once an eternity away, finally arrived. Upon finishing work, Anna rushed to Mrs. Byrne's boarding house. A potential disaster had been averted when Emma took a new job at the pants factory two days after Helms fired her.

"Watch your back," she had cautioned Anna, "lest he do the same with you, his best seamstress."

Somehow, the fear of losing a job, something that would have mortified Anna months ago, barely concerned her now. The acrimonious Supervisor Helms no longer scared her.

As Anna opened the front door, out of breath from her hurried pace, she found Emma waiting for her arrival. The two women hugged and giggled like schoolgirls. Long ago, in her youthful exuberance, she would have bounded up the steps, two at a time. But now she climbed up deliberately, her hand in Emma's, and made a joke.

"Hurry, we're behind schedule."

The hands on the grandfather clock in the hallway outside her room read seven o'clock. Emma took a seat on the bed as Anna unwrapped the new outfit she had purchased for this special occasion. Grover would be calling soon, and with Emma as a chaperone, they would walk to Tschopik's ice cream parlor. She held up each piece for Emma to evaluate.

"A silk crépon skirt—very fashionable," Emma said.

"This bodice is snug. Makes my shape appear like the women in those new advertisements. The drawings with no facial features and those thin bodies. The new woman."

She laid both pieces on the mattress. "Well?"

"Hmm." Without further comment, Emma continued to assess the clothing but offered no opinions.

"What do you think, Emma?"

"Not sure."

The serious expression and lack of comments worried her. Did she choose the wrong colors? The style must be wrong. On second thought, this might be a jest, a grab from Emma's bag of tricks. If so, she disguised the ruse well.

"Now you're scaring me, Emma."

Unable to continue the pretense, Emma's thin lips curved into a smile. Then she caved in. "This man Grover is a fool if he doesn't fall in love with you, right at Tschopik's. Come on; let's dress you. Afterwards, we can work on putting me together. That'll take a lot longer because I got less to work with."

"Oh, Emma, shush now. You're as fine as can be." Like a thief in the night, the self-doubt that plagued Anna tried to steal the excitement of the moment. "What if he doesn't like me?"

"He'd have to be a walking dead man. It will be impossible for him not to worship the ground you walk upon."

What would she do without Emma?

When Anna finished dressing, she waited downstairs for her friend to put the finishing touches to her outfit. One of the boarders played an uplifting tune on Mrs. Byrne's parlor piano. The jaunty bass notes and ragged rhythms brightened her mood and reminded her of the marches made famous by John Philip Sousa. As she waited for Grover's arrival, the music swept her back to last April when Papa had purchased tickets for the family to see Sousa and his fifty-man band of musicians at the new opera house where she first met Grover.

Sousa's concert performance sent her marching down imaginary streets that night, even as she sat spellbound, glued to the seat. Her magical conductor's baton waved high above her head, beckoning the tubas and trombones, and clarinets and trumpets to follow. All manner of other wind instruments, violins, and drums, all without players, marched behind them in her mind's eye.

The intermission brought destiny swirling into the lobby, where she bumped into Grover Biggs by accident. The stranger turned around, smiting Anna with his boyish good looks. He stood several inches taller than her.

"So sorry," she said, averting her eyes.

"No damage done."

She looked up in time to catch him staring. This time her eyes stayed fixed on his, a stunning hazel color set against a healthy crop of sandy-colored hair. She struggled to think of something to say. Words escaped her.

"Well . . ." She fidgeted.

He probed. "Your name?"

Her heart seized, and her mouth became dry. "Anna . . . Anna Gaines." Did she sound too anxious?

"How do you do? Grover Biggs is my name. New in town from Atlanta. Do you like Sousa's music? I bet you would like a new style the Negroes are playing. It's called ragtime. Much like Sousa's work, but with different rhythms. Are you familiar with the sound?"

What was happening? A handsome man talked to her; more so, he acted friendly, even a little interested. Caught by surprise, she measured every word she might say. What if she said something stupid? Precious moments passed with no reply.

The interlude concluded, and the call went out for everyone to be seated. As their eyes met again, Anna became distraught. The moment might be lost forever. Somehow, she needed to give this man some indication of her interest. There she stood, helpless, desperate not to appear woebegone as they parted. She had dreamed about a special moment like this, when a fine-looking, intelligent gentleman made her feel like a princess just by the way he gazed at her. And now, her dream began to dissipate, like a stream of smoke from her papa's pipe.

He blurted out, "Where can I find you?"

Providence shined down on her. "I work as a seamstress at Loveman's."

The pleasant memory lifted as the keyboard player at Mrs. Byrne's house completed his ragtime tune to the delight and applause of the other residents.

Since that day, Grover had shown up at Loveman's several times after work to walk her home, enchanting her with stories of baseball and horse racing, his involvement in the Chattanooga Cycle Club, and music. No talk of family or employment, other than to say he took a job at the Sawyer lumber mill on the river below the foot of Market Street. The private part of his life remained just that—private. A mystery.

Eventually, he had asked her father for permission to call on Anna, with an escort. Several days had passed since she last spoke to him, causing her to imagine the worst. Would he forget about tonight? He was fifteen minutes late. A knock at the door caused her heart to skip a beat. She stood tall, took a deep breath, and answered.

"Grover. Hi . . ."

"Sorry. Big gathering with all the bicycle riders." A bit snippy, he walked right in.

"Oh . . .?"

He pulled out his timepiece, offering no details about the assembly. "Where is our chaperone?"

Was he in a hurry to get this over with? "Be right down, I'm sure. Did anything of interest happen?"

"Regarding what?" He looked up the stairs, his right foot tapping the floor. He appeared nervous, distracted.

"The cycling group."

"Naw. Just planning for Labor Day and such." A thumb and finger pulled on his right earlobe. "A real bore."

Chapter Ten

SOMETHING WAS WRONG—VERY wrong.

The infectious smile that melted her when they met never appeared on Grover's face. He didn't bother to comment on her dress or how she looked. The silence during their walk to Tschopik's spoke volumes. Maybe his initial interest in her had waned over the last couple of weeks, or he found someone else and showed up tonight out of obligation. Did her limp embarrass him?

Emma had been following behind them, allowing them the chance to converse without someone else listening in. But now she wished Grover would trade places so she could ask Emma what was wrong.

Desperate for some interaction, she blurted out the first thing that came to mind. "I purchased this skirt for our time together. Do you like the style?"

He took a quick glance. "Yeah. Sure thing."

Approaching the ice cream parlor, a scaled-down version of Tschopik's original garden setting on Market Street, she reminisced about the old store, which had burned down in a devastating fire a few years back. At least once a year, her father brought his young family to savor Adolph

Tschopik's two delicacies—ice cream and cake. She recalled the wide steps leading patrons from the creamery to the garden area of the old store where she would rush to the goldfish ponds to watch them swim in their underwater domain. Meanwhile, her parents would tour the exquisite gardens or sit near the open-air stage to view the latest show or benefit. This never-to-be-forgotten place now existed only in her childhood. Tschopik never rebuilt on the same parcel, but she rejoiced when he opened this limited operation on West Ninth.

They sat upon arriving. Emma took a seat far enough away to grant the couple some privacy but close enough to maintain visual contact. Mr. Tschopik approached Anna to greet her. "My dearest Anna. I have missed you since your last visit. How is your family?"

She rose to hug him. "All are well, sir. Thank you. Papa and the boys are finishing up the wheat harvest. Soon we'll be picking our summer fruits."

"Wonderful. Give them my best." He turned his attention to Grover. "This is . . .?"

"Oh, I'm sorry. Meet my friend, Mr. Grover Biggs from Atlanta. He has taken temporary residence here in Chattanooga."

The proprietor offered his hand. "Mr. Biggs, you are most welcome here. A friend of Anna's is a friend of mine."

"Thanks," Grover said. A half-hearted response.

Tschopik turned back to her, a twinkle in his eyes. "Shall I bring you our specialty—ladyfinger cakes? They are . . ."

She joined in to complete the familiar description. "Baked today and very fashionable."

He chuckled. "Correct. Served with ice cream?"

"Of course," Anna said. "Thank you, Mr. Tschopik."

He reviewed the three flavors Tutti-frutti—his newest and most exquisite. Vanilla—the true favorite of his patrons. And the third one, maple. He claimed this flavor, featuring the syrup of Tennessee maple trees, could be found nowhere else in town. She mulled the choices.

"Let's see—I'll try the maple."

He turned to Grover. "For you, sir . . .?"

"Same." Again, he dispensed without any cordiality toward the owner. Tschopik winked at her.

"Coming right up."

Grover's mood had turned tetchy, but Anna couldn't figure out why. Did she anger him in some way? Without warning, he moved his chair closer to her and said, "Maybe it's not my place to say, so forgive me. But I'm concerned about all the attention you're drawing to yourself."

"Attention? What do you mean?"

He tugged his ear. "No less than half a dozen times in the last two days, I defended your character. People about town are talking about the woman who cycles, and I'm tired of trying to quiet them."

He had hit a nerve. The underlying message came through loud and clear: She must understand her place. A deepening relationship would require her to recant any interest in the wheel. She struggled to respond.

"People are talking? Who . . . where?"

"Are you blind to what's going on around you?"

"I thought . . ."

"Churches and business clubs. Social organizations. And much more. Petitions are being circulated to ask the City Council to ban women from cycling. You're bringing a nasty firestorm on yourself, Anna. The result won't be worth the heartache, I can promise you. What are you trying to prove, anyway?"

She averted her eyes as they began to well up. "I have nothing to prove outside of my need to . . ."

He remained silent, staring at her.

Intimidated, she couldn't stay focused on his face, but she wanted him to understand. As he stared, she pondered how misguided she had been. First Mama, and now Grover stood against her cycling. She had trusted Emma and Papa, their encouragements, but they must be wrong. After all, women were created to be wives and mothers first, to handle the domestic chores of the household. Matters of the community, politics, work, and sports had always belonged to men. The natural order should not be confused, least of all by her. She softened to his advice.

"Don't take to cycling to prove a point. Soon you'll be working on behalf of suffrage and promoting women's careers. Those things won't bring you happiness, Anna."

She nodded in agreement although, deep inside, those causes had called out for her to become involved.

"How about focusing on getting married and having babies?" he said. "Wouldn't such an honorable calling fulfill you?"

She took solace at Emma's presence as the cake and ice cream orders arrived. The confections saved her from having to answer his question. Was he telling her of his desire to settle into that kind of life, perhaps with someone like her?

Confused, she ate a couple of small bites in silence, reflecting on his words. She wavered because she wanted both. She longed for the day she would fall in love and be cherished. Other men of integrity like her papa, devoted to wife and family, must exist. Might Grover Biggs be such a man? He had shown her attention and treated her kindly, at least prior to tonight. For the first time in her adult life, she had begun to picture herself as an attractive woman.

"I appreciate your honesty, and I will strongly consider your advice. I enjoy riding the wheel, but maybe you're right."

The time at Tschopik's left her more in the dark about Grover and how to proceed.

⚜

As they walked toward the boarding house, Emma in tow, Grover's mood became more cheery, and the conversation was light and easy. She mentioned the opening of Charles H. Yale's newest production of *Devil's Auction* set for next Thursday evening at the opera house. Perhaps he would invite her to accompany him to what promised to be a sold-out performance.

He ignored the hint.

Anna and Emma sat on the bed, talking late into the evening—about Grover, their lives in Chattanooga, and the dawning of the twentieth century.

Walking over to the wall mirror, Anna unpinned her hair and began brushing it out. Two candles continued to burn, becoming more deformed with each drip and collecting at the bottom to take on a new and different shape. One candle sat at the side of the bed, casting a faint light against the side of Emma's face; the other rested on the small dresser below the mirror.

Anna stopped her bedtime ritual and locked eyes with Emma through the looking glass. "When you're famous—and you will become a woman who makes her mark on the world like Susan B. Anthony—remember your old friend." She shifted her gaze to her own reflection. "Anna, the forlorn spinster of Chattanooga."

Emma rose, took the brush, and ran strokes through her hair. She stopped, and they stared at each other through the mirror.

"To borrow the word, you'll be spinning all right, but it won't be the thread of an old maid," Emma said. "Many adoring grandchildren will sit at your feet while you spin tales of princesses and handsome dragon-slayers who live in faraway kingdoms and who fall in love. And your experience as a teacher will captivate them and build in them a love of learning."

Emma's optimism challenged her.

"I hope you're right."

"You're thinking of giving up cycling to satisfy Grover Biggs, aren't you?"

Anna faced her friend. "I don't know. Maybe it's time to grow up, to think about my future. Otherwise, I may never have all those grandchildren hanging on my every word."

She lowered herself to the floor, her back against the chest of drawers. Emma joined her, both of them gazing at the opposite wall. Anna pictured a waterfall surrounded by lush bushes and tall trees in the distance. For an instant, there she stood in the warm embrace of her faceless knight, his white steed beside him.

"How will I know when I find the right one?" Anna asked.

Her friend shrugged her shoulders. "Can't answer from experience. One thing's certain. You're hardly a spinster at nineteen."

"Why do I feel like one?"

"What about that young grocer, the one who attends your church here in town?"

"Peter Sawyer?"

It seemed like Emma already had Peter in mind given how fast she volunteered him as a possibility. Her past interactions with him had been pleasant enough, but he would surely hold the opinion that cycling was out of bounds for women. After all, she understood him to be the Cycling Club president. Having just learned of Grover's strong disapproval, neither man would be supportive of her newfound hobby.

"The grocer comes from top-quality stock." It took a moment, but they laughed at Emma's double entendre. "That is to say, Peter comes from a well-to-do family, one with means. Perhaps more important, character. So I'm told."

"True . . . and I've seen him working at the grocery," Anna said. "He's wonderful with customers. Seems kind and courteous and treats women with respect." One last meditation brought her to the same conclusion about Peter, at least for now.

"And so?" Emma seemed set on the match.

"Likable, even a catch, but not my type." She needed someone like Grover, whose presence coaxed her from her protective cocoon like Emma and Harriet did.

Emma hugged her. "Best we get some sleep then."

"Rest well."

Tomorrow promised to be a long day. She would attend the council meeting with Emma, but she tilted toward giving up the wheel. The disruption to the community—to her life and family—came with too high a price for a few fleeting moments of freedom. She prayed her friendship with Grover would develop into something deeper. A courtship with him might be worth the sacrifice.

Anna climbed into bed, exhausted. The evening brought little relief from the heat of the day, but she pulled her blankets up to her chest. The weight of the covers gave her a measure of security. She checked the bedside clock. Twenty minutes later, still staring at the ceiling and now overheated, she kicked the covers off. The air hung heavy as the open window brought no circulation into the room. She tossed and turned for over an hour before sleep arrested her, but her slumber turned fitful.

A distant rooster crowed its welcome to the new morning. She lurched forward and shuddered. The dark shadows in her life and the darkness in her room gave her pause.

Chapter Eleven

ON SATURDAY, TWO weeks after Anna had experienced another world on the Coney Island Cycle Path, she finished her work at Loveman's and caught an electric trolley to East Lake where her father waited. She carried her riding dress in a bag along with a few items needed for the overnight visit.

The tumultuous events at Loveman's had resolved themselves, for the most part. Emma had found new employment at the pants factory near Irish Hill two days after her dismissal, thanks to an inside contact who also attended Saints Peter and Paul Catholic Church. Hawkeye Helms, her boss's new nickname, continued to monitor her closely. To his frustration, which he didn't attempt to hide, Hawkeye discovered no fault in her work.

After church on Sunday, Mama and Papa rode east toward Ringgold to visit friends. Anna said her goodbyes and dashed into her old bedroom to put on her cycling dress. When she emerged and headed for the front door, her brother Harry commented on the outfit.

"Wow. I assume Mama and Papa approve."

"Oh, they've seen this." What would they say about the bloomers?

"I hope you're not inviting trouble on yourself—and on us."

Trouble? Anna sensed a fracas waited around the corner, but she didn't respond. The excitement of the ride trumped any misgivings she had. "Remember, you agreed to drive me back to the trolley station later."

She hurried to the barn, mounted her bicycle, and rode—energized as the spinning wheels carried her at speeds faster than ever before until she became giddy and steadied herself at a slower pace. How could anyone use supercharged words like *scandalous, indecent, reckless, uninspiring*, and *unhealthy* to discourage women from experiencing this independence? Cycling intoxicated her, but in a positive way.

The wheel turned into her freedom machine—her metal steed. She rode on, lost in her own world, before she realized her location—several miles up the McFarland Gap Road, almost to East Lake. Several travelers began to pass her along the way. Some were amused by the novelty of a woman astride a wheel. Others, appalled at her indiscretion, made deriding comments. She overheard some of the disapproving words meant for the inner sanctum of their carriages, but she didn't care.

Throwing discretion to the wind and disregarding the promise that she would only cycle around the farm, she pedaled farther along the base of Missionary Ridge, heading north on Dobbs. More than six miles on the bicycle and she did not grow weary. Well into the eastern parts of the city, she approached a church that had finished its last service and the congregants were wandering out the front door, intermingling.

As she passed, they all stopped talking and stared at the female cyclist. The word was getting around, and Grover would be quite disappointed in her.

Chapter Twelve

BERTHA MILLWOOD COUNTED herself among the original founders of the Kosmos Club.

Because she was a charter member surrounded by other women of exceptional abilities, Bertha's influence carried weight. They met in homes during the first years, but the collection of Chattanooga's most cultured grew in numbers and began gathering in various temporary locations including the room at Miller Brothers, the ballroom of the Read House, parlors of the Unitarian Church, and even the courthouse. These walls told stories about the Kosmos Club. The club soon invested in a permanent home at 900 Oak Street, about a block away from the Millwood residence.

For Bertha, meeting days included a pleasant stroll through Fort Wood. She rehearsed her talk as she walked to the gathering scheduled for Monday night, emboldened by the signatures obtained on several copies of the petition. If all went according to plan, she would present the documents and make an impassioned, clarion appeal to the City Council the next night.

The crusade fit well with the club's mission to examine the civic and moral concerns of the day. Ladies on bicycles, exhibitionists clad in shameful clothing, must be stopped in their tracks. The club would create the spark to ignite the flames of public indignation. A worthy cause might help Bertha to vanquish her own depression. Even if half the members circulated a copy of her call to arms through churches, social gatherings, and extended families, the mayor and Chattanooga Board of Aldermen would be compelled to take civic action.

The dominoes were falling in place just as she had planned. The plan included gaining the support of men's groups like the Cycle Club, the Chamber of Commerce, and the recently organized Young Men's Business League. One of her best allies enjoyed a strong voice among the wheelmen. But swaying these women to follow her would ensure that the message would spread like a wildfire. Taking on the responsibility for protecting the moral compass of her beloved city had fallen on her shoulders. Why?

Only God knew, but she rose to the challenge like Moses on Mount Sinai.

As she walked the pathway to the Kosmos front door, the face of her daughter flashed before her. She stopped halfway up, choking back the emotional pain that sought release. How she missed Constance, her first and only child, struck down at twenty years old. Why did she leave with that stranger? She had professed her love for him, a wild man she really didn't know. Bertha had tried to save her from the foolishness that resulted in her death. Edward, despondent over the loss of his daughter, quit communicating after the initial shock.

After taking several deep breaths, she pushed the ghost of Constance from her mind and put on her real face, that of the self-assured socialite. With her best smile, her head held high, and the gait of a refined lady, she engaged in polite greetings as she entered the home the club had purchased and made her way to the parlor.

As she took a seat, careful to arrange her hooped skirt, the moderator called the meeting to order. They worked through some items left from their last gathering, after which Bertha answered the call to address the group.

"Thank you for allowing me the fifteen minutes allocated for current events before we proceed with our program for the day. I so enjoy our studies of modern and medieval history, art, and science. This strengthens our community and each of us as individuals."

The audience nodded its agreement, and she became emboldened by their positive response. "Events beyond immediate control sometimes beckon us to discuss pressing issues, and unfortunately, this is one of those times."

Another one of her staunch supporters stood unannounced. Unable to contain herself, she blurted out the issue before them. "A female cyclist is riding the outskirts of Chattanooga. Every woman here must raise her voice before a trend develops. Before our daughters are all cycling in bloomers."

The tactless interruption elicited whispered conversations among the women. Delicate matters like this required discretion to avoid catching certain members off-guard. Bertha tried to restore order.

"Ladies . . . ladies. Now please. I agree this is troubling, but let's stay focused."

After the murmuring stopped, she restated the problem and began to detail the unintended harmful impacts the medical community attributed to female cycling—the destruction of feminine symmetry and poise, disturbance of internal organs, and the development of muscular legs. She then segued into the heart of issue, the promiscuous women who might abandon proper dress in public like many in the northern cities.

"Corsets, petticoats, hats and gloves, and long skirts that hide the ankles—the clothing of a lady. All may soon be replaced." Several attendees brought their hands to their mouths, shocked by the prophecy.

"Where will such a disintegration of social norms lead us? Just imagine, ladies."

Abigail Sawyer—Peter's mother—a longtime club member whose multiple family businesses included the grocery, immediately raised her hand. Respected in her own right, Abigail had resisted many of Bertha's ideas in past meetings, so she expected a roadblock to her current plan. Abigail rose as the chairman recognized her.

"Allow me to take exception to such dire predictions. The loss of modesty cannot be attached to something so innocent as riding a wheel. Dare I ask, wouldn't we all be more comfortable in some looser fitting styles? The media are already reflecting the shift in trends. The truth is, we are behind the changing times."

Two other members spoke out in agreement. The time had come for Bertha to switch to scare tactics. She told about her recent visit to Atlanta, and how she had attended the church of Reverend T. B. Hawthorne, a force for truth in the pulpit. The pastor made a statement that she wrote verbatim in her notes for a future occasion such as this. With a natural flair for the dramatic, she allowed Abigail to dangle, while she perused the crowd to spot-check the mood of the room.

She came back to her nemesis. "Mrs. Sawyer, may I share his ideas?"

"Of course. We welcome all points of view here, do we not?"

Bertha nodded to the naysayer, a woman she had grown tired of wrestling. "He said this, and I quote:

> If there is any object on earth, which makes jubilee in the realm of unclean spirits, it is a society woman in masculine habiliments, strad-dling a bicycle and prepared to make an exhibition of her immodesty on the thoroughfares of a great city.

The words hung in the air, and the women whispered about the religious indictment until an ally of Abigail's rose to challenge the pastor's assertions. "An alarmist viewpoint. I am aware of other pastors who invite parishioners, including women, to ride their wheels to services. They report an increase in attendees."

A handful of ladies chuckled, but their voices of disagreement faded and died. Determined not to be undone in such a righteous cause, Bertha hammered her opposition with another respected reference.

"Allow me to quote one more source, a writer from the *New York Times*, one of the nation's foremost newspapers. New York, you may be aware, is beset by this cycling craze. The red flag of warning is being raised even there."

While searching for the clipping, she explained that the story followed a vote by the board of trustees in the village of College Point, New York, to prohibit female instructors from wheeling to work. The room had become stuffy, or so she thought, but none of the ladies swooshed fans to cool themselves. Was it just her imagination? A droplet trickling from her forehead tickled her skin until it latched onto her temple, where she wiped it away.

"Let me . . . ah yes, I found the article here, and will again quote directly."

It is not a proper thing for the ladies to ride the bicycle. They wear skirts, of course, but if we do not stop them now, they will want to be in style with the New York City women and bloomers. How would our schoolrooms look with the lady teachers parading about among boys and girls wearing bloomers? We are determined to stop our educators in time before they go that far.

"End quote," she said with emphasis, spying the room for reactions.

"Oh, my!" exclaimed an older member who opened her hand fan in a vain attempt to cool her face. So . . . at least one other experienced the growing discomfort from the rising humidity.

Bertha placed the clip back in her jacket pocket. "I humbly suggest we follow their wise example. Thank you, ladies."

The group fell silent, absorbing the discussion. The moderator called for an official motion for the Kosmos to circulate a petition to outlaw cycling by women and public use of bloomers for any reason. Four members voted to oppose, including Abigail. With the majority voting yea, the moderator asked each member to take a copy of the petition to gain more signatures over the next several days. Abigail did not take one, but the other skeptics did.

"Tomorrow night, July 2, the City Council will present the second reading of a proposed ordinance to set a speed limit on cycling within the city," the moderator said. "Kosmos will seek time to submit our first petition and propose that language addressing our concerns be added to the current draft law. Bertha will speak on our behalf."

After they adjourned, Bertha offered cheerful goodbyes to several supporters. As she strolled home, a large patch of dark clouds threatened a downpour, and a wisp of wind bent the treetops lining Oak Street. She gave thanks for the validation of her cause, which of course was nothing personal against the Gaines family. Anna should not be maligned for her actions, but the indiscretion did bring potential peril upon the community.

Rather, Bertha wanted to nurture her and teach her the proper place for a Southern lady. Anna's parents had apparently failed in that endeavor.

She walked up the steps toward her front door taking stock of all her blessings—her home, her positions of influence, and even Edward's successful career. Yet a lack of fulfillment lingered and loneliness prompted many joyless days, darkened by events and words uttered in anger and frustration that could not be undone.

She turned and noticed a lightning bolt hammering down through the southern sky to the earth below. A rolling crash of thunder followed seconds later.

The rain began pelting down.

Chapter Thirteen

VISITORS POURED IN and out of the Read House on Ninth Street, a favored spot for holding business meetings and community gatherings. As Anna entered, her papa waved his hand from the corner table.

Early Monday evening, after finishing work, she had hopped a trolley to this legendary hotel to keep a time-honored tradition alive. Joseph took his daughter for a special dinner to celebrate the passage of one more year in her life. Just the two of them.

"Waiting long?"

"Not at all. You're worth waiting for. Grab a seat. And happy birthday."

Twenty years old now and no husband. Unthinkable two years ago, she'd begun to make peace with her lack of prospects. "Thank you. I'm starving."

The cigar and pipe smoke billowed up to form a fog above the patrons. Pulling his favorite corncob pipe and tobacco pouch from his jacket pocket, Joseph lit up and puffed long and deep. He sat back and blew his contribution upward to reinforce the thickening shroud.

While the family hammered him on the need to cut down on smoking, Papa could not resist the simple pleasure when surrounded by others enjoying their tobacco. She saw no reason to deny his enjoyment. Unlike the distasteful odor of burning tobacco leaves in cigarettes, Papa's pipe smoke was aromatic.

The low buzz of conversations and laughter from each table commingled like the smoke to create a noise that saturated the room. Even so, she overheard some talk about the female cyclist spotted east of town. She tuned it out, determined not to allow anything to spoil this time.

They talked about the farm and how more farmers had traded the rural life for big city living. She shared again how she dreamed of attending school and maybe teaching in New York like his sister. They reminisced about past Independence Day celebrations like the time one of the fiery rockets failed to explode high in the sky and came down into old man Prewett's wagon. The rig, parked too close to the display and filled with hay, ignited in flames when the rocket detonated upon impact. The vision, while not so funny at the time, earned their uncontrollable laughter whenever they recounted the tale.

As they prepared to leave, a gentleman stopped at their table. He was a towering man, with sunken eyes that accentuated his pallor. He looked ill.

"How are you, Charlie?" her papa asked.

"Under the circumstances . . .? I'm buried under profit and loss statements at the office and all manner of schemes at the chamber."

"Please, take a seat. You remember my daughter, Anna. Sweetheart, this is a business associate, Mr. Smith."

She nodded. "Mr. Smith. A pleasure, sir."

"Yes. Of course," Charlie said. "Been a long time."

Charlie's demeanor was guarded and his mood somber. He joined them, sinking into the chair, much to Anna's disappointment. Papa studied the man's face.

"Can I get you a drink? Coffee . . . or something stronger?"

"No, Joe. But thanks. Listen, it's fortuitous that I've run into you." He bit his lower lip and swallowed. "Something important I need to discuss. Can you spare a little time after your meal with Anna?"

The drive home would take longer in the dark. Although her papa always kept a lantern handy when he traveled during the evening, she worried about his safety and hoped he would decline.

"The hour is getting late. I'll be dropping Anna at her house and will head home from there. Sarah will worry if I dawdle. How about another time?" As they rose to leave, Charlie pulled his handkerchief and dabbed the beads of sweat from his cheeks and brow.

"Maybe I will have that drink after all."

Sitting down, Papa flagged the waiter, who took Charlie's order and left. They talked about the accountant's family and how proud he was of his daughter studying to be a nurse in Chicago at a prestigious university. Anna bit her lower lip. The scotch and water arrived, and Charlie took a sip. Her papa gave the man permission to speak freely. Instead, he tilted his head toward her father and whispered.

"This involves your daughter."

She overheard. Not surprised, she looked the man square in the eyes, a bold reaction for the old Anna Gaines. "I can wait for you outside the restaurant, Papa."

"No, Charlie, whatever you want to say, you can share with both of us." Papa treated her with the respect due an adult.

The man sighed and scratched the back of his head. "Well, how do I . . ."

"You wanted to talk about this bicycle business. Right?" Papa never danced around a hard conversation. Her ears perked up. Surprisingly, she didn't fear whatever he meant to convey. In the past, she would have been mortified to be the center of such a controversy. With each passing day, not so much.

"Not my choice, I can assure you," Charlie said.

Her papa took command. "Let me start. We are allowing Anna to ride her wheel around the farm."

"You're aware . . ."

"Yes, I am," Papa said. He began to get snappish, but caught himself. "Look . . . I know she's been seen cycling on the outskirts of the city. She's a grown woman, Charlie. As such, I can't dictate how she should live her life. She intends to act on principle here, and by gum, I mean to stand right beside her. Come what may."

Charlie fidgeted in his seat. The waiter saved him temporarily when he asked if Charlie would like some coffee. "I haven't had enough of my scotch to need coffee. But thanks." The businessman cast a furtive glance at Anna and turned to her father.

"Listen. We're friends, but I can't stall the executive leadership at the chamber much longer. Some members want to take the Mineral and Agricultural Resources Committee from you if this issue continues to spiral out of hand."

"So be it," Anna's father responded. "A petition is being circulated. Will the chamber collect signatures and submit them at the council meeting tomorrow night?"

She perked up. "What petition, Papa?"

Chapter Fourteen

EARLY TUESDAY MORNING, the Irish Hill section of downtown Chattanooga sprang to life. Grover Biggs walked toward the woman in a full-length summer dress as she dismounted her buggy. The structure housing the *Chattanooga Times* newspaper, at the northeast corner of Georgia Avenue and Eighth Street, towered before them, its dome made of sheet copper, gilded in gold. The iconic edifice stood for more than a free press. The *Times* building represented a source of community pride, a confidence that Chattanooga and her people possessed the grit to weather any storm threatening the South. To Grover, it was just another building.

"This should do the trick," he said, handing the woman an oversized envelope.

He had read, polished, and reread his prose. Mutual goals connected them . . . nothing more. Otherwise, he had no use for this pushy, overbearing woman. Both of them wanted to put a bridle on Anna Gaines, a racehorse with a mind of her own. Control her; rein back her misguided thinking about the role of a woman in the world, and he might consider spending more time with her . . . at least until he could leave Chattanooga. The larger mission of saving the city he left to Bertha Millwood for he would be moving on soon enough.

"Did you use the resource material I gave you?" Bertha asked.

"Yes . . . you can read the copy before you take it to the city desk, Mrs. Millwood. The *Times* will eat this stuff up."

"Wait for me," she said.

She walked back to her driver, gave him instructions, and proceeded to the entrance adorned with Tuscan pilasters and a keystone arch. Bertha emerged ten minutes later as the streets filled with the lifeblood of commerce—working people. Ready to move on, Grover became impatient with her self-righteous smirk.

He consulted the time. "And?"

"They promised to run the piece. I read the first couple of paragraphs on my way in . . . perfect. Quite a way with words, Mr. Biggs."

"Told you I can write." He mounted his wheel and turned his head back toward her. "See you later today as planned."

The woman couldn't be trusted. If any of her planned schemes failed, and she was brought to a reckoning, he would deny any attempts to incriminate him. He had a list of allegations against her, some true and some not. Fighting fire with fire came natural for him.

❧ ❖ ❧

The sun slipped behind the western mountain ranges as the buggy driver pulled up to the Chattanooga Driving Track on McCallie Avenue. Astride his wheel at the side of the road, Grover turned his bicycle and rode back to where Bertha sat.

"Are the wheelmen on board?" she asked.

She stared straight ahead, in all her arrogance, unwilling to make eye contact with him. So superior in her own mind. He did enjoy one serendipity from working with her: All this clandestine work put him in touch with some older citizens, people with money. Many of them were widows, potential leads for the scam run by an accountant named Mortimer Foxx. Soon he intended to leave all this behind. Especially Bertha Millwood.

"Yes," he said. "The Cycle Cub will speak out against the scorching ordinance. And when we present the petitions, a spokesman will make a statement in support of expanding the proposal."

"Excellent. What of the Young Men's Business League?"

"Also on board."

He began to loathe the woman and couldn't imagine how any man would want to live with her.

"Well done," she said. "Very well, indeed."

What was this . . . a compliment?

The buggy lurched forward.

Chapter Fifteen

AS PETER WALKED past the crowd, he was shocked to find so many people venturing out on a Tuesday night. And for a City Council meeting. The curious and the committed, around two hundred in number, surrounded the one-story brick building in Market Square.

Only a few gained access to the chambers where Peter took a seat another wheelman had saved for him. The rest milled about in front and on North Market Place and South Market Place—the twenty-foot-wide streets on the sides of the structure. Once the location of the public market, the only place by law where citizens could purchase meat, the block-long remodeled building now served as a city hall, police headquarters, jail, and engine house.

Mayor George Washington Ochs invited the clerk to present the first reading of Bicycle Ordinance 490. The wording was short and precise, covering speed limits, riding on sidewalks, and the amounts of fines for each infraction. He also warned the crowd that any unruliness would result in ejection from the proceedings.

The sixteen aldermen, one representing each ward, debated minor adjustments to the proposed fines and the method of collection from offenders, allowing compromise to define the session. With the board in one accord, Mayor Ochs opened up the forum for a public comment period.

"We received several requests from citizens who wish to voice their opinions for the record. Limit your time to three minutes or less to afford each person the opportunity to speak." The mayor reviewed his handwritten list, created as people had filed into the chamber earlier and indicated their desire to speak. "So . . . Mr. Peter Sawyer, President of the Cycle Club, is first. The floor is yours, sir. Three minutes or less."

"Thank you, Mr. Mayor and distinguished aldermen. My statement will indeed be brief." Peter examined the crowd, locking eyes with Anna Gaines seated three rows in front of him with her family and friend, Emma Kelly. "Allow me to enact a typical street confrontation between a cyclist and pedestrian and present an alternative solution to the one being considered."

He shared the idea of club members teaching cyclists and pedestrians how to avoid collisions, precluding the need for government involvement in the pastime. The plan that had been adopted at their last meeting.

Two other individuals stood to make statements after Peter. Hearing no other comments, the mayor informed the crowd that a second reading of the ordinance would take place at the council meeting in early August. The next order of business would be the submittal of signed petitions demanding the city to enact regulations against female bicycle riders and public use of indecent clothing, such as bloomers. The mayor looked to Peter.

"My understanding is that the Cycle Club will speak to this matter as well. Correct?"

Peter perused the room, perturbed by this revelation. Several members had signed the petition, but no one had informed him that his organization volunteered to make an actual presentation. All eyes locked onto him, while he peeked at Anna to catch her reaction. She turned and glared as the crowd waited for him to rise.

But he didn't dare, for he would not be boxed into a corner on this issue.

When woman wants to learn anything or do anything useful or even have any fun there is always someone to solemnly warn her that it is her duty to keep well. Meanwhile in many states she can work in factories ten hours a day, she can stand behind counters in badly ventilated stores from 8 o'clock to 6, she can bend over the sewing machine for about 5 cents an hour and no one cares enough to protest. But when these same women, condemned to sedentary lives indoors, find a cheap and delightful way of getting the fresh air and exercise they need so sorely, there is a great hue and cry about their physical welfare.

—Chicago Daily News, early 1890s

Why, pray tell me, hasn't a woman as much right to dress to suit herself as a man? [T]he stand she is taking in the matter of dress is no small indication that she has realized that she has an equal right with a man to control her own movements.

—Susan B. Anthony, 1895
(interview with a reporter)

Chapter Sixteen

THE ROOM WENT silent. Peter spotted Bertha Millwood standing in back as she nodded toward Gregory Jacobson, the Cycle Club Treasurer, and Grover Biggs. Jacobson rose, a pouch in his hands. "Honorable Mayor Ochs, may I approach?"

"Come ahead." The crowd parted to allow him through. As he came forward, Jacobson pulled out several pieces of paper filled with handwritten names. He addressed both the audience and the council.

"Name's Jacobson, sir. As an official representative of the Chattanooga Cycle Club, I present to you copies of the same petition circulated throughout the city and signed by more than six hundred citizens. These signatures include many of our prominent leaders in business. Also, some respected members of social and religious circles. All, and I dare say many who haven't yet signed, are united in this effort. Let us keep what infects many corners of this country from our city's doorstep."

The crowd broke into an uproar, ignoring the mayor's desperate efforts to quiet the room. After two minutes, the racket trailed off. This represented a symbolic smear of Anna, and any movement—however small—toward the emancipation of women. The bicycle happened to be front and center in this debate over a woman's right to choose. These were simple choices, like how to spend her leisure hours and the type of clothes she would wear.

Peter's teeth clenched, and his fists opened and closed. His anger boiled, but unbridled indignation would serve no purpose. Several organizations spoke on the various deleterious effects of cycling on women: Heats the blood and leads to certain complaints. Destroys feminine symmetry and poise and develops bulges on the arms and legs. Female riders suffer organ problems and make improper displays. They neglect their homes and try to dress as men in trousers. Loose morals displayed by unmarried couples going off unsupervised. On and on. Peter bristled at every allegation.

The mayor interjected, "The point is made."

Another citizen jumped up with a comment. "If you think we don't face a real challenge, a young woman in our city, a Miss Gaines, flaunts this kind of new-style independence right in our faces. She incites our community to participate in reckless behavior."

The room hushed. Mortified, Peter looked to Anna as she turned back to view her detractor. She trembled, her face drained of color. Peter looked at her parents: Mrs. Gaines with a hand to her mouth and Mr. Gaines consoling his daughter. As Peter started to rise, ready to lash out against the verbal lynching, Emma Kelly began to speak, seated at first, but rising slowly.

"This concern for women in our community is heartening. Should I take to the wheel anytime soon, I will be encouraged to find that both the men and the so-called proper women in our wonderful city will rise up to save me from myself."

Derisive comments rose from the crowd. "Boo."

"Take a seat, you Irish Bridget."

"Mick!"

"Settle down." Mayor Ochs pounded his gavel.

Emma appeared confident and unfazed, as a wide smile crossed her face. "A bunch of miscreants, the lot of ya."

She perused the crowd with a keen eye until the crowd quieted, many looking away. Then she continued.

"Meanwhile, I can't help but wonder why nobody expresses genuine worry about my hunching over a sewing machine for ten hours a day, with little time afforded for a break. There is little talk tonight about my aching back. Or my tired eyes. Will anyone here offer a fair wage for a day's work so a single woman like me can live? When my vision falters—what happens?"

Peter took heart in the fact that Anna possessed a true friend—a protector—in Emma Kelly.

As the council meeting wound to a close, a Cycle Club member stood and made a formal request. Anna cringed.

"The wheelmen ask this board to respond to our petitions." The crowd began to grow raucous, shouting out similar demands. "Add language to the ordinance banning any woman from riding the wheel and wearing bloomers in public."

The mayor conferred with the aldermen for several minutes. At first, the public's stern response to her casual bicycle rides surprised Anna. Her astonishment turned to bewilderment and finally to dismay. She had subjected her family to ridicule and shame. How foolish of her to be so self-possessed.

The mayor held up his hands to stop the grumbling in the crowded chamber. "The council decided, in response to the will of the citizens of Chattanooga, to add some additional language to the proposed ordinance. The new wording will be presented for public comment at our next meeting—the first Tuesday of August. This meeting is hereby adjourned. Thank you for your participation and enjoy the rest of your evening."

Anna's parents, Emma, and others around them rose. Anna remained seated, staring straight ahead. What happened here? She doubted her ability to recover from this public affront.

They filed out of the building and onto South Market Place. A difficult choice loomed from the darkness. Stand tall and proud, and don't allow people to bully her out of the simple right to ride a wheel. How she longed to become such a person, to possess the courage Emma displayed in the meeting. Or back away. Fade from the controversy. Let someone else take on this battle.

As they left the square, she spotted Peter Sawyer standing on North Market Place staring in her direction. Women wheelers somehow threatened him—so much so that he had organized a massive drive to quash the female cyclist before she ever took to the streets.

Who else could be responsible for the Chattanooga Cycling Club's complicity in this character assassination?

There was only one thing left to do. Confront him.

Chapter Seventeen

AFTER DINNER, ON the eve before the Fourth of July, Bertha peeked at the newspaper before Edward returned from his bedroom. Nothing on the front page, so she turned to the second. The bold headlines jumped off the paper.

"Beauty and Brawn . . . The Bicycle Leads Our Beauties into Amazonian Brawniness"

"The Girl with the Round, Slim Waist, Sloping Shoulders, Small Wrists, and Nether Limbs Molded on the Flowing Curves of a Greek Goddess. Not So with the New Woman" - (Written for the *Chattanooga Times*)

"What the . . .?" Edward said.

Excited by the coverage, Bertha jumped out of her skin at her husband's comment. "Honestly, Edward, you shouldn't sneak up on people, peering over my shoulder like that."

Without responding, he grabbed the daily edition from her hands and reviewed the headlines. His face and neck turned pink, as his fists crumpled the paper.

"Oh, Lord Jesus, help us," he said. Reading no further, he threw the *Times* on the dinner table, still strewn with the dishes from their silent meal together, and he retired early for the evening. As he climbed the stairs, his eyes were cast down, his lips pinched.

Bertha wondered what would become of their marriage. A tinge of guilt replaced her initial sense of accomplishment. She forced the emotion into one of her mental compartments where it would not distract her from the ordained task at hand.

Peter reluctantly accepted the invitation from his father and mother to join them for dinner at the St. Elmo home of Frank and Rosie Devlin. The day had been long, and he preferred to unwind before the holiday. He decided to forgo a relaxing evening on the patio, where he had planned to sip some wine and read the newspaper, in favor of social time with old friends. The Devlins were his godparents, and he owed them the respect of a visit.

While the men transitioned to the parlor for cigars and brandy, Frank inquired about the Sawyer business holdings and how Chester's other two sons fared in New York. Small talk ensued as they toasted each other's family and enjoyed their smokes. The newspaper sat on the small table. Peter assumed Frank had already read it.

"Anything noteworthy in the paper today, Godfather?"

"Interesting you ask. The business about women on wheels has us concerned. Where do you come down on the idea?"

A raised eyebrow and a glance from his father—a sign he would defer the question to his son. The reply would not be so simple. He had no indication of Frank's position and did not want to offend his host with opinionated rhetoric.

He stumbled. "Well . . . I . . . ."

"Peter, we're family here." His godfather gave him permission to speak freely, but Peter still refrained, unsure he could contain his anger. Thankfully, Frank offered his judgment first.

"The discourse in our city has fallen to a disgraceful level. I must read you the story appearing in the *Times* today. We don't see a problem with women enjoying a Sunday ride in the country or around town."

Saved. Peter spoke his unabashed belief. "Agreed…one hundred percent. After all, shouldn't ladies be granted equal rights?" He glanced at his father, who nodded his agreement.

"Yes, they should," his godfather said, turning the page of the newspaper. After reading the headlines out loud, Frank skipped to the second and third paragraphs. "Listen to this."

In the early spring, the woman in question procured a bicycle, joined a club, and soon learned to use her wheel with delightful proficiency. She made records for the mere fun of breaking them, boasted of always pedaling up the steepest hills, grew as slender and vigorous as a young Diana. On the first morning of rehearsal for a comic opera, she was relegated from her high position as the leader of the dancers to a bit player in the back row of a crowd of village maidens who comes on stage only in the last act.

The bicycle played her a trick, for where otherwise faultless outlines made her figure admired and renowned, even under the regulations and swathing of close, silk fleshing, now appeared a series of curious looking bumps and lumps, bulging ridges and knots, with billowy risings and sinking, calculated to outrage anyone's sense of statuesque symmetry. To guess the cause of this unusual development was easy enough.

Peter flinched with each reference, thinking of Anna and imagining how she would react to this indirect but vicious attack on her.

"The work of Bertha Millwood, according to my Rosie," his godfather said. "Pretty certain she's behind stirring up the Kosmos ladies to circulate the petitions."

Silent so far, his father weighed in. "Best be wary, son. Mother gave me the same report."

Peter reviewed the actions taken at the Bicycle Club's recent meeting and the underhanded comments from Grover Biggs. "The long arm of Mrs. Millwood extends into the Cycle Club, I suspect, through her henchman, Mr. Biggs. You recall, Father, he's the one we are looking into."

His father frowned. "Strikes true. The Millwood woman is a lost soul."

Duly noted. Both culprits targeted Anna at the center of their crafty schemes.

⚜

Anna sat on her bed, aghast, as Emma read the article to her.

If she is an enthusiastic rider, as most women are, within a few months her knees will be increased a half inch in circumference, above and below the joints and the tendons running along the back of the leg, from knee to ankle, begin to swell and harden. The woman hurts at first from the unusual exercise. Now the bigger and harder those sinews grow the more ease and pleasure does the rider find in using her wheel, and if she is a woman with a genuine love of outdoor sports and games to balance her development, she will turn to the golf sticks and also swing a racquet. The systems are unsurpassed for the purpose of acquiring health and endurance, but are the deathblow to beauty.

Emma stopped. "Do you want me to read more?"

"Skip to the end."

Folding the newspaper in half, she dropped down to the bottom. Anna locked onto Emma's eyes, a tear dripping down her face to match the hurt that her best friend felt. The story got worse as she read.

But in proportion as our women gain in bone and brawn and increased health, too, the loss of grace increases over time. Rosier cheeks and brighter eyes steady exercise brings, but every day grows more difficult, say the artists, to find the proper models, and for the ballet masters to draw suitable recruits to their service. Unless the standards of ladylike beauty are readjusted to meet the ideas of the modern woman, the feminine element bids fair to disappear from the painter's canvass and vanish in an ornamental capacity from the stage. For with a strong right arm, the damsel of the future means to rule.

Emma laid the paper on the bed, as Anna fell into her embrace, sobbing. "Why is this happening to someone who simply wants to enjoy being outdoors on the seat of a wheel?" Anna asked.

"Sometimes . . . to want something is not enough," Emma said. "A fight may be necessary to achieve the desire of our heart. The struggle can help us to grow if that desire is pure."

With a deep sigh, Anna pulled back to look at Emma's face, to view the resolve so evident in her voice. The affair turned personal with the publication of this wretched piece in the *Times*. With a renewed determination, Anna decided to take the tussle to the likes of Peter Sawyer and his ilk. Papa would cheer her on, but she expected Mama to quarrel with her intentions.

First, she would go to Peter at the grocery and seek an explanation. Then she would begin riding through the city streets rather than confine herself to the farm. Once more, she would wear her bloomers, if the desire struck her.

The following day the nation celebrated her birthday. The family led her to believe this as a child and reinforced the honor well into her adolescence. On this Fourth of July, the occasion of her twentieth year, she still enjoyed the notion. The community turned out to picnic and witness the fireworks show. The country's first display, twelve months after the signing of the Declaration of Independence, could not have been grander in Anna's eyes.

The rockets fired over Chattanooga exploded high in the sky, raining down brilliant multi-colored flashes of light that extinguished before hitting the ground. Afterwards, on the trolley ride back to the boarding house with Emma, it occurred to Anna that a different kind of explosion between neighbors would follow in the coming days. A non-lethal, much smaller-scale American Revolution, centered right in Chattanooga, loomed on the horizon. And Anna, forced to become a patriot in the struggle for independence, braced herself to become the war's first victim.

⥹❖⥼

The buggy ride from East Lake through McFarland Gap to the Chickamauga Valley featured a magnificent mixture of dense forest, open meadows, and farmlands. Papa's company usually vanquished Anna's stress. This time, she rode in a contemplative mood gripped by the rhythmic sound of Winnie's clopping hooves and a dark foreboding.

The events of the last three weeks had begun to spin out of control. How did she arrive at this place? She tried to shake free from the nagging voice in her head, warning her again of a violent storm about to rip the social fabric of Chattanooga to shreds.

The oppressive heat and humidity further dampened her outlook. A confrontation with her mama would make matters much worse.

A tense, loud Saturday night at the farm with Anna and her mother shouting verbal assaults and Papa entering the fray turned into a stormy Sunday morning. At this rate, they would never set out for church.

In a moment of brooding, she thought—*How could I have spoken to Mama like that?* Lashing out, interrupting, storming away. The justified disobedience bumped heads with her deep respect for the brave woman who gave her life, nursed her all those months in bed, and comforted her later when many children shot arrows of scorn into her heart. But now equally insensitive adults were launching the arrows, and Mama seemed to have abandoned her corner. The confrontation crushed her.

The family tried to settle into the Sabbath, seeking rest. Anna joined Papa on the porch, watching as he pulled some tobacco from his pouch and stuffed it into his pipe. She nudged the rocker back and forth; the creak kept time as he hummed "Amazing Grace." The situation at home had landed her into the eye of the hurricane, that peaceful core hidden within violent, swirling winds.

The sweet smell of his pipe grounded her. As he puffed the contents into a slow burn, Anna prayed for this strained family to remain strong and united. Determined about what would come next, she asked for guidance. Inside, Mama busied herself preparing the Sunday meal. The newspaper coverage about her cycling had thrown her mother over the ledge, causing a major rift between her parents. In her mama's opinion, the *Times* stories were Anna's fault, and she had brought all this negative attention on herself.

With clenched fists and butterflies flapping in her stomach, she tried to ease her frayed nerves. A few minutes later Papa began to nod off, so she retreated to her room and rifled through the clothes bag she had carried to the farm. She pulled the outfit out and changed. If Mama saw fit to join the townspeople and the newspapers in attacking her,

Anna would deliver a cold blast of newfound independence. The new woman inside of her, struggling to emerge, found the freedom to push aside her mama's ways.

As she walked down the stairs, their eyes met. Mama was aghast.

"What in God's name are you doing? Lord, tell me, who is this girl I raised, wearing such an . . . indecent outfit? Are you determined to ruin my life, to insult me and destroy our family? I forbid you to leave the house dressed this way."

"Sorry, Mama. But I believe that's my decision to make. In case you failed to notice, I am a woman. Not a little girl anymore. No disrespect to you or Papa, but I must do what I think is right."

Once again, they collided. The sharp words and forceful tones sounded an alert, as her papa entered the kitchen. "Whoa, both of you wild mares. Stop bucking. Calm down. Let's not say something we'll regret later."

Mama lobbed another missile. "Did you not read the *Times*? Are you not aware of how people are talking? How can you disregard the impact of your so-called independence on me and your father?"

Mama stared at him for support, but he said nothing.

"Please try to understand; I'm not doing anything bad," Anna said. "This is a practical sporting outfit, nothing more. If I wear a dress, the fabric gets tangled up in the bicycle chain. What can be so wrong with this?"

Mama's lips trembled. As the first cry began, she didn't respond to Anna's question. Might she be softening a touch? Mama stood speechless for a few more moments, until she wiped her cheeks dry. Anna braced for another salvo she prayed would not come, but the fit arrived with a fury.

"Here is what's wrong—it's against our Southern ways. And if this continues, I'll not allow you to come here, defying me and your father."

This time, overwhelmed by such an ultimatum, Anna looked to her father for sympathy. Again, he stood to the side, offering none save a pained expression on his face. Emptied, she ran to her room where she remained for an hour. When Anna descended the stairs, she was wearing an acceptable Sunday dress. With the bloomers gone and the wind removed from her sails, she joined Mama in the kitchen to help prepare the meal. They worked in silence for a while until Anna gently pushed one last time.

"As far back as I can remember, you both taught me not to concern myself with what others think about me. Also, to move forward if I believe something is appropriate and right. Are you now disregarding that advice?"

She waited for her mama's answer.

"The concerns I have go beyond what people are saying." She turned back to her cutting board, chopping vegetables and trying to stifle her whimpers. "Until you become a mother, I can't expect you to understand."

"Try me, Mama."

"Some itinerant worker or dangerous wanderer might . . ." Unable to continue, her mama retreated to the outside. Downtrodden, Anna would not be riding today.

Chapter Eighteen

ST. PAUL'S EPISCOPAL resembled a typical English village church. The building, erected and dedicated in 1888, featured an inspirational four-story brick tower that rose above the sanctuary. As Bertha and Rector Thomas Harden walked the grounds, the rector mentioned the need to fix the roof. In the recent rains, streams of water had leaked in several locations with well-placed cooking pots on the floors capturing the flow.

Building repairs depended on the generosity of the congregants in the church's pews, and Bertha considered herself among the top supporters of St. Paul's. So, she relied on her purse strings to gain this private lunch.

Rector Harden had spent many hours comforting the Millwoods, but not long after Constance passed, Edward stopped coming. When Bertha continued to seek the rector's time for many months, he tried hard to assuage her grief. Inconsolable, she could not carry on without the comfort of the church, so he continued to counsel her—until recently.

The conversation skirted around trivialities as they ate. Upon swallowing her last bite, she patted her mouth with the napkin. Time for the real discussion to begin. "A lovely meal. Thank you, dear Thomas. How wonderful to spend quality time with such a man of God."

"Always a pleasure," Rector Harden said. "May I say, you are in such joyful spirits given the burden you and Edward so gracefully carry each day."

"My Constance went to heaven two years ago now," Bertha said. "Not a day goes by without seeing her face in my mind or wondering if she suffered." She pulled out her handkerchief. "A difficult trial for us, as you are well aware. All your counsel during this time . . . well, how can I thank you?"

"Of course. Now, Bertha, can we do something specific for you today?"

She welcomed an end to the small talk. He listened to her concerns and the reasons for embarking on a holy mission to purify the city, starting with the petition drive. "These actions are not misguided, are they?"

The rector indicated he had heard about the campaign from other church members. Some congregants chose to sign, while others expressed worry about divisiveness within the church.

"Let me respond in this way. As you and Edward are aware, I believe God calls our flock to address the growing racial inequality befalling Negroes in recent years. We're not afraid to tackle causes involving justice and mercy as the people of the cross."

Her ears perked up, but he failed to answer directly. She asked, "But, Rector Harding . . . what is your position on this specific matter? The movement is a moral powder keg exploding across the land, don't you agree?"

The question gave him pause, and he took several moments to reflect. "The church should remain uninvolved—for now." A disappointing response, but now they were getting somewhere.

"This newfound freedom on the wheel and the resulting disregard for appropriate public dress are the designs of the evil one," she said.

The rector, usually more open to her leading, held his ground this time. "Perhaps. But I encourage you to examine your heart. Does the love of God motivate you to do His will, or are you engaged in a personal crusade? Look to God for your answer. He will guide you onto righteous pathways."

The veiled admonishment irritated her. Once again, she lifted the elegant napkin to her mouth, leaving the outlines of her lips on it. "I humbly suggest this is a matter for the church to address head-on," she said. "How better to discern our heavenly Father's will in such matters?"

"I will pray," he said.

She rose from the table. "Indeed, we all must seek God's wisdom." Back to her more formal demeanor, she decided to play her final trump card. "Well, I must be on my way. And thank you again for your time." The rector stood to bid her a proper goodbye.

"Always a pleasure, Bertha," Rector Harden said. "Please extend Edward our best."

She turned at the door. "By the way, Thomas. I assume you are still pursuing funds to repair the leaks threatening the structural integrity of our beloved church. T'was a nasty storm that battered our city."

"Indeed."

"I would hate for this important work to be delayed until another rainy season is upon us."

She smiled to seal her meaning and left.

⤞❖⤝

The relationship with her mother remained chilly as Anna lamented over her retreat from the wheel. More so, the seesaw she rode wearied her, from one decision about cycling to the next. She asked for courage, but God must have been on hiatus and missed the request.

During the week, she endured stares and snickers from strangers but received an occasional tip of the hat from the true gentlemen of Chattanooga. Her new celebrity, and the discord that followed, would grow if she pursued the bold plan to ride on city streets.

The next Saturday, July 13, Anna stayed in town. She closed the door of Mrs. Byrne's boarding house behind her and began the short walk to Sawyer's grocery between Broad and Chestnut. This would be her last purchase there, assuming the pipe she intended to buy for Papa's birthday had not been snapped up. After today, she would never set foot in this shopping place again. But before leaving, she would confront Peter Sawyer who at best was two-faced toward her newfound passion.

Who else but Peter Sawyer would have spearheaded the circulation of petitions and authored the horrid story in the *Times*? The man she once believed to be kind and sensitive didn't possess a caring bone in his body, and his cronies in the Cycle Club followed like sheep. What if she started a boycott of the grocery? She surrendered the temptation as such an action would make her no better than him.

She had begun to trust Grover who had showed up at Loveman's every day that week to walk her home. He turned out to be the understanding one. Even though he didn't believe women should cycle, she was certain that Grover would never have signed the unrighteous petition. Peter's name probably occupied the first line.

On a recent stroll, Grover had proposed that they take the Chattanooga & Lookout Mountain Railroad to the top on the following Sunday. An escort would not be necessary because Grover acted like a gentleman toward her, not like her sneaky nemesis, Peter. She was certain an outing to the famous battlefield, surrounded by visitors, would be innocent enough. Besides, she had tired of Emma's cautions about him. Her friend had misjudged Grover.

After walking north on Broad Street, she turned left on West Eighth and set foot in the grocery. The clean displays of food and sundries spoke well of the proprietors. It irked her to think well of Peter, the manager. Determined to end her patronage, she would miss the easy access from her residence and the high customer standards. A steep price to pay.

She picked up the pipe at the front counter; thankfully, another customer had not purchased it since her last visit. She walked through the store, hoping to spot Peter. As she returned to the front, a Negro woman dragging three sacks of groceries had beaten her to the counter. The young clerk attempted to explain something about credit policies. The poor woman looked embarrassed. Anna stepped back several feet and eavesdropped on their conversation.

"So sorry, Madam, but as I said, you are short one dollar. Perhaps you should replace some of what you wanted to buy."

"Can give you two dollars and fifty today. Got three young mouths to feed. This month been hard, with me being sick and unable to tidy houses like I do. Will the grocery give me a credit? My word that I'll make things right soon as I come back on my feet."

Anna's heart broke for the woman. The tattered clothes and shoes with holes indicated she possessed little means to obtain the basic necessities. One more reason on her list not to support the grocery; an uncaring attitude toward the community's most needy. As soon as she paid for the pipe, she would ask to speak with the store owner.

The clerk insisted. "This place requires cash. I'm afraid I can't help you."

The interchange continued as another woman entered the otherwise empty store. She wore a full-length bustled skirt and tight-fitting bodice, finished with a fashionable hat. Her face streamed with sweat, unleashed by the hot weather outside and no doubt assisted by her layers of clothing. The discomfort that some women experienced on such days, all to maintain appearances. To gain some relief, the lady waved her hand-fan with a frown plastered on her face.

She stopped to note the interaction at the front.

As the woman began to interject, Anna stepped forward and offered assistance. Out of the corner of her eye, she noticed Peter observing the scene from a distance. Would he intervene and assist the colored woman? She predicted not, or hoped not, as her negative opinion of the man might be turned on its heels. Besides, such compassion would be out of character.

Anna opened her handbag. "Sir, I would like to pay the remainder of this lady's charges. I believe you said she needed one additional dollar. Correct?"

The offer caught the clerk off guard. "Pardon me? What? I mean . . . yes. Very kind of you." Anna handed over one dollar.

The colored woman's penetrating eyes and warm smile moved her. The haggard woman took her hand. "Thank you, young lady. You a fine example of God's grace."

The other shopper objected. "These people should not be given something for nothing like this, or they won't learn the importance of working hard. Soon they will expect everything for free."

The clerk became tongue-tied, stuck in the middle of a dilemma that exceeded his training. "All due respect, Mrs. Millwood. I'm not sure . . ."

"Let her buy only what she can afford, like everyone else," Bertha said. "She must be an example to her children about the value of money and hard work."

Anna's surprise at this heartless woman left her without words. Peter stepped up from the shadows. "Trouble here, Frederick?"

The clerk, relieved by the presence of his boss, explained the circumstances. The other woman impatiently tapped her parasol on the floor, waiting to see how the proprietor would respond to the standoff.

The colored woman had no choice but to place her dilemma in the hands of kindness. She said nothing more.

Anna imagined the dinner table in the woman's home. Hungry children to feed and little sustenance to go around. Would her need for food go unfulfilled? After assessing the situation, Peter responded to his assistant with a solution.

"Well, Frederick, why didn't you give her store credit? As I taught you?" Anna stared at Peter, shocked by the unexpected suggestion.

The clerk also looked at him, perplexed. "Sir?"

Peter gave the money back to Anna without comment. She found it hard to believe the clerk had received such training and didn't recall the policy. In a gentlemanly fashion, Peter accommodated the humble patron.

"Allow me to offer my sincerest apologies for creating such an uncomfortable shopping experience. Would a sixty-day credit suit you?"

The old woman seemed to be the only person not shocked. "How wonderful, sir. Thank you."

"Why, I never . . ." Bertha stormed over to the fabrics and began viewing the latest displays, muttering.

Still confused by Peter's actions, Anna paid for her papa's pipe. With her free hand, she helped the woman carry her sacks, brimming with only necessities, out to the street. Frederick opened the door for them as Anna turned back for one more glance at Peter. The discussion would have to wait for another day. Meanwhile, she and the colored woman proceeded to the walkway outside.

"My name is Anna Gaines."

"I'm Hattie Washington. Leastwise, Hattie is the name my massah done give me on the plantation when I a child. Figured on keeping it once we all freed. Got my last name when I married Raymond. The massah give him some other name, but he changed when he given his freedom. Wanted a proper American name. None better than the first president, I guess."

The woman suddenly stopped talking.

"What's wrong, Hattie?"

"Been going on and on like a chatterbox. Sorry about that."

They began walking. At least she would help the woman carry her things home. "Where do you live?" Anna asked. "I'd like to help get these items to your home."

"Over in them Negro tenements on East Ninth Street. But my place be too far out of your way, I'm sure."

"Not at all. Please . . . I'm living close by, and you'll not be able to tote all these items on your own."

They walked in silence for one block until Hattie stopped and faced her, laboring to catch her breath. Anna almost called out to the man who passed ahead of them, certain that Hattie was unable to continue. But Hattie surprised her.

"Young lady, you is kind for white folk, like the manager back in the store. His heart be right."

Still breathing hard, she turned and started off again.

Baffled by what she had just witnessed, Anna stood in place a moment longer, contemplating Hattie's remark. Did she misjudge Peter? The man she encountered moments ago, who exhibited authentic Christian charity and concern for the woman's dignity, didn't resemble the ogre she had conjured up in her mind—the monster named Peter Sawyer.

Something didn't add up.

Chapter Nineteen

AS THE TWO women walked south on Broad and east on Ninth, Hattie told her story.

After the economy took a sharp downturn, Raymond, her husband, left home to find work. He went to Atlanta and got along fine, sending money to Hattie whenever possible. But something changed along the way. Raymond wrote that he would be moving farther south to find more work but didn't indicate where. Almost two years passed without hearing from him. The family lost their house, so Hattie took a unit at the tenement. She feared something horrible had happened to her man.

Moved by the woman's misfortune, Anna put the groceries down, took Hattie's bag from her grip, and released it to the ground. She hugged the old woman as tears welled up in her eyes. Hattie returned the show of uncommon love, holding her tight.

For the first time in weeks, Anna's focus turned away from herself and toward another less fortunate than she was. The heart she had gained for others in need while visiting Aunt Harriet lay dormant, like a butterfly waiting to break free from its cocoon. Hattie's courage fueled her reawakening.

"Hattie, you mentioned your children back at the grocery. How are you making ends meet?"

"Some days be hard, Miss Anna. I got three young ones under eleven years. I cleans houses and do sweepings around our building. But I got the beginnings of something in my chest. Can't breathe easy no more. Almost impossible for me to work. Charles, my oldest boy, he be ten year old. He finds a corner on Market or Broad every day after school. Leastwise, he says he goes to class."

"He must be an extraordinary young boy."

She nodded. "Yeah. Like his daddy. Anyways, he plays his old beat-up guitar and sings, collecting coins in a tin can. He don't bring home much, and most weeks we short on cash. Hard to pay living expenses. Not sure what we gonna do, but we still got our faith."

This soul needed help. Anna decided she would provide it. But how and what? "You are a brave lady. I hope you can continue to carry on."

They reached the three-story Negro tenement. Upon entering the narrow apartment-like dwelling, Anna gasped in shock. An oppressive wave of heat carrying a mixture of foul, noxious smells almost pounded her against the interior wall. The long, dark hallway received no ventilation, leaving the air stale and the temperature stifling. They inched their way to Hattie's front door, the visibility being near zero and her eyes slow to readjust to the darkness.

Some residents wandered about, coming in and out of the rooms. Some had lanterns inside that momentarily lit the hallway until their doors closed. This grimy, depressing place represented the final stop for the poverty-stricken. From here, the residents would be forced to find shelter at the mission. Or move to the streets.

Hattie, struggling still to draw full breaths, unlocked the door, and they brought the groceries to the kitchen area. Once inside, Anna's shock turned to anger. She became furious that anyone in the city would be forced to live like this. One framed photo and a thin rack to hang jackets and sweaters on, decorated the four cracked, peeling walls in the one-room squalid apartment. An old shredded mattress with no sheets or blankets, a worthless, banged-up guitar, and a dirty splintered table rounded out their possessions. Anna ran her right hand across the small table, shoved in a corner to make room. As she did, a spider marched to the edge and stopped, waiting for the giant intruder's next move.

She imagined Hattie and her young ones seated there, in the only real gathering place, with the two-foot extensions on both sides lifted to create more eating space. The meager portions offering little nutritional value; the children going to bed on empty stomachs.

Charles's old guitar—cracked and missing two strings—sat upright in the opposite corner. Anna guessed that the three kids slept on the one dilapidated bed, leaving Hattie on the floor where an extra blanket had been laid out. The smell of urine permeated the space, no doubt the failed effort of her youngest to hold the urge until morning.

Behind the guitar, a rat scampered through an opening at the base of the wall. A shudder wiggled its way down her spine as the rodent's tail disappeared. She turned to face Hattie, marveling at the woman's peaceful manner in the midst of such circumstances. Would her own courage and faith be so unshakeable if she stood in Hattie's tattered shoes? So far, with only her basic rights under fire, she had disappointed herself.

She strained for something to say. "Where is the . . .?" She hesitated. "I mean, where do you . . .?"

"Got one privy for some forty people in the shed out back. Got all we need here."

Hattie introduced Charles, Raymond Junior, and Herman, the youngest at five years old. All lined up and greeted Anna with a warm afternoon welcome and a handshake. With little to show for a lifetime of hard work, this woman possessed a treasure trove in her children.

"A pleasure to meet you all."

They spoke for a few minutes longer about Hattie's illness and what little assistance she received from the local Baptist church. Many congregants found themselves in similar circumstances, and the church's resources were spread too thin. The woman did not complain. Rather, she bemoaned the fact that she could no longer cook and deliver meals to others in more dire straits like she did before Raymond left.

Could the story get much worse than this?

As Anna moved toward the front door and began saying her goodbyes, something weighed heavily on her mind. A trivial matter compared to Hattie's health issues and her living situation. Rather than setting her own issues aside, she decided to seek perspective from this wise person. Hattie, of all people, wouldn't judge her.

"May I confide in you?"

The sick woman nodded, but began coughing. She struggled to breathe.

"Hattie, are you all right?" Anna walked her over to the table where they both sat. She worried that Hattie's condition might be more serious than a simple chest congestion. Pneumonia, or worse—consumption. She would speak with her father about getting Hattie some medical attention.

The coughing subsided. "I'm afraid my forty-five years is catching up on me. You wanted to say something."

Anna didn't understand why, but she took comfort in Hattie's presence. She bared her heart to a total stranger, something she had never done, looking down at the ground the whole time. She shared about her trouble in the community, and how her relationship with her mother had suffered. About being drawn to Grover but still uncertain about him. And about her confusion over Peter. She asked for advice.

"What should I do? I'm not sure who I am anymore or who I want to become. Someone inside is waiting to bust out and experience the world beyond Chattanooga like my Aunt Harriet in New York. Sometimes I fumble for the words to express what I'm thinking."

Hattie nodded. "Uh-huh. Go on."

Anna walked across the small room, her hands clasped together. She turned around and said, "I'm paralyzed, unable to make decisions. Back at the grocery, I wanted to give that horrid woman a piece of my mind. But I couldn't speak the words. And I have a lot to say to Mr. Sawyer."

Hattie came to her side and stood close. She stroked Anna's hair, her warm but weary eyes revealing the physical toll of her illness and stress. The lines in her forehead and around her mouth and her solid gray hair made her appear much older than a woman in her forties. Anna turned away again, ashamed she had switched the focus to herself.

Hattie and her children lived with trials she could never imagine. Yet this woman's smile, which revealed that several of her teeth were missing, spread warmth, goodwill, and a sense that she had lived a hard but good life. So many others, like Mrs. Millwood back at the grocery, thought little of letting out their anger on the world. Anna wanted to grasp what made Hattie tick.

She turned again. "How do you do it, Hattie? How do you keep going on?"

The woman pondered the questions and delivered her answer, speaking to her three children.

"The temple on the outside be crumbling from the hard times. But the foundation on the inside still be standing strong and true. Never gonna wither."

The two younger children giggled with a confidence that their older sibling didn't share.

Hattie came close and pulled Anna's chin up. "Look at me . . . here, in my eyes, Missy. You be a caring person; only wants other folk to give you a chance to do things the world say is okay for them, but not for you. Believe me, Anna, I understand."

Anna's heart welled up with respect. "I'm sure you do, Hattie. I'm sorry. You possess such assurance, such . . ."

"Peace?"

"Yes. Peace. How did you find this elusive gift?"

"Oh, that's easy. From my mama, when I turn five year old. She say to me, you got to rise each morning and make the day better than the one before—even when things is looking grim."

That sounded way too simplistic for her complicated life. Case in point: The men around her were confusing enough. But her inability to stick with a decision about cycling made matters worse.

Hattie continued. "Now, this Grover fella, he'll show his true colors, one way or the other. Guaranteed. Some time from now, the truth be revealed. Trust the instincts the Lord done put into you. It was my faith led me to Raymond."

Anna let her deepest insecurities rise to the surface. "Maybe my limp embarrasses him."

An adventurous spirit before her accident, she now considered herself a cripple. When people stared at her, she heard them laughing on the inside. She wanted to change, but she continued to view herself through the distorted prism of her youth.

Hattie flashed a toothless grin. "You got a limp? Didn't notice."

Anna got the message. Maybe she assumed people thought a certain way, and they weren't pondering her limp at all. They both chuckled, but Hattie's laugh brought on a minor coughing attack. When the attack subsided, the strangest thing happened. Still watering, Hattie's eyes sparkled bright, like the waters of East Lake glistening in the morning light.

Who is this remarkable woman? Anna wondered.

"Here's my word to you, Miss Anna Gaines. We all slaves to who or what we bow down to. People make everything their god, except God his self. If the wheel is becoming your massah, you are its slave. If people are living their lives always trying to control you, they got the wrong massah too. They be the ones in chains. So, I'm asking, what do you worship?"

"I'm not sure I understand. The one I bow down to, the Creator, is a who, not a what."

"All right. If it be something, or someone, bigger than the wheel and larger than what you gonna do with your life or what things you possess, then you be okay."

She began to follow Hattie's meaning. When the thing one seeks after becomes an idol, all is lost. After Anna said goodbye to the children, Hattie came to the door with her.

"You find the source of all things righteous, and you be fine no matter what you trying to do."

❧⚜☙

Emma knocked on Anna's bedroom door.

"Come in." Anna relaxed on her bed, resting before Mrs. Byrne called for dinner.

Emma plopped down next to her. "So, what did you do all day? I tried to catch up with you."

She shifted toward Emma, eager for her response to Hattie's prescription for peaceful living. "Do you know the true source of significance and value in life? At least in your life."

Emma mulled the question. "I believe I do. Why?"

Anna didn't wait for an explanation. She made a decision in her head and heart and wanted to share it with her best friend. After much reflection on Hattie's advice, she decided to do the right thing in this matter. Stand up to the bullies. They would continue to define her falsely, but she would dodge the slings and arrows.

"I'm not going to live my life as a slave to be pushed around at the whim of others. Tomorrow I will take the trolley out to East Lake and walk the rest of the way to the farm if I must. After I visit with the family, I'm going to ride back to the boarding house and store my wheel in Mrs. Byrne's carriage house, if she'll allow me. If not, I will find a place to live that will."

Emma giggled her approval. "Now we're getting somewhere."

Peter Sawyer and the wheelmen, or whoever decided to make this issue worthy of legislation, would get a true picture of a woman cyclist—up close and personal. Braced for the battle, she expected to be bloodied, but this time she would remain standing.

Chapter Twenty

AT THE FIRST crowing, Anna rolled over with her hands covering her ears. When that didn't blot out the disruptive sound, she ducked under the covers. No use. The daily reveille, courtesy of the city's proud cocks, roused her. Rather than lie in bed, she dressed for the day ahead. She wore the same skirt, boots, and corset as when she and Harriet glided over five miles past a hoard of onlookers on the new bike path to Coney Island.

As she descended the stairs and entered the center hall, Mrs. Byrne called out to her. "Top o' the mornin' to ya."

"And the rest o' the day to you."

Mrs. Byrne, standing at the entry into the dining area, ambled toward one of the wood-framed photographs hanging askew on the wall. She straightened the decoration and walked over to Anna. "Early to rise on a Sunday morning."

"I didn't sleep well. The call-to-arms from our feathered friends outside didn't help matters." She gave the woman her ritual once-a-day hug, a requirement of residency when Anna took the room. They had shared a growing bond in the intervening months, on occasion talking into the evening while the other residents enjoyed parlor games like charades and graces.

"Usual time for an old lady. Besides, I needed to help Mamie prepare breakfast." The faithful servant had been with the house for over a decade and tended to the day's first meal in the summer kitchen. "Are you off to church at this hour?"

A regular every week, either at First Presbyterian in town or the small congregation her parents attended in Chickamauga, Anna would not be sitting in a pew this Sunday. Her worship would be in conversation with the Almighty as she traveled back to the farm.

"No, Mrs. Byrne. I need to handle some business back home, so I'll be taking the trolley out to the east end."

"What about the rest of the way?"

She would figure something out. "Not sure."

The proprietress insisted on hitching her horse to the buggy out back and giving her a lift. At her age, a spry sixty-two, Mrs. Byrne kept as active as her young boarders, doing as much around the house as any man might—with some exceptions. In this way, she reminded Anna of herself.

"I, too, will skip, and once we've finished eating, we'll leave. I insist."

"Oh no, I cannot impose. You go enjoy the Sunday morning mass. I will call on the Brody family, good friends of my parents out near Missionary Ridge. The Brodys are Jewish so their Sabbath is on Saturday. I'm confident they will be home and can transport me the rest of the way."

"Come then. Can't leave on an empty stomach. Mamie's bread is almost ready, and the combination of cheese and some of her homemade preserves is to die for. We'll put some coffee up." She grabbed Anna's hand and led her into the eating area. "First, help me set the table, then we'll talk."

They walked through the full kitchen, complete with a fireplace, a sink with running water, a cast iron cook stove with five burners and an oven fueled by wood, and an ice-box. Shelves and racks held the pots and pans, mixing bowls, and various cooking utensils. For the first time, Anna discovered that Mrs. Byrne stored her many sets of dishes, glassware, linens, and other tableware in the adjacent pantry along with food items. She dreamed of having a full kitchen like this someday.

White cloths covered the long table in the dining room that seated up to nine people. They made place settings for the seven people expected to sit, eager to satisfy their morning hunger pangs. Mrs. Byrne, who sat at the head of the table, always took meals with her guests. The area had caught Anna's eye as a comfortable gathering place the day she submitted an application for residency.

The crackling fire on the hearth six months before and the walnut-stained mantel that continued down the sides turning into wood panels on the lower half of the walls, created a relaxed space. A cheery yellow paint covered the rest with framed hanging photos sprinkled around the room. Cherry-stained, wood-planked floors and a colorful throw rug beneath the table added an additional layer of richness to the milieu.

The mealtime repartee amidst this cozy backdrop had turned cold in recent days. Two of the renters had left; nevertheless, she still enjoyed eating at the Byrne house. The room gave her a sense of home away from home.

"Come now. Sit, Anna." Mamie delivered a platter of warm bread and cheese to the table and filled their coffee cups. "What business, other than giving God His due, takes you to the farm on a Sunday morning?"

"Oh, Mrs. Byrne. My life is somewhat tangled at the moment. I don't think you want to talk about my concerns."

The woman would not be deterred. "Try me. And it's time you called me Rose."

They talked first about Irish Rose. Anna had never asked about her younger years or about her husband, Daniel. Whenever his name came up, Rose turned misty-eyed, so Anna didn't push.

"My brogue has faded with time. Just a hint of an accent now."

"Oh, I can hear it Mrs. . . . ." The proprietor waved a finger. "I mean Rose. Force of habit."

"Can you now?"

"When conversations around this table get interesting, you often become animated about some of the questionable goings on around town. The accent finds its way past your tongue. It fits you."

Rose talked about the Chattanooga Irish, who came from their mother country in the mid-forties in the massive waves of immigration to escape poverty, centuries-old oppression, and the Great Potato Famine of 1845. Her family arrived that year after her twelfth birthday. Daniel Byrne, eight years Rose's senior and the first child in his brood to be born in America, worked on the rail system that earned Chattanooga its distinction as the Gateway to the South.

One day, unannounced, her father, also a railroad man, brought Daniel to the house for dinner after a grueling day of laying lines. Both families resided near each other on Irish Hill.

"I met Daniel in 1850 when I turned seventeen. So, young love is familiar to me."

She winked, and deep crow's feet lined her sparkling eyes. Anna pictured a youthful Rose, wrinkle-free, the best of life before her. She couldn't resist. "Was he handsome?"

With eyes wide and lips puckered, Rose nodded as though the man of her dreams sat right next to her. "A real looker."

They married soon after and conceived seven children. Two died as infants and one as an adult. Anna reached out and tenderly touched Rose's arm. "To lose children must have been horrible."

"In fact, you remind me of Ida, our first who passed during an outbreak of Yellow Fever back in the seventies. She had just turned twenty when the Plague of Memphis migrated to Chattanooga and cut her young life short. Gracious Lord, we mourned for months."

After the war, Daniel became a successful homebuilder. He built their house in the late 1870s where they raised their boys and operated a thriving contracting business during most of the following decade until his unexpected death five years ago. They shared many happy years together, the last few eschewing involvement with Chattanooga's high-minded elites for time with the lower-class Irish immigrants—the men who had built the railroads in and out of the Chattanooga Valley and were disappearing from the scene on Irish Hill. Some went to their heavenly reward, others settled elsewhere. A remnant remained on the hill named after their people.

"When Daniel went to heaven, I decided to turn the home into a boarding house for single and widowed women, more for the social interaction than a need for money. Daniel left me well to do, enough to weather the economic storms that beset us and then some."

The house supplemented her income and provided her the opportunity to care for the unattached ladies of her community. Anna had been reflecting on what it took to be a pioneering woman, and Rose fit the bill perfectly.

"Rose . . ." Anna stopped and mused for a moment. "Hmm. I will like calling you by your first name. Been thinking a lot about change. Do you think people can change—I mean, inside?"

Rose recalled how soon after their marriage, she had wanted to change some things about Daniel. Like his hygiene after long days on the railroad and later building houses. Many nights he came home and fell comatose into bed without cleaning up a bit. He tended to leave his clothes strewn around the house, a bad example for his boys. She loved him despite his faults and stopped her efforts to transform him. As a result, he began bathing more.

"A willingness to adapt to new situations, like a marriage, is the key to personal growth." She chuckled.

"What's the grin for?"

"My body isn't what it used to be. Youth snuck away from me in a blink of an eye. Some changes are bad like the loss of a child. Yes, I believe people can reform themselves, if they choose. One person's efforts to change can alter history. Even the story of an entire city."

Anna concluded that becoming a better version of one's self took hard work. A metamorphosis never happens overnight.

Rose stood and padded around the table to examine the settings, each an example of order and class in a world of chaos. She adjusted the napkin at one place, insisting her table be a statement of perfection and excellence. The woman displayed a keen sense of Southern culture, one of style and refinement. Yet she imagined Rose kicking up her heels at a jig with the best of them.

"Rose, you're going to be exposed to some negative things about me in some circles. This uproar about me riding the bicycle." She had grown fond of the woman and did not wish to cause her trouble.

"Dear girl, those whispers have already flown into one ear and quickly exited the other. No surprise, given how everyone is talking about the stories in the *Times*. My other boarders have already threatened to leave if your attachment to the bicycle continues."

"Oh, Rose. I'm so sorry." She walked over to her friend and hugged her.

Two other residents came down the steps, chatting away as they entered the dining room. One of them made a derisive comment about the bicycle issue that hung in the air. The women clammed up the moment they laid eyes on Anna. They took their places at the end of the long table as Mamie offered them coffee. Rose walked Anna back into the hallway.

"Pay no mind to those magpies." She leaned in and whispered. "I told them, they're free to find new accommodations any time the mood strikes."

"What if they leave?"

The lady of the house took both of her hands, another assurance that she supported Anna's quest for personal freedom. "Daniel and I once pursued our own dream, to climb above the prejudices of narrow-minded people against the working-class Irish. We wanted only to be considered as Chattanoogans."

"You're an inspiration to me. Thank you for your encouragement. I will be cycling more in the coming days, and I predict life is about to become more difficult for both of us."

Rose pledged to buy her own wheel and start riding. An amusing picture crossed Anna's mind: the young agitator and her older accomplice, cycling in bloomers to the astonishment of everyone they greeted. Rose gave her permission to park the wheel in her carriage house.

❧

Mr. and Mrs. Brody planned to visit friends in Chickamauga in the early afternoon, so they dropped Anna at the farm. She bid them a good day and walked the last half mile across the field she played on many times as a child.

The sun sought cover behind a cloud, shielding her from its powerful rays. The air stood still, thickened by the July humidity. A few intermittent raindrops fell, but that often changed from one breath to the next. Immediate thunderstorms might loosen from the billowy skies without warning, so she carried an umbrella.

When she approached the farmhouse, the place appeared deserted. As she thought, the family would not return for another hour or so. This would allow her to avoid a confrontation with her mother. Her heart saddened when she pictured Mama's face. There must be a reconciliation—but not now. On this trip, she would gather her bloomers into a satchel, take her vehicle from the barn, and pedal her way back into the city to Rose's house.

She came through the side door and found her mama sitting at the kitchen table. "Mama . . . ?"

She looked up, her cheeks wet. "Oh . . . I didn't expect you to come today." She wiped her face with her hands. "Everybody's in church."

Anna walked over to the table and pulled out a chair next to her mother. "Why aren't you with them?"

Mama sighed, and a new wave of tears emerged from her eyes. She took Anna's hands into hers. "I guess I'm a bit melancholic today."

"I've been sad all week, too. The way we left things over the weekend."

Her mama's face spoke a hundred misgivings and a single need for reconciliation. "I'm sorry, Anna. Please understand—your happiness and wellbeing are the most important things. You are precious to me."

Anna's eyes welled up as she embraced her mother. "I love you, Mama."

"Maybe I am too overprotective and need to give you space to let you find your own way. I must remember you're a woman now. Forgive me."

"I do, Mama. Please forgive me as well."

Anna rose and stared out the kitchen window to where the hens in the nearby coop clucked and walked about. She missed feeding the chickens every day and collecting their eggs. Despite her complaints as a child, she fondly recalled milking the cows. Life seemed less complicated when she lived under her parents' protection.

She turned back to her mama who joined her at the window. Anna pulled the net and pins from her auburn hair. Mama gently wove her fingers through the locks, like she did all those years ago.

"Life used to be so simple," Anna said.

"You loved life and embraced each day with gusto. Until the accident."

Yes, she had turned into a different little girl, but she had changed again—for the better. She was beginning to like the new Anna more than the old one.

"I'm going to ride, Mama, but not because I'm defying you. And I will cycle in my special outfit made for the comfort of women cyclists." She stopped to gauge her mama's reaction, one of silence. "And I will take to the streets because I love the physical activity and the leisure that riding brings me; because the wrong-headed behavior of people must stop being judged as right by others."

Unrestrained now about her views on the bicycle, Anna no longer fretted about what people would think of her.

"I'm afraid." Mama turned pale, her elbows drawn to her sides.

"Me too, Mama. Certain people will not like that I'm breaking the rules. The country is changing, and the South should begin to change along with the times. All I can do is ask for your support."

Her mother's tearful nod showered assurances upon Anna. Now her whole family stood united. People must sometimes take principled stands even at their own risk. Mama, still filled with trepidation, now agreed, and that added an impenetrable iron to Anna's shield of courage. She hugged her mother, went upstairs, and changed into another outfit. One she had long waited to debut.

She mounted Choo Choo, the name she had given to her wheel, and began to ride.

❦

As Anna traveled the McFarland Gap Road toward East Lake, the clouds opened up and let loose a rain shower lasting for several minutes.

The droplets soaked her face and saturated her bloomers, but she didn't care. She rejoiced in the wetness, singing her favorite hymn, "How Great Thou Art," and pedaling at a moderate pace. Riding in God's creation would be her worship today.

By the time she passed the lake and rode north on Dodds Avenue and west on Chamberlain, the precipitation had stopped. The sky cleared, revealing the earth's own star in all its glory and power—one among the billions of stars she couldn't see, scattered like sand across the universe. The heat warmed her and began to dry her outfit.

She rode to McCallie and over to Oak Street where some of Chattanooga's wealthiest citizens occupied some of the finest homes. The roundabout route would expose her to the upper crust of society, the people who opposed her. So, she rode in plain view, head held high, to make a statement.

Anna pedaled slowly, sitting erect in the seat and looking at some of the city's most beautiful homes on both sides of the road.

Many people had returned from Sunday services, changed their clothes, eaten lunch, and now lounged on their porches, enjoying a casual afternoon. Children romped outside, and people strolled along the sidewalks. Farther down Oak, she overheard some of the comments spoken extra loud for her benefit. The stares from curious homeowners were obvious.

One house captured her eye, so she stopped riding to take a gander. The two-story structure sat on an oversized swath of land. The light-green wood siding, fanciful eaves, white-painted windowpanes, corner tower, and prominent porch gave the house a unique look, setting it apart from the other Victorian-era structures.

Scanning the front, she was surprised by whom she found. The stern, cruel woman from Sawyer's grocery the day she met Hattie Washington—the lady who had shown no compassion toward someone ill and lacking the money to buy food for her kids. The clerk had mentioned her name that day. The shock of seeing her again replayed in her mind the question she had just posed to her mama before leaving the farmhouse.

"Mama, what can you tell me about a woman named Mrs. Millwood?"

Her mama had turned white. With a blank stare, she muttered, "Bertha Millwood," and climbed up the stairs. The ominous response had given Anna pause.

Now, there she stood, elegantly dressed, drowning in all her opulence. The woman's unlined face and dyed jet-black hair gave her a youthful appearance. In fact, Anna found her attractive. Except for one disturbing detail.

Mrs. Millwood stared right at Anna, a dour expression engraved on her face.

Chapter Twenty-One

ON MONDAY, ANNA rode her wheel to Loveman's and locked it outside in a secure area. At mid-morning, her supervisor, Hawkeye Helms, marched over to her machine, perturbed about something.

"Miss Gaines, did you ride to Loveman's this morning?"

Unfazed by his imposing presence, she rose and studied the man's eyes. "Yes, Mr. Helms. The bicycle is such a convenient transport. The air invigorates me, prepares me for a day's work, and fills me with a positive attitude. Try out the wheel sometime and you'll understand."

Anna's confident response caught the supervisor by surprise.

"Well . . . I . . . received a few negative comments from employees and customers, and frankly, this can't be allowed. I'll admit you are a conscientious worker, Miss Gaines, but I must ask you to refrain from riding to Loveman's. Thank you."

He walked away. Anna peered at the women on both sides of her machine. Having stopped to witness the confrontation, they raised their eyebrows, beamed, and continued sewing. She sat, a grin plastered on her face. Victorious in the skirmish, but a war had been declared.

She exceeded her normal quota and took on additional orders in what promised to be a productive morning.

On Tuesday, she rode to work, and Hawkeye Helms gave her another stern warning, this time implying her job might be in jeopardy if the insubordination continued. The word spread, and more customers complained. In the evening, Emma encouraged Anna to stand her ground and said she would make inquiries with friends in other shops about possible employment. On Wednesday, having ridden a third day to work, Anna was preparing to take her lunch break when Hawkeye Helms lowered the boom.

"Sorry, Miss Gaines, but since you choose to ignore my warnings, you leave me no alternative but to dismiss you. Come by on Friday and collect your final pay."

Anna stared straight at him. This time, the supervisor cast his eyes downward; for once, the other person blinked first. Heartened, Anna took her calm response as a sign of personal growth. Something greater than a job stood in the balance. The cowardly manager walked off, mumbling under his breath. She clung to her courage, which wanted to seep onto the floor and dribble away.

"Until Friday, Mr. Helms, when I pick up my pay. Until then, I wish you well. And I thank you for the opportunity to work here." If he heard her, Hawkeye Helms chose not to respond.

She gathered her things, retrieved her wheel, and rode off to catch Emma at the pants factory before her lunch break. They sat outside and ate together. Emma listened to Anna's story and expressed little surprise.

"Oh, Emma . . . I'm worried. And scared."

"We expected this might happen," Emma said. "When we're finished eating, I want you to go across the street to the upholstery shop and talk to this man." She took a piece of paper and a pencil from her handbag and wrote down the name Robert McCausland.

"Do you know him well?"

"An Irish friend of the family. I spoke with him yesterday. As luck would have it, one of his seamstresses married a month ago and moved to Memphis last week."

Nervous about a future with no job, that afternoon she met with McCausland, who indicated he might have something for her, but she needed to come back next week for another meeting. A promising first step, but she must broaden the search. The experience in a respected store like Loveman's might bring her some cachet, but being let go after only six months would be viewed in a negative light. As she visited other shops in town, she developed a nuanced response to the difficult conundrum when it arose. After climbing a final trolley back to the boarding house, she considered the last alternative: doing private piecemeal work in homes. Inconsistent. Not her preference.

While she had nowhere to go on Friday, she decided that day would be her coming out party.

⇜❖⇝

Rose and Emma insisted on sending her off.

The plan was to ride the streets of the city, dressed in bloomers, for most of the day. She would stop on the corner of Market and Seventh for lunch and a soda in the Live and Let Live Drugstore, do some window shopping, and meet Emma at the pants factory before the sun fell off the western horizon. Anna descended the stairs, relishing her moment of glory and the collective look of approval on their faces. She giggled.

Emma blurted out her excitement. "Ha!"

Rose nodded her head and winked. A woman cycling the downtown roadways would, in itself, cause an uproar. But this—riding in such a revealing costume in front of the world—would add insult to injury.

Cooler temperatures the night before had brought much relief, and forecasters predicted lower temperatures would follow today, not quite as hot and muggy. But the weather was not the reason she would ride in unrestrained freedom. The principle of the matter egged her on. The time had arrived for her to rise up.

"What do you think?" She turned in a full circle as they examined her from head to toe.

"Scandalous," Emma said.

Rose bent down and pulled the elastic band that held one of the shortened pant legs to just below the knee. The old lady harkened back to her early adult years. "Turn the clock back forty years and . . ." A deep sigh followed.

The bottom half of this outfit revealed a lot of leg. An arrest for indecent exposure would turn her parents on their heels.

She pedaled her way east on Ninth Street, then over to Gilmer, and slowed as she approached the overhead railroad bridge. At the entrance to the pass, she waved to the conductor who blew the whistle twice to acknowledge her while the train barreled past on the track below. Billows of dark smoke from the engine's stack climbed to the sky. The pollution caused her to cough, reminding her of Hattie.

She crossed over to McCallie going west, then to Oak, wheeling beyond Chattanooga University and the First District School. People stared, astounded to see someone wearing such sparse clothing in public. She greeted them all, wishing them a fine morning.

One little girl playing in front of her house came bolting onto the macadamized street—right into Anna's pathway—when her ball got away. Anna swerved to avoid hitting the child and fell to the road. Shocked, she lay still for several moments while she took a mental inventory for any major injuries. She moved her legs and arms. Nothing broken, thank God, just some scratches on both hands when she broke the fall. One of Oscar's first lessons, how to take a safe tumble, came in handy.

Still in one piece, Anna sat up. She had ridden within the proposed speed limit for wheelers, another reason she escaped harm. Some bruises might show up later, but at least her outfit didn't tear. That would have upset her. None the worse for wear, she stood, brushed herself off, and walked her wheel to the side of the road. An examination revealed Choo Choo's first battle scar—a scratch on the handlebar.

As she sat to collect herself, the girl came over.

"Are you hurt?" The child appeared to be around eight years old, with brown hair tumbling beneath her bonnet in ringlets to her shoulders. She wore a white smock.

The fallen rider looked up. "I'm fine. Want to sit with me for a few minutes?"

"Okay."

"Like your dress." Anna ran her hands over the material, and noticed the girl's face had turned red, probably from playing ball in the heat. "Are you hot?"

"Yeah. Kinda." The girl goggled at Anna, who tried to place her face. From church? Perhaps they met at Tschopik's. They sat in silence for a full minute while Anna racked her brain to remember how she recognized the girl.

"Will you tell me your name?"

"Hope . . . Nichols." The name didn't ring any bells at first, but seconds later, she remembered. Gabriel Nichols, a classmate from her senior year in high school. One of the few young men with whom she had engaged in conversation during the semester. As she recalled, he was cuckoo over his little sister Hope. Anna had run into Gabriel and Hope about a year ago while shopping in town.

"Hi, Hope Nichols. I'm Anna Gaines."

The girl continued to stare at her. Her curiosity could no longer be subdued. "I've seen you before. Are you the person my mama always talks about? You must be, because here you are, riding a bicycle."

Anna Gaines, again the topic of suppertime banter. "Well, I guess so, little Hope." The untarnished innocence of a child, like a spotless lamb.

"She and my daddy argue about whether girls should cycle. He doesn't think there's anything wrong with females riding a wheel. My mama thinks differently."

"What do you think?"

She gazed back at her house, came to a swift conclusion, and flashed a dimpled grin. "When I get older, I want to be like you. Maybe I can wear a costume like yours."

Hope's mother ran out to the street, took her hand, and scolded her on the way back into the house for talking with a stranger. Wide-eyed, the little girl disappeared behind the closed door, but not before giving one wave of goodbye to the woman cyclist.

Would Hope Nichols ever get her wish?

Chapter Twenty-Two

ANNA MOVED ON to Market Street and passing the Fischer Evans post clock, she noted the time. Half-past eleven. Not quite lunchtime, but her stomach growled its unwillingness to wait. Her left hip ached from the fall, but Anna pedaled on toward Live and Let Live Drugstore.

She parked her wheel in front of the Central Block Building, careful to lock it securely. After climbing several steps to the third floor, she entered her second favorite place in the city, next to Tschopik's.

She missed the rush, set to begin in fifteen minutes. The forty-foot counter, replete with marble and bronze decorations and four drink dispensers staffed by as many young men, would soon be inundated by dozens of hungry patrons. She perused the wall-mounted menu above the counter. A sandwich from the delicatessen would do the trick, along with a soft drink and ice cream.

Ten people stood in line. Everyone turned toward her. Two women, fanning themselves in long dresses, brought their free hands to their mouths, surprised by her costume. Boisterous conversations suddenly turned to deafening silence, and some heads shook with disapproval.

Being the focus of attention and scorn in such small quarters began to shake her mettle.

Still, she took her place in line. By the time she reached the long fountain, she had lost her appetite for lunch. She requested a beverage and two scoops of chocolate. Hopefully the ice cream would ease her nerves. Herbert Beard, the young manager behind the counter, declined to take her order and asked her to leave. She refused to budge and repeated her request.

"Madam, you are disrupting our business here. Again, I must ask you to vacate." Both of them held their ground.

Many more people entered the line and witnessed the embarrassing scene. Anna's first inclination to withdraw gave way to a surge of courage. She forced herself to speak up. "I have done nothing wrong. I deserve—no, I demand to be treated like any other paying customer."

Mr. Beard leaned toward her and whispered. "Please, I don't wish to further embarrass you by having someone escort you from the premises." His hands shook, so he laced his fingers. His face revealed a panicked young man, out of his league in having to make such decisions.

Someone behind her stepped forward. The voice needed no face to be identified. "Sir, as the owner of a retail enterprise in town, may I offer you advice? Accommodate the lady. Avoid turning a bad situation into something worse."

Peter Sawyer gave her a tip of his hat. A quick peripheral glance at him revealed a man with equal parts charm, confidence, and sureness of purpose. At least, that's what she saw on the outside. She tried to fight off the allure of his undeniable appeal. A score still remained to be settled.

The manager resisted. "Mr. Sawyer, my instructions for difficult circumstances like this require me—"

"To use discretion. So please do choose to serve this woman. Sawyer Enterprises enjoys strong business relations with the founders of this wonderful establishment. It would be a shame for you to risk your job for so petty a matter. But make your decision quickly. As you can see, these patient customers are waiting. Thank you, sir."

Everyone in line had stopped talking to hear the encounter. All eyes were glued on the manager, whose hands continued to shake.

"Of course, Mr. Sawyer." He turned to Anna. "One soda and two scoops of chocolate. Coming right up."

The order came in time for her to take the last available table. There were four tables to seat a growing clientele, an oversight the owners pledged to fix within the next two months. The poster in the entrance promised this and other improvements as part of an overall remodel. She sat, reflecting on the bizarre interaction. What just happened? Peter's voice again shook her from distant thoughts.

"Excuse me. The poster on the wall promises that this eatery will soon be expanded. But my ice cream will melt if I have to wait for them to put in more seats."

His mere presence, as if by magic, drowned out the accusatory chatter and stares of condemnation from the people around them. She imagined that an impenetrable glass dome had been lowered over them. What did he want?

"Yes . . .?" He had ordered the same items as her.

"May I join you here?" Peter asked. "The other tables are full."

She squirmed in her seat. "I . . ." This was her chance, but she needed to speak up.

❧❖❧

"Promise I won't bite. Please." She looked up at him with uncertain eyes. He stood there, face to face with an enigma.

On the one hand, she seemed somewhat awkward, unsure of herself. But standing across from a woman dressed in bloomers, in full view of the community, did not square in his view with someone who was faint of heart. The meek woman he thought her to be only moments ago stood up for her right to be served under the scrutiny of many onlookers without any hint of embarrassment. What had changed?

"Yes . . . yes, of course, Mr. Sawyer. Have a seat. No one else will be seen sitting next to me."

Her initial restraint seemed to softened as her ice cream also began to melt. Unable to figure her out, he took a bite of his own dessert and let the tension at the table dissipate. Did she dislike him for some reason?

"Miss Gaines, please call me Peter. And by the way . . . their loss."

"Sorry?"

"Not having the pleasure of your company. They lose."

Anna gathered some ice cream on her spoon, but instead of eating, she swallowed a small swig of coke. She appeared unsettled by his comment. Not hard to imagine because he too had a fluttery sensation in the pit of his stomach. The compliment sounded too forward in his mind, but he gave voice to it anyway, perhaps overstepping his bounds. She moved the dessert around in her dish.

He took another run at breaking the awkwardness. "Perfect day for a refreshing treat, don't you think?"

The uncomfortable circumstances didn't affect his desire to eat. He took a man-sized portion, closed his eyes, and savored the taste. Lifting her napkin, she symbolically dabbed her own lips twice. He got the message. Some ice cream remained at one corner of his mouth.

"This is about my favorite thing in the world. I come around here often to indulge my weakness." He pointed to her bowl. "By the way, you will be sipping yours soon."

"Huh?"

"Yours is melting."

"Oh . . ." She took a bite. "Yeah. Tasty ice cream."

He put his spoon down and glanced around at the crowd. His eyes came back to hers. They magically came alive, piercing through her protective shell, like stabs of sunlight peeking through a sky shrouded in dark clouds. Hypnotized for several moments, he willed himself to break the spell he was under but found it difficult to avert his gaze. She unlocked and looked down. The welcome respite made him realize he hadn't taken a breath. He was acting like a star-struck schoolboy.

He tried speaking in soft, comforting tones. "May I call you by your first name?"

He and the ice cream continued to melt as he awaited her reply.

"I suppose so." Did he let out an audible sigh of relief?

"And you must call me Peter."

"Okay."

"As I tried to say before, you needn't be afraid of me. Most folks who make my acquaintance say I'm a decent guy." He felt the blood rush to his face. "Oh, my gosh, did that sound conceited?"

She beguiled him. "No. At least, I don't think so."

⭒✦⭒

Anna found herself venturing into dangerous waters so she sat back in her chair and turned more stiff and formal. Mr. Sawyer must be made to answer for his actions concerning the petition drive.

She issued her challenge head on. "No reason to fear you, or so you say. Why are you and your friends trying to turn the citizenry against me? All I want is the same freedom to ride that men enjoy."

The accusation obviously shook him. The whites of his eyes increased in size, and his brows shot higher. "What . . . ? Do you actually think I'm behind the petitions . . . and . . . and all the gossiping about scandals and ruining the Southern way of life?"

He appeared wounded. Of course, he would swear against any complicity; she expected as much. "This is what I know to be true. Are you denying your involvement?" she asked.

Dear God, she hoped she hadn't falsely accused him. She watched as the little boy in him surfaced, desperate to protect his name.

"Here is the truth," he said. "Most men in the club do not want you, or any other female, riding a bicycle in Chattanooga. But I'm not one of them."

Could this be possible?

"Tell me then, who is behind all this?" She examined his face to detect any hint of deception. He didn't bat an eye.

"Many culprits skulk around our community like spies—and we're surrounded by a lot of narrow-minded people stuck in the past. The Southern way of life offers many fine qualities, but empowering women isn't one of them. Far as I can tell, Mrs. Bertha Millwood is your misguided perpetrator. At least one of them. Best to steer clear of her."

The revelation sank in, but she suspected he was holding back. In hindsight, what he said made sense. She seemed a cruel, troubled woman, and Anna's previous interactions with the socialite had been tense. Anna discovered that some of the other clubs in town, like the Kosmos, had circulated petitions. Bertha Millwood cut a daunting figure in those groups.

"Mrs. Millwood. But why?"

He shared the gist of her tragic story. Some time ago her daughter ran off with a man and later turned up dead. Murdered. The information took Anna's breath away. She lamented the woman's misfortune but didn't understand what this horrible story had to do with her or bicycle riding.

"In some twisted way, maybe she's trying to protect you from yourself—to rescue you since she couldn't save her own daughter. My theory, near as I can make out. But who really knows?"

All things considered, maybe Mrs. Millwood deserved her pity, not anger and disdain. "Naturally, I concluded that . . ."

"Because I'm a man, and I ride the wheel almost everywhere, I must support all this nonsense. Right?"

She nodded her head. "I'm sorry, Mr. Sawyer . . . Peter. Perhaps I've made a mistake."

They stood to make room for other diners. "May I walk you to your bike?" he asked.

After a moment of contemplation, she nodded again.

"One more thing before we go, Anna. Be watchful around Grover Biggs. He also is not what he appears to be."

The ominous warning rattled her. She and Grover would rendezvous on Sunday at the train depot for a day on Lookout Mountain. She tried to banish any untoward opinions about him. He had proven that his intentions toward her were honorable, and she rested in that assurance. Why would Peter try to tarnish Grover's name? No longer willing to walk on eggshells, she came right out and asked.

"It strikes me as unfair for you to indict Mr. Biggs without giving him a chance to defend himself. Why would you do so?"

He seemed to be caught off guard, hesitant. "Yes, you're right. Ungentlemanly of me. Please, I do apologize."

She wanted to think the best of him. "Apology accepted." As they walked, she spoke about Hattie Washington, the colored woman in his store. "The way you handled the situation impressed me."

She shared the rest of Hattie's story about how Raymond, her husband, had disappeared while looking for work two years before. The subject captured Peter's attention. Talking about Hattie reminded her to mention the basket idea to Rose. Hattie's family needed food, and Rose's kitchen overflowed with provisions. A long-term solution was also necessary, so she would seek her father's counsel about Hattie's medical condition and how they might help her.

Peter maintained a steady gaze straight ahead, his eyes squinting. "Did she mention anything about Raymond's last location?"

"Atlanta—according to his final letter. Said he would head deeper south to find more work." She gave him a description—height, weight, and the scar across his forehead, the handiwork of some plantation overseer's knife soon after the war ended. "Why the interest?"

"Oh, no reason. Just curious."

When they reached the area where she had left her wheel, Peter sensed something was out of place. They found the bicycle crumpled on the ground. The spokes on the front wheel were destroyed, and the tire's frame was bent out of shape.

"Who would do such a deplorable thing?" Peter asked. Despite his earlier apology, he answered his own question, but refrained from mentioning Grover's name. He needed proof.

Under other circumstances, this act of wanton vandalism would have incensed him. But with Anna here, he wanted to be part of the solution, to provide a sense of calm. She brought out the best in him. He unlatched the tire repair kit attached to his own bicycle and removed the battered wheel. They walked the short distance to Graham's on East Eighth Street to purchase a replacement.

The vandal's intention was to send a message to Anna.

Stop riding the wheel.

Chapter Twenty-Three

PETER HAD ATTACHED Anna's new bicycle wheel and returned to the grocery. Seymour, the sleuth, entered the store from the back door and proceeded to Peter's office where he gave three rapid knocks, followed by one. Peter opened the door a crack, allowing the gentleman to enter.

The man tipped his hat.

"Greetings, Seymour," Peter said. "Read your earlier account and assumed some additional information would be forthcoming." He invited the Atlanta man to take a seat across from him.

Peter didn't mind his cramped quarters. His tastes were simple, his needs few. The area contained a desk and a couple of chairs, some file cabinets, a safe, and a few photos on the walls. One photo pictured his father and him after he had placed first in an amateur race in Atlanta the previous fall. A great day with his father cheering him on. A small throw rug covered much of the wood-planked floor, adding a touch of warmth to the otherwise drab space.

Distracted, Peter's mind wandered almost immediately.

Most Cycle Club members held him in high esteem—until recently. The membership pressed him to be more vocal in representing the club's opinion about women cyclists. Before long, he expected some associates to launch a revolt to push him out. The unrest in the city, and now all this sleuthing around Grover Biggs, took him away from his passion—riding the wheel. One pleasant diversion did remain. Anna Gaines.

"Yes. More intelligence." The detective's faint voice pulled Peter from his distraction.

"Pardon?"

"My business, Peter, is observation. You asked if I found something new. Yes, I did, and I can give you a verbal rundown if you want to save all the particulars for your reading pleasure." The investigator handed him the written notes.

"Summarize for now. But first I want to make sure I understand the facts of your initial account." He recounted what he had learned.

A defrauder, Grover Biggs had been run out of Atlanta and pursued his schemes around Memphis and Nashville before landing in Chattanooga. One swindle involved posing as a Catholic priest from New York. With credentials appearing authentic, he gained the confidence and hospitality of the head clergyman for a couple of days. He would scout the local jewelry store and request some diamonds and other choice stones be taken to the head priest's residence, as he ostensibly sought a gift for a cardinal.

When the jeweler arrived, the swindler answered the door in a priest's garments, and asked to take the precious cargo into another room to display the gems to other men of the cloth waiting there. Before anyone became aware of the plot, the fake exited out the back.

"Nasty business," Peter said. "Did I accurately capture the ruse?"

The sleuth shook his head in agreement. "Well done, Peter. Indeed, an accurate summary of my original detailed write-up."

Many people called Peter savvy for his age, a perfect model for younger boys to emulate. Everybody's dream son. Such praise would swell anyone's head, but he worked hard at practicing humility, to the point of self-deprecation. Sometimes he failed, but he acknowledged his shortcomings, and his mother helped to keep his ego in check.

"The Sawyer family is paying you top dollar, sir. Better do my homework well and at least read your reports."

The former policeman relit his smoke. "Agreed."

"So, what is the reason for this visit?"

"This man in question is in the employ of your father at the lumberyard. Somewhat of a newcomer here who actually hails from my hometown, Atlanta."

"Yes. That much we knew . . . but this information supports our suspicions about him." The link that he hoped and prayed did not exist, despite the tension between them. "Go on."

"Appears he and others are now working a bigger con twenty-five years in the making. Details about the local players are sketchy, but the scheme goes beyond this fair city. Accusations of fraud have abounded in recent years, but the business has never been proven false. The likes of J. J. Astor and other investors—doctors, lawyers, bankers, and businessmen—have been associated with this outfit called . . . let me find the name here . . ."

One thing Peter's father had taught him early on: Patience is a virtue. "Please, take your time."

The Atlanta man thumbed through a small notepad. Peter admired his attention to detail. "Yes, here. The Keely Motor Company out of New York. Been around more than twenty years. Several millions collected from investors to bring a new energy contraption to market. Many stockholders still think this guy, John Keely, is the next Thomas Edison."

Fascinating. "So, what is this mysterious machine?"

The investigator searched his pad again, and when he found the page, put his finger on the reference.

"Ready for this—the hydro-pneumatic-pulsating-vacu-engine. Designed to bring cheap power to the world for the next several centuries if you believe such bunk. I guess many still do, including a few of Chattanooga's wealthy widows. At any rate, you'll read more details in this update. We'll continue our probe."

Peter rued the day he was put in charge of this nasty business. The clandestine investigation had dumped Peter at the front door of a den of thieves. Soon he must update his father about the inquiry.

"Keep me posted." He accompanied the man to the door. As he began to leave, the private detective turned back to Peter.

"One more thing. I witnessed who vandalized the woman's bicycle today. The hoodlum is named in the report."

⁂

The Millwoods sat on the porch, Bertha reading by the light of a lantern. The day when electricity would be installed in every home could not arrive soon enough for her.

Introspective during his favorite time of day, Edward tapped his foot and sighed. He checked his antique pocket watch again, evidently bored in her company as if stuck at an unimportant gathering that dragged long into the night. The fatigue in his eyes made her long for the days when he found comfort and rest in her.

The heat began to moderate, a welcome shift, and the twilight slipped off as they whiled away the minutes. Shades of orange, red, purple, and lavender lit the western horizon, the sun disappearing behind the ridges and peaks encircling the valley.

On this occasion, she took stock of the routines he enjoyed. Friday nights had always been sacred to him after a long week at his accounting practice. A hearty dinner, a smoke afterwards, and a peaceful time outside where he read his paper and took in the sights and sounds of the neighborhood. The passage of two decades together had brought them a happy and healthy family. Or so she had thought. But tonight, he seemed impatient.

The core unraveled two years ago. Now they lived separate lives together, as the marriage faded with each passing day. The death of Constance chipped away the tiny bits of happiness that lingered. The cycling controversy added fire to their season of discontent. She didn't mean for this to happen. After she accomplished her holy assignment, they would piece together the jigsaw of their broken union.

The outgrowth of her campaign placed undue pressure on him, but his duty as a faithful husband required him to stand with her. She swallowed hard, hesitant to engage. "You're anxious tonight. What's troubling you?" A long pause, the silence broken only by a nearby cat's yowl and another feline scream.

Shoulders slumped, he yawned and rubbed his eyes. "If you insist. Chamber officials are responding along with other city groups to your vendetta."

She bristled at the word. How dare he describe her work as such? "How unfair of you and not the term I would—"

"Believe me, I understand how you characterize the situation. You asked me a question. Do you want me to finish?"

The tone chastened her. "Please do."

"While I argued strenuously against their decision, most of the board said they would try to strip Joseph Gaines of his chairmanship of the Mineral and Agricultural Resources Committee at our next gathering."

An unintended consequence she regretted. "Sometimes these things must occur to achieve a greater purpose."

He disagreed. "Joseph doesn't deserve this political fallout."

Edward indicated he would challenge the vote, which would bring them at cross-purposes. This would force them to confront their personal problems head-on, sooner than she expected. Pride had imprisoned them both for far too long.

An ominous premonition distracted her. Might the future include a solitary life as a divorcee? Such unbearable shame would kill her.

⚜

The two friends lay on Emma's bed lost in conversation about work and life and love.

"By the way, a position finally came through at the upholstery," Anna said.

"Wonderful. Congratulations."

She had taken a bit less money for longer hours, but Mr. McCausland said he didn't give a hoot if she rode a wheel or an elephant to work, or if she came in bloomers or a ten-foot-wide hoop dress. As long as she brought strong sewing skills and a work ethic, he'd be whistling "Dixie." She imagined him and Papa performing a duet.

In several days, Anna would accompany Grover on a day-long outing to Lookout Mountain. She tried to shake her misgivings, born out of Peter's statement, which he had so quickly retracted. The two participated in the same association. Did Peter discover some information about Grover that led him to believe she might be compromised?

She probed Emma. "What are your true feelings about Grover?"

The question caught Emma by surprise, and she struggled to formulate a response. "Well, he's still . . ." The gap spoke volumes, as Emma always found words to express her thoughts.

"Please, Emma. Speak freely."

"Since you met him at the opera house, you turn all flush when we talk about him. As I started to say, he's a mystery. I also understand you believe he respects you, and you feel the same about him."

Her reply did not answer the query. Anna needed Emma's approval, but she had dodged endorsing Grover as a suitor. She framed the question in a different way. "Should I allow him to call again?" Anna's more specific question presented little wiggle room.

"Don't you think until he states his long-term purposes, chaperoned meetings would be wise? At least for a while."

First Peter, and now Emma, had raised concerns about her wellbeing, but she still didn't believe an escort would be necessary. Grover would act like a gentleman toward her. They would be surrounded by plenty of people on Lookout Mountain. Despite her reasoning, the doubt crept in again. She found judging a person's character to be hard work.

Emma changed the subject. "What about Peter Sawyer? From what you told me today, he sounds like a wonderful man. Not the contemptible guy you made him out to be." Emma had always held a more favorable opinion about Peter. True, Peter had been somewhat redeemed, but she would remain skeptical about him for now. Besides, he showed no real interest, except a desire to be friends.

"You are right about Peter. Perhaps I misread him. He seems a genuine person. But are you asking if I would entertain any romantic involvement?"

Peter did come from a hard-working, respectable Chattanooga family, and he earned his own reputation as an upstanding member of the community. Grover, a transplant to the city, remained an unknown. No apparent financial prospects, other than his job at Sawyer's mill. Both may be honorable men, but Grover struck her as the better match.

Anna anticipated her best friend's response.

"Might Peter already be showing his regard for you?"

"Think so?" Despite her own opinions, she still trusted Emma's intuitions.

"Just going by what you told me," Emma said.

The two lay together in silence for several minutes. They experienced no awkwardness in these moments of companionship. Emma understood the deep emotions beneath the mere words, and she never judged her. Neither of them needed to fill the gaps of quiet with idle chatter.

Emma gave Anna much to think about. A friendship with Peter might be enjoyable, but she doubted his interest would ever go further than a platonic relationship. This made things easier as Grover held her heart hostage. If he insisted she give up riding, she would consider his wishes again.

They had not spent any time together all week, but Grover had left word at the boarding house—he would meet her at Union Depot next Saturday morning at quarter past eight to catch the 8:25 train to St. Elmo.

After she and Emma said goodnight, Anna dressed in her nightclothes and slipped into bed. The crystal glass night lamp on the table by her bed threw beams of light to the ceiling as a pesky fly bounced against the outside of the lamp's chimney. The insect's frenetic demonstration in futility made her wonder whether the effort to clear a pathway for women cyclists would prove equally pointless. To put an end to the racket, she blotted out the light. Maybe this would save the buzzing nuisance from pulverizing itself. Both of them might gain some rest.

Sleep eluded her at first. Why didn't Grover show up at the upholstery to walk her home?"

Chapter Twenty-Four

ON MONDAY, BEFORE they left for work, Emma led Anna to the carriage house in back.

"Stand at the doorway with your eyes closed," Emma said.

"What is this mystery, Miss Kelly?" A bump and a clank caused her to jump.

"Sorry," Emma said. "Knocked over a hammer. Keep your eyes shut."

"Hurry. Do you wanna have me fired?" A more familiar sound moving toward her almost made her peek.

At last, Emma gave her permission. "Now you can open 'em up."

Did this vision deceive her? To the side of Rose's two beautiful carriages stood the proud owner of a new bicycle. Speechless, Anna stood in the same spot, her mouth agape in disbelief. "When . . . but you said . . . wait a minute. What about the asthma?"

"Yeah, well . . . we get one life . . . on this earth anyway," Emma said. "May as well do all the living we can while we're here."

"What a beautiful wheel, Emma."

"Tá, I know. Ain't she top banana? Figured I'd do some riding with you. Don't want to cycle arseways, so maybe you could give me some lessons."

The prospect of cycling with her trusted friend thrilled her—long rides on Chickamauga Valley roads and through green meadows and forest-covered paths. Talking about the things they talked about but doing so side by side out in the fresh air on a wheel. Taking excursions through the city, over the Walnut Street Bridge to Hill City, and short rides to Tschopik's for some tutti-frutti ice cream. So many possibilities.

The obvious suddenly shattered her daydream, yanking her back into a hard reality. Emma would face the same criticism and scorn that Anna endured on a daily basis. The mood swing was dramatic and swift from excitement to clammy palms and dizziness. "But what about . . ."

"All those people, so riled up about how others go about their lives, they don't recognize that their own lives are spinning out of control?" As usual, Emma operated two steps ahead of her.

"Yeah. Them."

The ends of Emma's mouth lifted. "Let them spin. We'll ride."

After work the next day, Anna and Emma rolled their bicycles onto a crowded trolley headed toward East Lake and Dodds Avenue. A second woman standing with a wheel did not go unnoticed. The jerky motion of the trolley made it difficult to stand with both hands holding the wheels upright. At one juncture Emma almost fell forward on top of hers, but Anna reached out and steadied her. None of the gentlemen made the proper gesture of offering the lady a seat. Many whispers accompanied the darting looks as they stepped out of the car at their stop.

Walking on, she searched for the perfect spot. An open field with some brush that would provide a gentle landing pad, for Emma would undoubtedly take her share of tumbles.

"Over yonder, Em." When they reached the patch, Anna laid her wheel on its side. "Are you prepared to tame this magnificent beast?"

"More than ready."

"First, you must name your bike."

"Ha! Are you serious?"

"Very." Anna explained.

Dubbing her steed would give their relationship a certain intimacy and make them a team. Emma would provide a safe, clean resting place for her bicycle and regular maintenance to extend its life. The wheel promised new and exciting adventures, pathways to explore, invigorating exercise, and Sunday afternoon picnics in the countryside. They would function as a unit, each looking out for the other. All this would begin with a name.

The idea amused Emma. To prove her sanity, Anna told her of women's rights leader Francis Willard who wrote a book about learning to ride at age fifty-three. Willard named her wheel Gladys who became her metal mount, a metaphor for her life. So, Anna had adopted Willard's motto: The woman who succeeds at mastering the bicycle will master life. The wheel required the hardiness of spirit to begin, the persistence to continue, and the patience to start again when failure struck the rider down. The feminist author had named her bicycle, inspiring Anna to do the same.

She remained straight-faced.

Emma got the message. "You are serious. So, what do you call your wheel?"

A giggle emerged, followed by a wide grin, laced with a little bit of embarrassment. "Choo Choo." Both of them erupted in laughter. Emma's face lit up.

"Okay, Choo Choo. Meet Irish."

An appropriate name, something already in common between Emma and her new friend.

"Now we can start," Anna said. "Are you prepared to tame Irish?"

The two drilled on the basics: mounting, dismounting, pedaling, and turning. Over and over, Emma practiced and Anna encouraged her on. By the end of the first forty-five-minute session, Emma rode in circles for several minutes, unassisted. The two times she tumbled to the ground, Emma sprang to her feet, heeding her instructor's words—get back up after you fall. Her battle scars were minimal—a scrape below her left elbow and a sprained index finger.

The wounds to her ego far surpassed the physical injuries. Recounting the force of gravity on her dismounts led them into a fit of disruptive giggles on the trolley ride home. Some passengers glared at them. Again, they stood with their bikes, ready to battle the laws of motion.

"Quiet," Anna said, working hard to suppress her own laughter.

Poor Emma. Irish already owned her. Soon it would be difficult to tell who drove whom. If Emma practiced twenty minutes a day this week, by Saturday a longer journey might be in the cards. Maybe Oscar would come up for the weekend and ride with them.

She decided to share another bit of news, certain in advance what Emma's response would be. "A note addressed to me came to the boarding house. An invitation from Grover to be his guest at the opera this Thursday night. I'm going to accept, so please no lectures."

"Not meaning to lecture you, but something is not right with the man. He's up to no good. A bad vibration runs deep inside my bones."

❧❖❧

Anna marveled at how quickly Emma mastered her newfound sport. The two women, with Choo Choo and Irish at their sides, boarded the trolley after work hours and headed for the riding patch. The sun remained aloft long enough for a few short practice rides, but Emma's confidence on the wheel grew exponentially each time she sat on Irish.

New faces took notice on the public transit, ensuring the word would spread that Chattanooga's ranks of female cyclists had doubled overnight.

After Wednesday's session, Anna proclaimed the new cyclist would be ready for an outing in the Chickamauga Valley. She had sent word to Oscar, and he agreed to come for a visit. On Saturday, after they both took a lesson with Oscar, Anna would lead the party of three on her favorite ride.

In the meantime, her night at the opera with Grover the following evening loomed as a possible turning point. The attachment would either become something more serious, based on his behavior toward her, or she would heed Emma's cautions and avoid any future contact with him.

A friendship with the other man in her life became equally complicated. The grocer had all but disappeared. Peter must be avoiding her.

⋙❖⋘

On late Friday afternoon, following a thirty-minute practice ride along Dodds Avenue, they stood at the trolley stop. The cycling bug took its bite as Anna expected would happen, and Emma welcomed the fever.

Earlier concerns about her asthma had never materialized. Instead, Emma proclaimed, "Riding Irish energizes me. Tomorrow's ride can't come soon enough."

"For both of us."

Emma's face went flat, no expressions, but her eyes shifted back and forth between Anna and the empty space ahead. As they waited, Anna could tell that her friend was busting inside.

She too was anxious to share details about last night at the opera house but had purposely not said a word, a ploy to keep Emma wondering as they often did to each other in a teasing way. Then again, what if Emma didn't care to hear about her glorious night with Grover, that things went well, appropriately so, and that the friendship may have

165

been advanced further? A possibility, but out of character for Emma who wanted her happiness. So, Anna abandoned the thought and waited.

Moments later, Emma blurted out her curiosity. "Since you obviously are not volunteering any information, I will dig around until you do. What happened?"

Another chance to play coy, so Anna took it. "Why, Emma Kelly . . . I'm not at all sure what you're talking about."

"Okay, I understand. You're going to make me suffer until you're ready."

Anna let Emma's frustration settle for a few more moments.

The trolley rolled up. Anna paid her fare and boarded, Choo Choo in tow with Emma and wheel close behind. "Oh, are you by any chance referring to my time at the opera with Grover?"

"What else? Well . . .?" A paragon of patience most of the time, Emma nodded her head. "Out with the details."

"The evening can be summed up in one word: enchanting." The dinner before, the performance, and the walk home—all perfect. And the good night peck on the cheek, as she had envisioned.

"Sounds like he behaved . . ."

"Like a true Southern gentleman, Emma. Never brought up the subject of cycling or anything related. I think he now accepts my riding."

Emma might find her trust in Grover's best intentions to be naïve and say a leopard can't change its spots, an ancient truth that many through the millennia learned the hard, painful way. Anna loved Emma Kelly, but in the afterglow of her dream night, she didn't want to hear any of this. To her relief, Emma held her tongue and pivoted to another topic.

The trolley reached their stop as the sun disappeared. As they rolled their bikes off the coach, Anna glanced at a man sitting at the other end of the trolley car taking notes.

They mounted their wheels and pedaled toward Rose's house. Just before arriving, Anna asked one question about a habit of Grover's that bothered her. One she noticed first at the Tschopik's ice cream parlor and again last night. Repeatedly.

"When someone tugs at their ear all the time, what does it mean?"

Chapter Twenty-Five

SATURDAY ARRIVED, AND Anna awoke earlier than usual, ready to ride Choo Choo through the forests and fields of the Chickamauga Valley. The light of day began to filter through her curtain-covered window. Cracking her bedroom door, she peeked out. Dark and quiet—nobody else stirred, so she plopped back into bed but couldn't fall asleep. A half hour later, she arose again and dressed for the day.

The plan was for Oscar to arrive at the depot late Friday afternoon and cycle out to the farm. She and Emma would catch the trolley out to East Lake, where Oscar would meet them. When Anna came downstairs, Rose lifted her hand over her mouth, as her eyebrows raised and forehead creased.

"Oh!" she said with a snicker and handed her a cup of coffee, but she made no mention of the bloomers.

The darkened sky over the city dropped moderate rainfall as they took their breakfast early in the dining room. The once boisterous atmosphere in the boarding house had turned quiet in recent days as the two friends were the only residents now. She missed the parlor games, the joyous music, and singing at the piano after a satisfying meal and lively exchanges. And the scuttlebutt about who got jilted or the business deal gone bad.

Dressed for her virgin journey, Emma bounded down the stairs to find the two ladies dining at the table. "Oh, so sorry I'm late. Did I get the time wrong?"

"No. I woke up early, thinking about the fun journey Irish and Choo Choo would be taking together."

"Did I hear you say Choo Choo and Irish?" The confusion on the landlady's face required an explanation.

"Our wheels, Rose. Mmm . . . that food looks good. The noise you hear is the loud rumble from my midriff." Emma sat down and spooned some of the eggs, ham, and bread onto her plate.

The landlady laughed. "Now we're naming our vehicles?"

Emma embellished. "Both of us are forging bonds with them."

Anna nodded her head, battling the urge to laugh at Rose's serious expression as she stood. "Sometime soon, I want to ride Irish or Choo Choo," Rose said. "Pick the most patient one and give me a lesson. Now that'll give this city and all its roosters something to crow about."

"I can just see us turning heads together," Emma said. "All in bloomers, the three musketeers. All for one and one for all."

⨯⟡⨯

They disembarked the trolley at the last station on the line, out by East Lake. As planned, Oscar came forward to greet them, grinning when Anna stepped down in her bloomer costume.

"If your Aunt could see you now."

"If only . . ."

After a hug, they headed southeast down the McFarland Gap road. The thunderstorm had moved on, leaving some puddles on the ground and a partially gray sky yielding to the shining sun. They rode three abreast at a leisurely pace, with Oscar offering encouragements to the neophyte among them.

"Appears you've been well taught, Emma."

Emma teetered, as she turned slightly to reply. After a few jerky movements, she gained control. "Oops. Not my best moment."

"Be careful," Oscar said. "Fall into one of these mini-lakes on the ground, and your ride will be over for today."

They planned to cycle until around noon and head back to the farm in time for lunch. The trio did not cross paths with any other riders or passengers. At one point, Oscar spotted swift movements just inside a heavy patch of trees and pointed out the area to the others. When they looked closer, nothing moved, so he attributed the distraction to a deer or some other animal.

The multitude of animals and birds in the valley provided the perfect backdrop for cycling. As they continued, several deer grazed in the meadows. The summer brought countless species of birds—woodpeckers, horned and barred owls, red-shouldered hawks, and varieties of songbirds—into the valley. Muskrats, raccoons, opossum, and ground hogs roamed the land. Butterflies and dragonflies darted through the landscapes. The treetops swayed, and the slow-moving clouds added their touch to the vibrant panorama. Some of Anna's favorite secluded pathways beckoned her forward.

Amidst nature's dance, a day like this turned magical. Anna noticed Emma marveling, like she had the first time she watched Oscar performing fancy maneuvers, like resting his legs on the handlebars while he glided along, and balancing the bicycle without touching the grips. A circus acrobat on wheels.

"Don't try these moves any time soon, if ever," he said. "Some call me a showboating cyclist . . . an exhibitionist. So be it for them. Bottom line: These are dangerous moves for a beginner."

Anna understood him better and sloughed off the disparaging, jealous remarks of others. Her cousin shared his skills with budding cyclists to encourage and entertain them and because he took joy from people who appreciated his ardor for cycling. Innocent fun—that's what motivated him.

Emma also admired his riding. "How did you become such an accomplished cyclist?"

"Simple, Emma—I get to practice several hours a day, six days a week while I work. Been doing this for the last five years." A barrage of questions followed.

"How can you spend that much time? What kind of work do you do?"

"Let me explain."

Druggist Avram Kaan, a wealthy and well-known Russian Jew with a penchant for sports gambling, hired Oscar to deliver medicines to his customers and messages to shady men staging cockfights and other events. The matches were held in isolated locations, some of Atlanta's seedier quarters. His pocket filled with wads of cash, Oscar would weave through congested streets, avoiding people and animals.

"Come rain or shine, I did the bidding of Kaan and developed the abilities to think quick and ride fast. In the meantime, bicycle racing became the new frontier."

Schools like Harvard and Yale fielded teams, and the new spectator sport began to rise in popularity. People paid to attend meets, and more riders vied for fatter payoffs. Oscar rode a fixed gear safety wheel with no brakes and started competing as an amateur in both official and unofficial contests around Atlanta. He planned to participate in the five-mile group events at the upcoming Labor Day races.

In no time, the threesome pedaled all the way south to the Chattanooga and Chickamauga National Military Park, the first such memorial in the country. Both valleys anxiously awaited the opening ceremony scheduled for September 19, the thirty-second anniversary of the horrendous clash of armies on this hallowed ground. Planners braced for some forty thousand spectators.

Emma began to tire, so they decided to head north to the Gaines spread. Along the way, Anna guided them through a backwoods trail she'd discovered weeks ago. The broken beams of sunlight filtered through the variety of oak and pine trees, casting picturesque variations of shadow and light against the ground. A stunning backdrop for the last part of their ride.

Anna pulled alongside her cousin. "Breathtaking, don't you think?"

"Umm . . ." A non-answer, unlike Oscar.

Eyes darting from right to left, he ran one hand through his hair. "Listen, I don't want to ruin the end of Emma's maiden ride, but I can't shake this sensation that we're being watched."

"From where?"

"Not sure. Like someone or something is lurking beyond the next turn, waiting. Over the last couple of years, I've learned to be sensitive to my surroundings."

"Now you're scaring me."

"Sorry. Some of the districts I ride through back home are quite sordid."

As they approached the bend, they found the path blocked by part of an old felled tree. No dead trunks nearby, and a deep indentation in the ground, revealed that the rotting wood had been dragged into place.

Out of nowhere, some ruffians raced up behind them and obstructed their retreat. The scowls on their faces sent a clear message: This was not a chance visit. The three stout malefactors intended to do harm, but why? Small in stature himself, Oscar showed no fear. But outnumbered and outsized, Anna concluded he would be no match for the rough riders.

He placed himself between the gang and the women. "Perfect day for a ride, don't you think? Been down to the military park site, and we're about to meet up with several others from our party. Can you husky men give us a hand with moving this dead tree out of the path? So all of us can pass."

No answer, but plenty of over-confident smirks. Oscar had nerves of steel.

The men dismounted, the leader careful to pull a paper bag containing a bottle from the basket attached to the front end of his wheel. The boss pulled the cork with his teeth and took a gulp. He passed the near-empty container to his fellow hooligans, who drank the rest of their liquid courage. The third man tipped the flask above his mouth to gather the last drop before passing it back to their leader.

Oscar moved forward. The ringleader broke the bottle over the horizontal crossbar of his bike, causing shards of glass to fly in all directions. The remaining jagged edges created a formidable weapon, and the wielder took an aggressive posture as the other riders shifted to Oscar's left and right flanks. The leader moved toward him, as his cohorts closed the space on their sides. The man in front stood three or four inches taller than Oscar, and his muscular build indicated he would be difficult to bring down.

Oscar tried a last bit of diplomacy. "Now, friends, no cause for trouble here. Say we go our separate ways and enjoy the rest of this fine day."

The hooligan's posture confirmed that he hadn't come to chat. He veered to Oscar's left, waving the sharp instrument of destruction in small circles. "This trouble is your own doing. After this, you'll go back down to Atlanta and stay with a few visible reminders of why you better not return."

How did he know where Oscar lived? Emboldened, the second man at his left made another threat. "Yeah. Now you're gonna bleed."

The leader shifted his eyes over to his cohort for a split second. Oscar charged his adversary, who swiped the bottle toward his head. The sweeping motion left an opening for Oscar's strong right hook, taking the man by surprise and throwing him off balance. A follow-up right to his ribs stunned the leader, leaving him gasping for breath.

The second man snuck behind Oscar, and with his fists intertwined, struck a mighty blow to the back of his head, sending him to the ground. Dazed, his eyes followed Emma as she darted forward and jumped on the man's back, her arms around his neck, choking off his windpipe. Armed with a thick branch of wood sitting nearby, Anna joined the fray. A swing into the man's stomach took him to his knees. When Emma released her grip, Anna brought her club down on the man's head. He dropped to the ground, unconscious, reducing the odds against Oscar. The third man, hesitant to engage, remained outside the circle of battle.

The leader rejoined the fight, lurching toward the women. Oscar also regained his senses and rolled into the man's pathway, tripping him three feet in front of the women. The man ended up on top of Oscar and crashed the jagged bottle on his head. The blow failed to take Oscar out of the fight. In the struggle, they changed positions, allowing him to hammer several sharp punches to the man's face, disabling him again and causing him to release the weapon.

The third man moved a few steps to engage the scrappy ladies but thought better of the idea and backtracked. With no stomach left for the fight, the three men managed to stagger back to their bicycles and escape the scene of violence. Oscar stumbled over to Anna and Emma. "Are you both okay?"

Blood streamed from his scalp, behind his ears, and down his neck. Anna's eyes shifted to the top of his head. He touched the wound and brought his bloodied fingers down to view.

"Let me take a gander, cousin. On your knees." He stooped down. "Ouch, you have a nasty gash, about two inches. Sorry, but you're going to need some stitches. Why did this happen?"

"Not a clue," Oscar said. "But I do know one thing. I'll never tangle with the likes of you two."

"Yeah, well, you're pretty talented with those fists. Where did you learn to box so well?" Anna pulled the scarf from her neck, a last-minute clothing selection, and used the material to apply pressure to the cut on Oscar's head.

In addition to the cockfights, Oscar placed wagers on some boxing matches for his boss. At one point, someone goaded him into the ring, and he handled himself well, making a tidy sum when he bet on himself to win. Several other contests followed, increasing his fighting skills and landing him and the druggist Kaan some fat purses. Along the way, his bank account had fattened as well.

Anna checked his scalp again. Most of the flow had been staunched, but blood still collected in smaller amounts around the wound. "All right, I'm going to tie this scarf under your chin so the material on top is tight over the cut. Time to get some medical attention. If you bleed to death, Harriet will hate me."

❖

Later, in the dark shadows behind the city auditorium on East Ninth, Grover met with three men. An exchange of money occurred.

A conspiracy had culminated in an ambush earlier in the day. Grover, the money man, perused the leader's facial cuts and bruises and questioned who had actually taken the licking. The face-swollen leader ignored the question and promised that Oscar would not be giving cycling lessons in Chattanooga any time soon. The other two brutes nodded in agreement.

"You've got your money," Grover said. "Now leave the city and don't show your faces again unless I send for you."

As they scattered, he shifted his club from his left hand to his right and tiptoed toward the shed behind him where he had heard rustling noises. The conversation and exchange of money could not have escaped the attention of the intruder. The person in hiding snapped a branch that echoed into the night. Grover circled to one side of the shed and waited for a moment, his breathing shallow, indiscernible. He stepped quickly around the corner, expecting to surprise the interloper.

To his disappointment, he stood alone, except for a stray cat that began rubbing its head against his leg. The feline dropped to the ground and rolled on its back, purring and waiting for a rubdown.

The conniver from Atlanta left to some disappointed meows echoing into the night.

⨝❖⨞

Back at the farm, they had gotten Oscar all stitched up and put to bed. Anna sat outside with Emma, listening to the shrill song of the cicadas.

"A harrowing day," Anna said. "Here's hoping future rides on Irish won't be quite as eventful."

"A day I'll remember for certain." They sat in their own silence for a while. "Anna, you'll be going to the mountaintop tomorrow. Have you sorted through your feelings for these two men?"

Truth be told, she didn't know what to think. Men confused her, and she began to think she would never understand them. Maybe never understand Anna Gaines. Just when Grover shows himself unworthy, he turns around and acts like the perfect gentleman. And Peter. After a pleasant interaction at Live and Let Live . . . nothing. Her transition from childhood to adulthood had been delayed by a horrible accident. The trauma must have stymied her personal growth and hindered her judgment. Now she found herself in an adult world, floundering, stuck between old and new ways of thinking. Unsure of which desires of her heart to pursue. Trapped in the middle of a controversy forcing her to make difficult decisions that brought more uncertainty into her life.

"This is all too much for me, Emma. Ride or don't ride. Grover or Peter, or wait for the perfect man who may never come my way. Pursue college and a profession or raise a family."

"Give yourself time. The answers will come."

"I wonder."

Chapter Twenty-Six

PETER ROLLED UP to the grocery and walked his wheel over to the sidewall where he saw a man in a tweed coat and a black, soft fur fedora. The man, broad-shouldered and medium in stature, held one arm close to his side. With eyes focused downward, apparently lost in his thoughts, he muttered an indistinguishable comment. He turned away, missing Peter's presence, and paced in the opposite direction. A thin, winding stream of smoke arose from the man's long pipe as he mumbled to himself.

"Come now, Detective," Peter said to the man as he checked his own pocket watch. "It's just a little past eight, and I'm only ten minutes late, fifteen at the most. A bit of a predicament with a pedestrian along the way."

The detective turned around. "As Ben Franklin taught us, time equals money. Please remember, I charge by the half hour. The waiting also goes on your bill."

One of the best in the business, the detective ran a tight ship. No matter how much work Peter threw his way, each thirty minutes spent, including time in casual talk about family, was entered into the ledger.

No grace time was allowed. A businessman himself, Peter took no real offense.

"Understood." They entered the front of the store, where Peter lit a large lamp.

"Let's talk in my office where we can sit."

Seymour updated him on the energy scheme. Two other prominent Chattanooga families had met with key investment agents in the city, but Seymour didn't know if they had snapped up the bait. The sleuth had found nothing new on the Catholic priest crimes. No further attempts had been made. Two of his associates monitored the other Tennessee cities while he snooped around for any suspicious activities in town.

Match in hand, the detective rekindled the tobacco and blew rings toward Peter, who attempted to stifle a cough. Seymour took notice.

"Do you smoke, sir?" Calmness had replaced Seymour's anxious demeanor of a few minutes ago. The creases in his forehead relaxed, and his scowl faded.

"On occasion I'll enjoy a cigar with a spot of brandy but never in such cramped quarters. Too much of the habit may pose a danger to one's well-being over the long term, don't you think?"

After some thought, he raised his shoulders. "Hmm . . . not so sure. Puts a man in a better frame of mind all around but especially when doing business. The ritual relaxes one and reduces stress. Less strain can only advance our health, I'd say." He puffed and enlarged the hovering cloud at the ceiling.

Peter ignored the statement and pivoted the conversation to another, more pressing subject. "Are you staffed to conduct a quest for a missing person?"

"Depends on the whereabouts."

A white stream blew directly into Peter's eyes and nose. This time, he let loose a couple of full-throated coughs and waved his hand in front of his face to sweep the nuisance away.

"Oh. Sorry again, Peter. Most men I deal with engage on a regular basis, so I don't tend to think the smoke might be bothersome. I'll try to blow elsewhere."

"Last location, Atlanta—your neck of the woods," Peter said. "Name's Raymond Washington, Senior, a long-time resident of Chattanooga. Here's a quick sketch."

Raymond had served as an alderman for some time in the 1880s. When things got complicated a couple of years back, he went to Atlanta seeking employment. Not long after, he wrote to his wife that work had dried up and he intended to move farther south, perhaps to Montgomery, or as far down as Savannah. Hattie never received any further word and suspected foul play might be involved.

The detective stroked the whiskers along his upper lip, which were curled and jutting outward at both ends. He took several puffs, concentrating.

"Yes, I have friends in those towns, and I believe they can cover the surrounding areas. Any description?" He pulled a pencil and notepad from his coat to jot down the details.

"Around fifty years old. Five foot eleven. Two hundred pounds, or at least that's what he weighed when Hattie, his wife, last saw him. A knife scar all along his forehead, courtesy of some slaveholder when Raymond was a child. Did I tell you he's a Negro?"

Seymour's brow furrowed at the mention. "Continue please."

"Three kids named Charles, Raymond Junior, and Herman. The man's reported to be a hard worker, committed to his family."

"When shall I begin?"

"As soon as possible." As they left the store, Peter locked up and gave the man his last instruction. "Leave no stone unturned, no path undisturbed. We must discover what happened to this man."

"One more question."

"Yes, Mr. Leland." Impatient, Peter glanced at the time. He needed to cycle home to the special meal his mother had promised.

"Why are you so interested in finding this man?"

"My reasons are my own. Why do you ask?"

On the way home, Peter decided a letter of explanation would be appropriate. After all, he couldn't very well drop by the Byrnes boarding house unannounced. The unanticipated trip to Memphis at his father's request had taken him away for several days. Upon his return, he had worked at the grocery during normal business hours and at night helped the staff at the lumberyard comb through months of transactions, looking for anomalies in the accounting. The extra work would not end anytime soon.

The absence and long hours made it almost impossible for him to connect with Anna. He pined for her presence. But that day when they ate ice cream together, while it seemed to end on a high note with him coming to her rescue, helping to put her wheel back together, he parted company with a troubled heart. How could she think him responsible for efforts to malign her? He had tried, somewhat ungracefully, to warn her about the real culprits, but she had challenged him when he mentioned Grover Biggs, and so he shut down. The ironic disclosure that Grover had played along with Mrs. Millwood must be handled delicately, but he must act soon or lose her. Since she had not frequented the grocery since his return, a written communication would have to do.

After dinner, he took pen to paper and wrote. He sealed the missive, dropped it into a desk drawer, and wondered, *Will this seed of a friendship ever have a chance to grow?*

Maybe finding Raymond Washington would help.

Chapter Twenty-Seven

WITH A FULL picnic basket in hand, Anna walked to the depot. The early morning church service helped her to move beyond the terrible attack by the three men on Emma, Oscar, and herself the day before.

She wore her newest day dress, chartreuse and black patterned silk with a thin machine-made cotton net lace running from her shoulders down to her chest. Leg o' mutton sleeves with huge shoulder puffs narrowing down at the elbows, distinguished the dress among the latest fashions. The purchase set her back several weeks of savings.

Today, Grover Biggs would be treated to her more feminine side, as she quieted her bloomer-wearing, tomboy instincts. Perhaps her more traditional outfit and the food would win his affections. She spotted him as she approached the ticketing area for the Chattanooga & Lookout Mountain Railroad. He was tall and handsome, and his shirt, blazer, and informal trousers made the perfect ensemble for the athletic man on a day-long outing.

"Been looking forward to our time all week," Grover said.

He tugged his earlobe . . . again. The nervous habit had not gone unnoticed. Should she say something to him? He made no mention of her outfit.

"Almost time to depart. May I say, you are quite well-groomed, Mr. Biggs."

Without responding, he purchased two tickets. They climbed aboard a coach with about a dozen other people to make the fifteen-mile trek toward St. Elmo, the oldest Chattanooga suburb built at the foot of the mountain's east side and the first leg of the trip.

Soon after the train rolled forward, Grover turned inexplicably moody. Unable to contain herself, she peeked at him from the corner of her eyes. "A dollar for your thoughts, Mr. Biggs."

He turned his gaze back to the window, resting his head on his palm. She shrugged. Sometimes he clammed up and said almost nothing, and other times he chatted away without leaving any breaks for her to respond.

The locomotive picked up its speed for the fifty-minute excursion. After several minutes, she attempted again to converse. "How are things going at your job?"

"Fine." He pulled his ear, eyes fixed on the outside. At this rate, the trip would be long and quiet.

"Train rides thrilled me as a little girl. I loved watching the countryside roll past, eager to reach its destination while the passenger car stood still. Leastwise, it appeared so through my youthful eyes." She sighed at the memory.

Nothing. To change him might be near impossible. What made her think she could?

"Grover, I packed us a hearty lunch—fresh bread, cheese, a chunk of ham, and lots of fruit. Maybe we'll find a spot to eat at the Point while we gaze out over the valley."

The talk about food caught his attention. "I expect that meal will do. Didn't eat much this morning, and I'm already starving."

Without another word, he crawled back into his own world of silence. She wanted to learn about Grover's life, about his family and how his parents had raised him. Every time she asked about siblings, he changed the subject. Perhaps he had suffered a trauma in his growing years like she had. He hailed from Atlanta, and that's about all she had gathered. To avoid ruining their day, she decided the topic would remain off limits. Curiosity would bide its time.

Instead of forcing the conversation, she decided to join him. The scenes outside the train were grand. The Tennessee River wound its way below the hills. The alternating fields and forests extended southward, and the long ridgeway was to the east. The train pulled into a switchback and came to a stop. Lookout Mountain towered before them.

"Quaint little place," she mumbled, focused on the country store and the few scattered cottages and gardens.

The passenger across the aisle overheard her. "Yes, I agree. Called Mountain Junction."

In the past, such a casual exchange with a stranger would have never taken place. She welcomed the distraction. "Mountain Junction?"

"This is where the engine gets detached and rolls away. A second climbing steam locomotive is hitched to the rear of the train for the ascent." As a resident of the city, she didn't know this.

The passenger struck her as a jim-dandy, by all appearances. Well-dressed, refined, and quite handsome. Mid- to late-twenties in age. She straightened in her seat and engaged him.

"Interesting. This is my first time taking the railroad up the mountain. Been to the top once before, about five years ago for a family reunion at the Mountain Inn—months after the hotel opened."

The gentleman's eyes and nose crinkled. He traveled alone and appeared pleased by her attentions. "Most likely, you ascended to the inn by way of the first incline railway."

"Yes. I found the steep grade over the open gorges frightening. I guess they would be to a fifteen-year-old girl. Today I would find the views breathtaking and the climb exciting."

She peeked over at Grover. With arms crossed and eyes rolling, he cast his attention out to the foothills of St. Elmo as the train began to chug up the side of the mountain.

The train now headed north, ascending high above the track for the incline railway.

"Hear tell the second one is due to open around November," the stranger said. "Bound to give this old railroad a harder time staying afloat. Too bad as I rather like this line."

The passenger's lament struck her, and Rose's comments about changes echoed in her ears. The view of the river below, Walden's Ridge at the north and northwest, and the city and Missionary Ridge to the east began to disappear as they scooted across the front side of the mountain and over to the west side. Farther on, the train made a sharp turn and again headed northward.

The stranger shot a glance over at Anna and pointed to the outside.

"Below us is Hooker's battlefield—the Battle Above the Clouds as they called it. The battle on Lookout Mountain paved the way for the bloody fight at Missionary Ridge the following day. The Rebs lost, and that opened the route for Sherman's infamous march from Atlanta to the sea."

She glanced at Grover and smiled. Quite a history lesson.

"A coward, that man Sherman." These were Grover's first words, spoken as he leered at the stranger. On the topic of the war, he held nothing back. The gentleman nodded.

"Most Southern men and women at the time would agree, sir."

"And your thoughts now, sir?" Grover asked. The war stirred passionate opinions within him; about the humiliation the South had endured and Lincoln's legacy of granting full legal status to the coloreds. At least Jim Crow laws had begun to reverse that mistake.

"Time for the war to be left to the judgments of historians, I say," the passenger said.

As he expected—a gutless non-answer.

The train moved across the eastern slope again, traversing over the New Mountain Road, and later—after another bend—under the same road and up to the Lookout Inn. The panorama and beautiful vistas on the way up appeared like landscapes on a canvas, rich in color and definition, without artificiality. Paintings captivated Grover and became his singular appreciation for the arts in recent years. He ignored the annoying chatter between Anna and the passenger as they exited the train.

Anna beheld the spectacular structure on the eastern brow of the mountain. They climbed the flight of steps leading through the lush green lawn, up to the inn's stone pillars. At the entrance, she craned her neck to view all four stories and the two extra five-story towers. She scanned the huge network of porches and verandas.

"So . . . it appears you brought a picnic lunch," the man said. "You are not staying at the inn?"

Grover spoke up. "No. This is a day visit—just popped in for the tremendous views."

"Well, sir, I am currently a resident at the hotel, and I insist you and your companion join me in the dining room. Be my guests, of course."

"Oh, no, I . . . "

"To dine with you would be an honor," Anna said. "Thank you for asking." With Grover acting childish, this invitation might reset the course of their day.

"Wonderful." He extended his hand, first to Grover. "Name is Alexander, after the famous American patriot of the revolution. Last name is Philips, hailing from Birmingham, Alabama."

Resignation passed over Grover's face. "Grover Biggs, from Atlanta. A pleasure, sir."

The unexpected surprise thrilled her. "And I'm Anna Gaines from Chickamauga, now living in Chattanooga and working as a seamstress."

"Well, Miss Gaines, I say thank God for the seamstresses of the world. Without them, none of us would be properly clothed."

She tittered. He gave her a flirtatious wink.

Alexander led them on the thick red carpet with gold accents, past the billiard tables, reading nooks, lounges, and smoking rooms to the wood-floored dining area. He said, "The lovely place where we will feast—thirty-eight yards long, finished in quarter sawn southern maple."

He winked again at Anna, causing her breath to quicken. Tight-lipped, Grover dragged his feet toward the table that Alexander picked out. A host led the way.

"Quite impressive, Mr. Philips," Anna said. Perhaps her attentions toward the gentleman would draw Grover out of his cheerless, self-constructed shell. A little competition for her affection might be a perfect antidote for their shaky courtship.

"Not so impressive, actually. Please, do call me Alexander. I'm not smart enough to figure such calculations in my head, although I do possess a knack for building things. The grandeur of the room struck me, so I asked one of the waiters."

As Grover sat, apparently without recognizing his ungentlemanly conduct, Alexander pulled a chair out for Anna.

The tactical gambit worked as she had hoped. While they ate, Grover became frisky, engaged in the conversation. Perhaps the sustenance lifted his unpleasant mood, or the realization a stranger had gained her attentions. Or the talk about his favorite subject—the post-antebellum South, her resurgence on the national stage, and her march into the brave new world of the twentieth century. Whatever the reason, his participation pleased her.

The bill arrived. Upon making the payment, Alexander invited them to further tour the grounds with him. Grover stood up and raised his hand to shake. "No, but thank you, Alexander. We've a few sites yet to explore before heading down the mountain. Thanks for your fine company and hospitality, but we best be moving on."

Alexander rose and returned the gesture. "Understood. Well, sir—a pleasure." With savoir faire, he took Anna's hand, gave the top a gentleman's kiss, bowed, and rose slowly, studying her eyes. "Dearest Anna, dining with you—a sheer delight."

One last coquettish wink, and he left them.

The flirtatious gesture caused Grover's face to turn a light shade of green. A man should treat his lady like this perfect stranger had behaved toward her. With a little luck, a stranger's minor lesson in romance would rub off, and her courtship with Grover would take a turn for the better.

⚔️

Anna left the picnic basket with one of the inn attendants, and, at Grover's urging, they strolled a short distance to Point Lookout. They ventured onto the solid rock, which rose like a palisade more than a hundred feet above the slope of the mountain. They stared out at the city and beyond, awed by the same landscapes and vistas compelling none other than General Ulysses Grant to scale the mountain following the historic local battles.

The cooler temperature at the higher elevation, combined with the mild breeze, brought welcome relief from the valley heat. As they viewed the spectacle, Grover took her hand. She didn't resist. The warmth of his touch, his flesh against hers for the first time, almost made her gasp. Did he observe her chest heaving or how she trembled? She prayed the avalanche of sensations she was experiencing on the inside were not somehow obvious to him on the outside. A bead of sweat formed on her forehead; she swiped the perspiration away with a handkerchief before a stream trickled down.

His focus remained outward at the panorama below. "An apology is necessary for my behavior earlier. Too many things on my mind. In case you haven't already guessed, my feelings for you are strong." No eye contact to support his warm words, but he did pull his earlobe.

"Please know that I care for you as well, Grover." Despite her profession of fondness, a woman's intuition advised her to proceed with caution. Her own desires concerned her as much as his. They stood a few minutes longer until Grover wanted to move on.

In an uncharacteristic display of openness, he told her about the first time he came to the mountain two years before with some friends. How they hiked many of the trails and visited all the unique rock formations. The men later abandoned his friendship, one reason he hesitated to get close with people. For him to share this little piece of his life made the day worthwhile.

The Point Hotel, competition for the Lookout Mountain Inn, sat several yards below them. "Hey, Anna, let's go to the front desk and ask where the narrow-gauge railroad track leads."

They descended the small path, bought tickets, and boarded the train, which skirted along the west side of the mountain a short distance to a popular visitors' location called the Natural Bridge. On the way back, they would make one last stop at Sunset Rock before ending up back at the Lookout Mountain Inn.

The Natural Bridge formation stood fifteen feet high and spread sixty feet across. To the right, they stared at The Old Man of the Mountain, an outcrop resembling the face of an aged man, jutting twenty-five feet into the air. A few people milled about nearby. Like a boy, wide-eyed and ready to explore, Grover seemed at home on the mountain.

"Come on," he said. "Let's take a quick hike."

A walking adventure sounded innocent enough, but her dress would limit any climbing. How ironic—bloomers would be the perfect outfit for this activity. She checked her pocket watch. Two-thirty. Plenty of time left in the afternoon to catch the five o'clock train back to Union Depot. The end to an excellent day.

"Sure. Let's go, but not too far."

Chapter Twenty-Eight

THE GROCERY WAS closed on Sunday, but after church Peter took a ride there to review some files. On the way, he stopped at the boarding house. He knocked on the front door, hoping Mrs. Byrne could deliver the letter to Anna. Nobody answered, so he tried again. Nothing. Had the landlady not returned from church? Rather than leave such a personal correspondence on the porch and risk that it might not find its way to the intended reader, he hopped back onto his bicycle and proceeded to the store. He would try another time.

The disappointment had distracted him, so he dwelled instead on a positive development. Frederick, the apprentice who turned seventeen two days before, had managed the store while Peter helped his father in Memphis. Each day, Frederick had taken on more responsibilities and shined, giving Peter the confidence to leave him alone with a temporary assistant while he was away. The young man had proven his value to the grocery and made his mentor proud.

Settling into his office, Peter pulled the investigator's report from his desk, withdrew the eight-page document from its folder, and began his second scan. This time he focused on the Keely scheme and perused the snippets he had marked the first time through.

Excerpt from *New York Times*, September 22, 1884 (quotes Keely following demonstration of his vapor gun). Allow me to strip the process of all technical terms: take water and air, two mediums of different specific gravity, and produce from them by generation an effect under vibrations that liberates from the air and water an inter-atomic ether. The energy of this ether is boundless and can hardly be comprehended. The gravity of the ether is about four times lighter than hydrogen gas, the lightest gas so far discovered.

Notes to Mister Sawyer: Confusing and strange. Reports of Keely using musical instruments (flute, harmonica, violin, etcetera) to activate machines . . . iron bars destroyed, bullets penetrating twelve-inch planks, and other demonstrations of machine's power. Company stalls patent filing each year . . . to avoid piracy of his invention until its etheric forces can be unleashed in a moneymaking machine. So Keely tells his investors. Seeks board issuance of new shares to raise additional capital . . . chance for old shareholders to strengthen their positions and new ones to benefit from creation of the world's first perpetual motion device. Many millions invested. Mrs. Clara Bloomfield-Moore, a widow, his most ardent supporter . . . holds investments worth six figures . . . provides him two thousand a month in living expenses. Stock public since January 1890 . . . trades at a steady rate, no bubbles and no collapses. Some scientists claiming his results can be achieved with compressed air. Might this, and not some etheric force, be the explanation?

He skipped down to one of the targets of his investigation—Grover Biggs. Anna's infatuation with him blinded her judgment.

Grover volunteered little about his family other than that his father, James Biggs, owned a thriving wholesale lumber concern in Atlanta. The investigator found this part to be true but with an interesting twist. The two men had been estranged yet Grover came north under the pretense of doing market research for the family business—thus his interest in working at Chester Sawyer's lumberyard.

Peter's concern heightened. After placing the report in his files, he leaned back to digest the information. At some point, after briefing his father, he needed to inform the authorities, but timing would be critical. Had a crime been committed? At the least, an alarm should be sounded to keep any unsuspecting marks from being bilked out of their life savings.

Now fidgety, he stood and walked to the calendar on the wall and stared mindlessly. What would the next several days bring to Anna? To Chattanooga?

To him?

⚜

"This isn't right, Grover."

Wild-eyed, he tried again to kiss her. This must stop—now. But he wouldn't take no for an answer.

"Please, Anna. I just want to . . ."

"Stop."

"But . . ."

"Enough!"

She fought to free herself from his firm grip and dogged determination to subdue her and slapped him across the face, turning his cheek pink, infuriating him. Frustrated, he pulled back with a condescending sneer and launched into a rant.

"Learn to submit when a man cares about you. Quit trying to be a new woman because you're not. Forget these crazy visions about cycling in bloomers, practically in the nude. These antics on the wheel have gone far enough. You need to be shown your place."

As he took two steps toward her, hikers on the old footpath interrupted him—two men, well-built and young. Seeing part of the altercation, one of them squared off with Grover, his icy stare indicating he meant business and stood ready to rescue a woman in distress.

"Is this man bothering you?" The stranger's steely eyes remained fixed on the attacker who backed down.

She composed herself, shifting her intense gaze from Grover to her deliverers. "Yes. In fact he is, sir. Might I ask if you and your friend could lead me back to the hotel so I can catch the next train into the city?"

"No problem. Pleased to help out."

As the hiker approached her attacker, prepared to teach the coward a lesson, Grover slid to the ground against a tree, his jacket bunched up to his middle back. "Not worth the energy," the hiker said, and he turned back to lead Anna back up the Natural Bridge Trail. As they walked, she turned to see Grover lifting his hands to cover his face. He called out to her.

"Forgive me, Anna. Such behavior is reprehensible. My life is in turmoil, starting with parents who want nothing to do with me. They blame me for my brother's death."

She stopped. "Get some help, Grover. I cared for you, and you betrayed me."

"No matter how hard I try to earn their favor, I fail. Sometimes I can't bear the loneliness."

He covered his face again. Did she dare believe him? The apology came across so real, the confession heartfelt. Then one hand grabbed an ear.

Chapter Twenty-Nine

ANNA LEFT GROVER behind. As the train chugged away from the inn, she realized she had also left the picnic basket in the lobby of the hotel. Maybe someone would discover it and eat the food inside. The screech of metal on metal and the rattling of bumping cars as they rolled down the mountain distracted her.

After the train pulled into the depot, she walked to the boarding house, shaken by what happened on the mountain. Rose met her at the doorway. Staring into each other's eyes, Anna broke down. The kind woman drew her into a motherly embrace. Without asking any questions, Rose directed her to the rocking chair out front and delivered iced tea and a dish of dessert cakes. As she turned toward the door, Anna grabbed her arm.

"Won't you join me?" The last thing she wanted was to be alone.

"Of course. At a time like this, I think you need Emma. Let me go fetch her."

Minutes later, Emma emerged and took a seat beside her friend. The three women nibbled on cake and drank Rose's libation, a welcome relief from the valley heat. To be with them, hushed in the calmness of the night, brought her solace. In her own time, she began to recount the day's events. Emma and Rose sat in continued silence, absorbing the story, shocked at the conclusion. Both women, having already expressed their doubts about Grover, withheld judgment.

After Anna finished, allowing the account to sink in, Emma asked one question. "Will you let him call again?"

"Why me? If God loves us, why does He sit back and do nothing, like He doesn't much care?"

It was the question that had puzzled the faithful throughout the ages. A moment of silence passed. Not expecting a reply to her query, she took a last sip of tea and began to rise.

"Dear . . ." At the sound of Rose's voice, Anna sat back down. "About Grover . . .?"

The answer tumbled from her mouth as the tears collecting at the bottom of her eyes trickled. "Of course not. But I would be lying if I also didn't say that I'm heartbroken. Don't get me wrong. What he did to me was horrible, but I'm saddened that true love has passed me by."

Her friends sighed at the same time.

The landlady gave her own eyes permission to moisten as she took in the moment. "When I lost my Daniel, the deep hole in my heart ached something terrible. A discomfort no tonic or pill could ever soothe burdened me for a season. Believe me, we are not alone, and the suffering eventually becomes a distant memory. There is a strength to be gained in such times of trouble."

Did Anna think herself strengthened by the experience with Grover? Not much. More like violated and taken advantage of. However, in thinking about the controversy erupting over her cycling, she found some truth in Rose's words. The Anna of today did not resemble the woman who returned from New York weeks ago, yet she was still not the woman she aspired to become.

The mysteries of heaven would remain mysterious. At least for now.

"Rose, whenever I spend time with Grover, he pulls on his earlobe. Is that some kind of nervous habit?"

The old sage's eyebrows drooped like a white lily after being picked. After giving the question some thought, she entered the house without answering.

＊＊＊

After dinner, they relaxed in the parlor room. Anna sat back into the couch with her eyes closed as the landlady performed an old Irish folk tune, "Red Is the Rose," on the piano. Surprises never ceased as she learned for the first time that Rose played the piano . . . and well. The haunting melody rang out from the Steinway upright that Rose had purchased a few years before.

As she began to coax the keys toward the chorus, the music stopped with no warning. The abrupt silence pulled Anna from her trance.

"Are you all right?" she asked Rose. Had the ballad tapped some hidden vein of emotion inside the old gal?

Emma joined Rose at the bench, and Anna followed to find her benefactor staring at the walls. Her eyes remained fixed on something off in the distance, not confined to the house. A long ago remembrance? A tear blossomed. She breathed in, followed by a long, deep, audible exhale. The moment had arrived unannounced and departed with no fanfare. Rose placed her age-spotted but still nimble fingers on the keyboard. She resumed the chorus, not acknowledging the two women standing by her side.

She sang the words out, written in the sheet music. Emma crooned with her.

Red is the rose that in yonder garden grows,
Fair is the lily of the valley.

Clear is the water that flows from the Boyne,
But my love is fairer than any.
Come over the hills, my bonnie Irish lass,
Come over the hills to your darling.
You choose the rose, love; I'll make the vow,
And I'll be your true love forever.

A penetrating silence held each of them captive. Rose lifted her gaze. "Daniel's favorite song. Sorry. Not sure what came over me."

Even at Anna's young age and limited background, she understood the answer. "The reminiscence of a one-and-only lover."

"Whenever I played the melody for him, he'd say—you make my heart open its petals." Now Anna heaved a sad sigh.

Rose started to rise, but instead she responded to the unrelenting demands from the two women. She launched into another more upbeat danceable folk tune with her name in the title. "Here's 'The Banks of the Roses.' My man loved this one, too."

As she played and belted out the lyrics, Emma taught Anna one of the newer Irish céilí dances. They covered the entire floor in the parlor. The reverie banished Rose's melancholia, and she cackled with glee. Some time had passed since the sounds of joyous music and dance filled the gathering places in the Byrne house. At the end, Emma and Anna collapsed on chairs, out of breath, having frolicked with abandon.

Chapter Thirty

PETER WAITED FOR Detective Leland at the Read House restaurant. He glanced at his pocket watch. Fifteen minutes late. A perfect opportunity to score some points at the sleuth's own game. As Seymour entered the establishment, he spotted Peter at his reserved table in the far corner and walked over. The detective handed his cane and tall crowned bowler hat to an attendant, signaling his appreciation with a nod as he sat.

"Seymour, you're late. Call us even. What did you say before . . . time is money?"

"Touché, my friend. I concede. Our revolutionary Doctor Franklin succeeded in teaching us both something new. However, since you called me away from my existing plans on a Saturday evening, I must charge you extra for this time."

"I see." Outsmarted at his game.

The detective flashed a mischievous smile and a wink. "And . . . you invited me here during dinnertime, something which I have forgone to honor your urgent request. So, I'll assume we will be eating, and that you will be paying the bill."

Peter liked the detective. The man spoke his mind and excelled in his field. In their first meeting to discuss the possibility of working together, he had inquired about Seymour's early life. He joined the Confederate army as a sixteen-year-old in the spring of 1864 and served under General Hood in the defense of Atlanta. Allegiance to Georgia had compelled him to fight, not preserving the institution of slavery. A minie ball shattered the detective's left arm during the final battle for Atlanta, leaving him with limited use of the limb.

"The sawbones almost took it, but I promised to shoot him if he did," Seymour told him in that first appointment. "My other arm worked fine. Still outfought and outworked most guys. Also wooed some of Atlanta's finest belles in my heyday until I settled down to raise a family."

Now a widower with three sons and two daughters, he had opened his business after spending twenty-five years on the Atlanta police force. Two of his boys had joined him in the agency.

"This dinner is mine to buy," Peter said. "But Seymour's Private Detective Agency will handle the bill next time."

"Agreed."

Reaching into his pocket, Seymour pulled out his pipe and tobacco. As Peter resigned himself to a smoky table, the detective reversed himself and placed the items back into his frock. "Lost my desire for a smoke."

The small talk during their meal turned to business. The investigation into the disappearance of Raymond Washington had yielded some early results. Peter perked up, ready for the smallest bit of positive news. Had his private detective picked up a trail?

Seymour leaned forward, sitting on the edge of his seat. "Listen, Peter, I assume you're pursuing this gentleman for personal reasons, and I'm guessing the connection is this woman bicycle rider. Your business, of course. If you find him, that may save whatever's left in your relationship with her."

"Such is my hope, Seymour. And I do want to reunite this hurting family. Any guesses about where he is?" He sat on the edge of his seat.

The detective grinned. "I—"

"Hello again, sirs," the waiter said. "Brought coffee and cream with me."

Much to Peter's chagrin, the server asked if sugar would be required and whether the gentlemen would be ordering desserts. When he began reviewing the selections, Peter declined dessert for both of them. As the waiter innocently chitchatted, Peter requested the check, anxious to hear the detective's update. Seymour took a swig of coffee. He seemed to be enjoying the delay.

"No guesses," the investigator said. The buildup turned into a huge letdown. "Well . . . maybe."

"Do you know where he is . . . yes or no? Pick one."

"Both." The investigator spoke in riddles.

His associates had traced Raymond Washington's movements from Atlanta to Birmingham, Alabama, but the trail went cold there. The hunt would continue until they found him or uncovered information pointing in a new direction. Police and hospital records, hotel registrations, and lists of railway passengers would all be checked. One of the first stops would be the Jefferson County office to examine files on the local prison inmate population.

Peter began to lose heart when he calculated the minuscule chance of finding Raymond after all this time. "Tell me, what's your experience with these kinds of cases?"

"All depends on the paper trail and the willingness of people to talk. My associates possess certain, shall we say, skills. When put to use, individuals are quick to confess what information they hold. Mind you, they will not bend the law too far. Assuming our man never left Birmingham and we can't find him, chances of picking up his trail become slimmer."

Tickets on major transportation routes to another city or town would also be traced. If they found evidence he had moved on, they would follow his movements and start again. But there was one possibility they might never uncover—foul play.

Nefarious deeds were being perpetrated against the coloreds—on the highways and byways between cities and towns, in open fields, and on the rolling hills and mountainsides where witnesses turned away like nothing ever happened. Hundreds of Negroes were lynched or burned to death throughout the South, never to be found.

"If Mr. Washington fell prey to scoundrels, he might be resting in some unmarked grave," Seymour said. "A search would require a massive effort at a cost way more than your family should consider bankrolling."

As a businessman, Peter liked to think about outcomes in percentages. "What are the chances of something bad happening between towns, where nobody comes forward to tell the story?"

The detective sighed and shook his head. "From what I'm told, many more men meet their maker at the end of a dangling rope. The majority of these victims are never accounted for."

A mound of dirt with no marker, in some backwoods where nobody would think to look might be where Raymond Washington would rest for all time.

Chapter Thirty-One

IN WHAT SEEMED like a wink of an eye, Sunday had gone and come again. Anna rode her wheel to First Presbyterian on Seventh. Along the way, men and women in buggies and walking on the sidewalks sneered at her, some hurling insults and epithets. Young children—some sitting, some ambling beside their parents—waved in their innocence.

She rolled up to the sanctuary. The attenders in line, greeted by the reverend at the front door, turned toward her. A few moments later, more like a millennium to her, they turned around and marched into church. Walking to the side of the building, she found a place to secure her wheel. The trip had ruffled her blouse, so she tucked the top into her skirt and smoothed away the wrinkles. Straightening up, she looked around and walked over to the back of the line.

How would the pastor greet her? The procession of many turned into one. She moved forward. This man of God gently took both of her hands and uttered five simple words of comfort. "I'm glad you are here." The organist's prelude, a Mozart composition, resonated through the pews and out the door where they stood.

The judgment she anticipated never came. "Thank you. To be honest, I expected . . . well . . ."

"Take heart, young lady, we are about to be knit back into community. Now, go take a seat."

She slipped into the last row. The congregant next to her stood and took another place. As more people noticed, whispers crisscrossed the aisles, mutterings loud enough for her to understand.

"Corrupting our children."

"Actions inconsistent with one who follows Jesus."

"Doubt she's a Christian."

"What must her mother think?"

The old man now in the space next to hers dressed in tattered pants and holding an equally worn straw fedora, scooted closer. His eyes remained on the organist.

"Pay no mind to those old crows. Be surprised to find one authentic bone inside 'em."

Taking her hand, he gave a reassuring squeeze. She pressed the man's arm and whispered. "Thank you for your kindness."

At least one worshipper practiced Christian charity. The liturgy continued with the prayers of the faithful, hymns sung by a fifteen-person choir, and greeting one another. A female congregant two rows up came to Anna. "Peace be with you," the worshipper said.

A comforting statement from someone brave. "And with you."

"Do not be afraid. Not everyone in this assembly is mixed up. Stay strong, and you will prevail."

Two grace-filled believers and counting. Others around the kind woman avoided her, so Anna returned to her pew. As the collection plate circulated, many of the pious and upright, judgers and condemners, checked to see who noticed when they dropped in their contributions. When the offering passed by Anna, she placed her tithe inside.

A hush fell as the expositor took his place on the dais. Before beginning, he patted his jacket pocket and withdrew a pair of spectacles. Next, he opened the oversized Bible to the chapter and verse containing the backdrop for his homily as he did every week. He surveyed the packed room.

"Beloved, I've stood by and listened over the last few weeks as one of our own endured the slings and arrows of ridicule and scorn from her brothers and sisters. I chose to say nothing, but after much reflection and prayer, this morning I will speak on these matters. Do you remember when our Lord fended off trick questions and legalistic tests from the Pharisees and elders? The Jewish leaders asked Him, 'Which is the greatest commandment?'"

Pausing for effect, he turned his head to each side of this holy place. "Do any of you recall His response? More importantly, are any of you attempting to follow Jesus' teaching in this passage?"

The words came to her: Love the Lord, your God, with all your heart, soul, strength, and mind. And the second part about loving your neighbor as yourself. The ultimate message—one she and the congregation needed to hear. After reading the Scripture, the pastor turned the pages and read another passage.

"John 8:7 says . . So when they continued asking Him, He lifted Himself up and said unto them, He that is without sin among you, let him first cast a stone at her."

The murmurs stopped. The pastor's discourse struck the committed with the truth of the gospel and left the parishioners with an almost palpable conviction.

⇜❖⇝

Across town, Peter and his parents attended services with family friends. Secretly, he wanted to worship in his own community, but he accepted his parents' invitation to join them. The churchgoers settled into the pastor's inspired word for the day.

"The Savior is speaking through me, saying, wives are to submit to their men. Make them masters of your households. The design of creation puts man in submission to his maker, and likewise the weaker sex should yield to their men. But what happened in the garden is proof that the first man and woman got the commandments backward. These new women of today, wanting to cycle, or play golf and tennis, or vote—doing the things men are uniquely designed to do—these misguided souls seek to take control. This is nothing new. Look to the first woman for the results of emancipation. Like Adam's wife, the original new woman, today's liberators vie for dominance."

The preacher stopped. Many heads bobbed up and down, but Peter muttered under his breath in disgust. Several times, his father made subtle gestures to keep his blood from boiling, like a tap on the knee. The religious diatribe continued.

"Or maybe they want to be like men. Pray for these confused humans, for as Eve disobeyed her husband and Adam defied his Father, they are being led astray by the serpent and will face God's harsh retribution. Do not be fooled by these false teachings around this debauched country, for they are creating a cesspool threatening to drown us all."

Peter cringed.

❖

At another place of worship in downtown Chattanooga, Bertha Millwood parsed every phrase Rector Harding spoke. He addressed the subject on the minds of many congregants—the casting off of biblical truths guiding societies for almost three millennia. He bellowed about decency being abandoned across the nation. Now the scourge of evil tapped at the doors of Chattanooga and the South, waiting to infest the last bastion of principled life.

"Some provocateurs who clad themselves in suggestive ways cause men to entertain lurid thoughts and to take physical liberties. Reports abound of many females being forced to fend off unwanted advances. Some of them attract the attention and sneak away to rendezvous with men on their two-wheeled contraptions, riding unsupervised to isolated spots where sinful relations take place. The seats are proven to give women unhealthy sensations, creating friction in the pelvis areas with every revolution of the pedals. This city may be our own modern-day Masada, a stronghold where we, like Israel, will make a stand against unrighteous invaders. But make no mistake, beloved—we will fight to the end rather than succumb by our own hands."

The worshippers in the service responded enthusiastically. The church's roof would be repaired after all.

⚜

Anna bounded down the street and up the steps where Rose and Emma appeared steeped in conversation. "Did you enjoy mass?"

Each waited for the other to answer. Rose fanned herself in the shade, and Emma threatened to take residence atop Lookout Mountain where cooler weather made the days more bearable. But neither responded to the question, so Anna pressed them.

"Saints Peter and Paul Catholic Church? Did you not attend this morning?"

"Yes, we did," Emma said. "The sermon was engaging, to say the least."

Code words for a disaster.

"And yours?" Rose asked.

"Fantastic," Anna said.

With a spring in her gait, she moved to the kitchen to finish gathering food for Hattie's care package. The truth preached that morning had set her free. The rest of the day would be about giving back to someone less fortunate.

⚘

With a basket full of bread, meat, and vegetables, Anna and Rose began the short walk east on Ninth to Hattie's tenement. Rose's hand fan did little to agitate the air. When they reached the hovel, Rose stood with a dropped jaw, aghast that a woman alone with three children resided there. "This horrid building is where she lives?"

"So many people pass by every day, including me, and never consider what life is like on the inside."

"True for most people, but I understand all too well."

The comment stopped Anna at the entrance. "Have you been inside?"

"I lived here. After we married back in the 1850s. An almost unlivable place, even in those years."

She cautioned Rose to brace herself for the worst. Complete squalor. A place infested with sickness. Through the hallway door they entered into total darkness. A hand reached for hers. She grabbed hold and squeezed, stepping extra slowly to avoid a tumble. Halfway into the hall, Rose stepped on an object, causing her to lose her balance.

Anna cried out, panic-stricken, steadying the woman with her other hand. "Are you okay?"

"Fine. Keep going." If not for Anna's iron grip, she might have lost her footing and fallen to the ground in the dark.

"This way. The room is down a little farther. This family needs a helping hand. Hattie is in a bad way, and I'm worried she might die. The children are hungry, and little Charles is brave, but he can't hold things together much longer."

They stopped at the door and knocked. The door was already open a crack, so Anna pushed it forward and walked in. The putrid odor inside made her gag. The sick woman lay prone on her blankets, pale and quiet, while the three boys sat at the table. Dangerous illness festered here, and none of them, especially the young ones, should remain. Taking charge, Rose laid out all the food. The ravenous children attacked their plates while Anna gave Hattie water and tried to clean around her makeshift bedding on the floor.

"Curiosity killed the cat, but satisfaction brought it back," Rose said without warning. The youngsters stopped eating and looked at her for an explanation.

Anna also had never heard the saying. "What does this phrase mean, Rose?"

Without answering, she walked to the corner where Charles's guitar sat propped up and moved the instrument to the side. She stooped low, while making sure her feet stayed planted on the ground. "The wall will tell all."

Another cryptic reference. Anna stood next to her, unsure of what to look for. Suddenly, she understood Rose's riddle. As she also bent down, the etching became clear, riveting the old woman to the spot. The initials were DB & RB. Anna made the connection: Daniel and Rose Byrne. A young couple had carved a memorial to their love for all who followed them into this space.

Rose straightened up and became misty. Anna comforted her. "Let the emotions out."

Rose reached into her clutch for a handkerchief and dabbed her eyes but quickly regained the composure and determination that Anna respected so much.

"Tears of joyful memories and some hard times," Rose said. "This place holds no joy for its current occupants. Time to move these innocents out of here."

When Anna needed Choo Choo the most, her mechanical friend sat parked at the boarding house. Left with few options, she would run back to Rose's place, hop onto her wheel, and ride like the wind to collect her father.

"While I'm gone, pack up the children and gather anything useful you can find for Hattie. Some additional clothes if she has any."

"Okay . . . then what?"

Papa would bring them back in the wagon to Chickamauga to stay at the farmhouse for a time. At least to figure out the next steps. Some kind of doctoring, if such would do any good at this point. And a normal, healthy environment for the young ones.

A good plan unless Hattie lay dying on her bed, hacking up a dreadful, fatal disease like consumption over all who came into contact with her. The attempted rescue might lead to a death sentence for her family. She shuddered and imagined nasty bugs burrowing their way through her body.

Chapter Thirty-Two

THE JAUNT TO the boarding house turned several heads. Strolling women in tight corsets and heavy, full-bodied dresses, crowned with all manner of stylish hats, and some carrying parasols to ward off the sun's bright rays, raised their brows as they crossed paths with Anna. The long skirt she wore limited her stride, but still she made decent time. The hours of riding had increased her stamina.

Like a whirlwind, she ran through the door and up the stairs. The skirt came off first. No time to worry about getting tangled up in the rotating chain. The bloomer outfit would allow her to pedal unhampered.

She rapped on Emma's door. "Answer, Emma." Another knock. "Please, I need you."

"Coming." The door opened and Emma peeked out, her eyes half-open. "A bit drowsy from a nap. Let me wake up and . . . "

"No time. Go to the upholstery first thing tomorrow morning . . . "

"What is happening?" The urgency in Anna's voice brought Emma back into the land of the living.

"Listen, Hattie is deathly ill, and I have to take her and the kids to the farm. Tell them I can't come to work. An emergency or something. Tell them I'll make up the time and how sorry I am."

"If they ask, should I say you'll be back on Tuesday?"

After a moment of contemplation, she shook her head. "Honestly, Emma, I don't think so. No way to determine how many days I'll be gone."

"Okay, I will do my best, but they won't be happy," Emma said. "What about the community meeting? The ordinance?"

Both had been forgotten in the drama of the moment. Would her absence be taken wrong, that she had given up? The health of her friend took priority. "More than likely, I will not be able to attend. Trusting you to be my proxy. Have to go now."

The thought crushed her spirit. After turning away, she stopped in her tracks. "Emma . . ."

"Yes."

"Thank you for being there whenever I need you." They hugged.

In the backyard, Anna climbed aboard her wheel and barreled through the neighborhoods of eastern Chattanooga. An accident would result in devastating injuries. Keeping her eyes peeled for rocks, she amazed herself with how fast she arrived at the farm. The normal forty-minute ride took only thirty-two.

As she pulled up to the house, she jumped off the bike, letting the vehicle fall to the ground in one continuous motion. Once through the front door, she called out. "Is anyone home?" Frantic, she darted toward the parlor and this time yelled out. "Where are you?"

Both of her parents flew down the stairs, apprehension lining their faces. Papa reached her first. "Are you okay? What's wrong?"

With her breathing unsteady, only phrases trickled out. "So sick . . . must help . . . need to bring the kids here . . ."

"Slow down, Anna. Start from the beginning."

The face of her father encouraged her. "Oh, Papa, I'm so frightened for them."

He put his hands on her shoulders. Like the times as a child when he kissed her bruises or settled her into bed, Anna centered herself on his touch and soothing voice. Once she explained the immediate need, her papa swung into action.

"The wagon should be big enough. Let me hitch the team, and we'll put a makeshift bed together. We'll gather Hattie and her boys. Let's prepare the room at the end of the hall. We can isolate her until we understand what we're dealing with."

Anna caught his rhythm. "The kids can take the other rooms."

"Oh . . . and Sarah, whip up some of that miracle soup you make."

Anna and her father looked at each other, and both turned to Mama. Sometimes people must throw caution to the wind, and this life-or-death situation qualified. An unshakeable faith often prompted him to take risks to come to the aid of others. Mama would need coaxing to move into uncharted territory.

Sweat on her brow, Mama moaned in agony. "Dear God, I pray we are not inviting a plague upon this house."

The trip into town took three times as long as her race into the Chickamauga Valley. The slower pace stressed her. They stopped first at the boarding house to remove her wheel from the wagon bed. After parking the bicycle inside, Anna returned from the house with two blankets. She bunched the loose straw in back, and threw the heavier blanket on top to create a resting place for Hattie. The second one would cover her.

Satisfied, she climbed back up to the bench and took her place at Joseph's side. A surprise kiss on the cheek made him turn toward her. "Thank you, Papa. This is asking a lot of you and Mama."

"No. This asks little of us. We should do whatever we can for this family." As they rolled up to the tenement, Papa took in a deep breath.

"Whoa . . ." The team obeyed the verbal command and his tug on the reins. At a complete stop, he removed his soft felt hat and scratched his scalp, pulling on his untended hair. "Oh, God, any building but this one. Yet here we are. Let's go collect these people."

The situation inside remained the same. All their belongings amounted to little, fitting into a tattered suitcase nearly as old as Hattie and the basket that was filled before with Rose's feast.

"Nothing else, Rose?" Anna scanned the room.

"This, some other things not worth toting, and what they're wearing on their backs."

And a battered guitar.

On the floor, Hattie lifted her head to determine who had entered the room and dropped back down to the old clothes bunched together as a pillow. She moaned. "What . . .? Tell me who's here."

"Don't worry. My papa's going to lift you into our wagon, and we're taking you and the children to stay at our farm for a while."

He scooped her into his arms. Upon leaving, Charles viewed the room one final time, his guitar in hand. The lad muttered, "Pray I never be in this place again," as he shut the door behind him. Life in this unbearable pigsty would advance any child well beyond their actual years or destroy them. Despite what the boy had gone through, he appeared strong—healthy in body. But he seemed distant.

Outside, Anna embraced Rose. "Are you sure you can walk home on your own?" The humid air lay thick, and a gray cloud cover blanketed the city.

Nodding yes, she answered with a quip. "Might be in my sixties, but I'm not dead yet. Go on now and stop your fretting. All will be well."

"You are my hero, Rose Byrne."

By the time they reached the farm, the sun sat hidden below the western ridges, heralding twilight. Mama met them in front when they rolled up, taking charge of the three children while her papa lifted Hattie from the side of the wagon and carried her upstairs to the bedroom. The cross draft between two dormers, although minimal, provided ventilation in the room, something the patient needed.

Perhaps a complete change from her previous dark environment would serve as a natural remedy. Once Papa laid her in the soft bed, with clean sheets and real pillows, Hattie uttered "Blessed Jesus" and fell fast asleep.

Anna kept a vigil through the night. Except for one violent coughing attack, Hattie slept. In the morning, the open windows ushered nourishing sunshine to the patient. Mama entered the room carrying a small bowl of chicken broth. "Morning, Hattie. I am Sarah, Anna's mother. Now, I need you to eat as much of this soup as you can."

The familiar voice started to pull Anna from a dreamy vision involving Peter. They rode together somewhere in the countryside, laughing and challenging each other to race. The fantasy faded. Crunched in a small chair, she woke up with a crick in her neck. One of her feet tingled, so she stretched the leg in and out until the numbness subsided.

"Good morning, Mama. Here, let me feed Hattie."

Mama put the soup on the bedside table and gazed down at Hattie. "Don't worry. Either we are going to nurse you back to health or find someone who can. In the meantime, your kids are safe with us and will remain so until you are back on your feet."

Mama rallied to the cause. While her mama fluffed up the pillows, Anna wrapped her arms around the sick woman and inched her upwards. This way she could spoon the broth into Hattie's mouth.

With each bite, more color returned to Hattie's pallid face. Out of nowhere, as Anna lifted another spoonful, a terrible coughing spell hammered the patient with a vengeance. Hattie grabbed the towel at her side and expelled a glob of phlegm. The attack subsided, but the noxious odor of the expectorant invaded Anna's nostrils. She said nothing about it.

"Can you take a couple more sips?"

With a raised arm, she groped for Anna's hand. "No more. My babies?"

"All three are eating quite well." Hattie laughed, causing her cough to return, but nothing near her previous spell. "Now you must sleep more. Later, I will bring more tea and another bowl of soup."

She linked her arms under the patient, and with a gentle movement, Hattie lay prone on the bed again. Anna repositioned her pillow and kissed her on the forehead. "Rest well."

The woman was skin and bones. Anna took the soiled towel for washing and placed a fresh one at Hattie's side. As she opened the bedroom door, three children took a step back, startled. The best medicine for Hattie stood before her.

"Follow me," she said. Herman, the five-year-old, hugged her. Anna marched them to Hattie's bedside, where she stroked the woman's forehead until she lifted her eyelids. "Three little people desperately need to hug you."

Two stepped forward, but Herman, the youngest, called out. "Mama . . .?"

"Come here, my baby."

Hattie opened her arms, giving the boy permission to advance. He buried his head into her side with one arm draped over her blanketed stomach. The boy became tearful. Touching Hattie's face, he voiced the fear of a child faced with an imminent loss. "Mama, is you gonna die?"

The sick woman stroked his cheek. "Naw, honey. Look here. My eyes is open, and I ain't dead. Nothing to worry on. Everything be in God's hands."

Downstairs, Anna found her parents preparing the first meal of the day. The aroma of coffee stimulated her senses, and the frying bacon caused her mouth to water.

"I'm starving. How can I help?"

Papa poured a cup. "Sit here, and this will wake you up. Breakfast is almost ready."

"What about the children?"

"The children ate in the first shift. I showed them the coop—how to feed the hens and collect eggs. When it came to cleaning the pen, Charles decided he would supervise the younger ones."

After the feast and the idle chatter about family, work, and the increasing community tension over bicycle riding, the conversation took a long pause. Her parents cast knowing stares at each other. Anna had learned early on how to read her papa. "Something is brewing here besides the coffee."

"Listen, Hattie is pitifully ill, a tiny sparrow of a woman," he said. "But my guess is she doesn't suffer from consumption. I have seen my share of this plague up close, but I can't be certain."

It was welcome news. "What do you think ails her, Papa?"

"Some kind of chronic chest infection for sure. Like bronchitis, but I'm no doctor. At this point, Hattie needs a real physician and some facility where she can receive the best treatment possible. There's only so much we can do for her, and that's not enough."

"Where?"

He shrugged with raised eyebrows and palms up. "Not sure I trust any facilities or doctors in Chattanooga for this kind of illness."

Mama's face lit up. "What about contacting Bradley Lynch down in Atlanta? Isn't your cousin still practicing in the new public facility? What's the name?"

"Grady Hospital. Yes, Bradley may be able to help, depending on whether he's still on staff. He's been threatening to retire for the longest time. No harm in asking what he can do."

A seed of hope took root.

Hattie ate more soup and sipped on other liquids. She suffered throughout the day with fever and chills, shortness of breath, and chest discomfort. A train ride would be difficult on her.

⤝❖⤞

The following day, Papa hitched a team to the buggy, and he and Anna headed for the Chattanooga telegraph office. He dictated a quick message:

Hello, Bradley. Desperate. Need bed for one indigent Negro woman with bad lung infection. Can arrive tomorrow, Aug. 5, with patient. Plan on 3 p.m. arrival. Will wait for reply. Affectionately, Cousin Joseph.

Anna began to pace the floor, her hands intertwined and turning white. "Oh, Papa, how long must we wait?"

"Patience." An hour later he received a response:

Perfect timing. One bed available. Pulled some strings. Come ahead. Will arrange for an ambulance to be waiting at the station. Been far too long. Bradley.

After purchasing train tickets, Papa decided to maximize his time in Chattanooga, so they headed over to visit Charlie Smith, his fellow chamber board member and close friend.

Charlie was working at his desk, hunched over some papers, as she and papa entered the office. The businessman raised his eyes from the stack.

"Joe and Anna. Please come in and take a seat. To what do I owe the pleasure?"

After a quick handshake, they sat in the leather chairs across from him. "Came to town to fire off a telegram to my cousin in Atlanta, a doctor at Grady Hospital," Papa said. "Thought I'd drop in and catch up."

Charlie appeared anxious. He removed his glasses and rubbed the crease that the pads left on the bridge of his nose. Papa didn't beat around the bush. "Give me your update, Charlie."

"Bad news. The opposition has enough votes to snatch your committee chairmanship."

"Yeah, I figured as much. Just a matter of time. A small price to pay for supporting my daughter. Besides, you know I would never bend to their kind of pressure."

The businessman stood and walked over to the liquor and cigar table. "The situation gets worse. Can I get you a drink? A fine Southern-made cigar?"

Papa waved him off, so he reached in the box and took one for himself and poured a brandy. Lighting up, he pulled several deep puffs. "Sure you won't join me, Joseph? Most pleasurable. Oh, Anna, do you mind if I . . ."

"Not at all, Mr. Smith."

Her papa tried to appear unconcerned, but Charlie left him dangling off a steep cliff. He fidgeted in his chair. "Please continue."

"Sorry?"

"Something about things getting worse. Come on, Charlie. Give it to me straight."

Charlie took a sip of brandy and pulled again on his cigar, the smoke billowing out around him. "Here's the latest: Now they're talking about revoking your entire chamber membership."

Since their last meeting at the Read House before Anna's birthday, the chamber leaders had received political pressure from certain elected officials and influential money interests. Either lean on Joseph Gaines to convince his daughter to quit making a spectacle of her bicycle riding, or advantages might be withheld from some business members.

"For the record," Charlie said. "I voiced my opposition to such a move."

⁂

As the rubber-wheeled, single horse-drawn ambulance made its way toward Butler Street in Atlanta, Anna and her father rode behind in a buggy also arranged by cousin Bradley. They arrived in front of a towering three-story silhouette that stood out from all the surrounding structures.

Carved granite framed the dark red brick building. The round arch of the entry portico featured egg and dart molding and a sculpted keystone. The attendants took Hattie into the facility on a stretcher, and as they followed, Anna gazed upward at the frieze above the entrance. The Grady Hospital. Bradley greeted his cousins at the doorway.

Anna hugged him, the pungent smell of tobacco emanating from his clothes. She whispered in his ear. "How can I thank you?"

His bewhiskered face tickled her cheeks. Bradley was on the rotund side, and his suit jacket, at least one size too small, stretched across his chest, pulling on both sides where it buttoned. The bottom of his coat flared out like a pair of wings. She guessed his age to be mid-sixties or so. Her father and Bradley shared a slight family resemblance for first cousins.

"A pleasure, Anna. In the time since we last visited, you have grown into a beautiful young woman."

"Thank you, Bradley," she said. "Are you well?"

His voice sounded gravelly, more so than she remembered. Too many cigars? Maybe he suffered a throat ailment of his own.

"Not recently. I've been meaning to be examined myself, but time always gets in the way." He shook Papa's hand. "Good to see you, Joseph. I hope Sarah and the boys are doing fine. Please, let's go in."

A wide hall divided the first floor into two sides, and another hallway crossing the building north and south separated the front entrance from the rear of the hospital.

"Everyone's okay, Bradley. Busy keeping up the farm. Like always."

Bradley led his family members on a quick tour of the hospital. "Opened our doors in '92 with four doctors, including myself, twelve nurses, male and female, and a handful of cooks and engineers. Now we've got over fifty physicians on staff."

They made the rounds on the second and third floors. People receiving medical treatment were placed in wards by race and sex. Colored patients on one side, whites on the other, joined by a crosswalk between the wards. The structural design resembled the letter H. Bradley took them to visit Hattie on the Negro side. As she rested, Bradley said she would remain under observation to determine her illness and would be treated as needed.

"If she suffers from something like chronic bronchitis, we will treat her for several days with inhalations, stimulating medicals, tonics, and different sprays. Of course, good diet will help. This sickness comes and goes with the seasons and may stay with her for the rest of her life. The solution is to keep the ailment under control with proper treatment."

"What about consumption?" Anna held her breath.

The doctor gave no immediate answer. "We'll walk that bridge if we come to it."

Chapter Thirty-Three

BACK IN CHATTANOOGA, the big meeting would be underway in a couple of hours, and Peter's thoughts meandered like fireflies aglow. Earlier, his second attempt to deliver Anna's letter had also failed, but this time Mrs. Byrne had come to the door. When he asked her to hand it directly to Anna, she indicated that her boarder was out of town and had not specified when she would return. Discouraged, he left again with his explanation in hand and headed home.

"You haven't touched your food, son."

Abigail Sawyer had learned the way to Peter's heart, and she had planned the most direct route—fried chicken, mashed potatoes, greens, and fresh-baked bread, his favorite meal since childhood.

"Huh?"

Father cleared his throat, attracting Peter's attention. "You wandered far away the moment you sat down." The real point sank in when he caught his father's signal, a nod of his head toward Mother.

"Oh . . . Mother. So sorry." He took a bite of the juicy chicken breast on his dish. "This is wonderful as usual. Thank you."

Still, his thoughts shifted to the upcoming spectacle, and he considered the remarks he would make. The Read House extended the full length of Ninth and Chestnut streets. The bike ordinance covering excessive speeds, fines, and now a ban against women cyclists and wearing bloomers would receive the standard second reading at the hotel. A huge crowd was expected.

He dug into the mashed potatoes, not out of hunger, but to honor his mother. The sharks would encircle Anna, and he decided she would not be railroaded into abandoning her hobby, nor would she stand before a hostile audience alone. In the end, he would rise as her champion.

"Are you thinking about tonight's forum?" His father could read his mind, a talent that presented problems on those few occasions when he told a little white lie, as young boys will do. But now he loved the bonds between them.

"Yes, sir. About Anna Gaines and how she will fare against the naysayers. Some people in town can be brutal, Father. This woman doesn't deserve the treatment she is getting from so many. Like the men in my own club."

Father nodded his understanding. "As the leader, they're expecting you to take a strong position against women cyclists, right?"

"Pretty much, you got the picture."

His father gave Peter the respect to work through his own dilemmas without telling him what to do. He briefed his father on the investigation into Grover Biggs and the stranger's involvement in various schemes to bilk money from unsuspecting marks. The topic of the mysterious disappearance of Raymond Washington also arose. His parents had raised Peter and his older siblings to extend a helping hand to those in need and to give voice to the voiceless. When he shared his desire to find Hattie's husband, his father had sanctioned the search. More than business partners, they were family. They trusted him.

He dove into his dinner, his lost appetite no longer missing. A glance at the majestic, handcrafted mahogany grandfather clock in the dining room suggested little time remained.

"If you both will excuse me, I need to collect my ride and be on my way."

Following Peter to the back door, his mother gave him a hug and his father a firm handshake. "All the best, son. We'll wait up so you can tell us all about what happened."

His mother handed over his hat and asked the dangling question. "What will you do?"

"What you and Father always taught me. The right thing."

That night, Cousin Bradley led Millie, his wife, on his left arm into the dining area where an elaborate table had been prepared. Papa followed with Anna also on his left arm. Both gentlemen stood until the ladies sat. They removed their gloves at their places, and the men took off theirs before sitting down. Punctual and proper. As the first courses were brought to the table, Bradley set the pace with a light repartee, and Anna's papa joined the banter. But Anna rubbed her eyes and stared into space.

By half-past seven, she had succeeded only in moving her food from one side of the gold-rimmed, bone china plate to the other. Someone at the table addressed her, but she had drifted to a place more than a hundred miles away where a brouhaha would soon begin. Her papa's voice brought her back into the conversation.

"Anna . . .?"

She looked up, somewhat embarrassed at having missed the question. "So sorry. Afraid I am not the best company. Please, come again."

Millie spoke up. "No problem, dear. I'm sure you are focused on your friend at the hospital. Harriet, I believe."

Bradley corrected her again. "Her name is Hattie. You remember, Mother."

"Yes, of course. Didn't I say Hattie? I meant to. Anyway, I asked about your future plans now that you've graduated high school. Do you have any prospects?"

The question threw her into a deeper state of depression. The automatic assumption was that she should be thinking about marriage next. "I am distracted by my friend's predicament. A bit of a stomach upset is also intent on ruining my evening. So sorry, but would you all mind if I excused myself early? Sleep will be my cure, I am certain."

Sliding their chairs out, Bradley and her father stood. "Of course," Bradley said.

"I so appreciate all you are doing for Hattie and will be forever grateful. Papa and Millie, sleep well." Both bid her a restful evening in return. She bobbed a curtsy and left.

When she reached her room, she stepped onto the small balcony and gazed up at the moon. Beneath the same celestial body at the same moment, a highly-charged assembly in Chattanooga had commenced without her. Although she would not trade locations—Hattie's illness being her highest priority—the issues to be determined at home would impact her and others for years to come.

The cast in this drama was as diverse and multi-dimensional as any playwright ever conceived. She turned the pages of a script about wheels, women riders, and scant clothing in an imaginative flight of fancy.

The curtain opens and act 1 introduces her antagonist, Bertha Millwood, who makes an impassioned plea for the lawmakers to do their moral duty. A raucous group, not to be denied a good show, bellows its encouragement. At her beck and call, Bertha's busybodies, an army of self-proclaimed reformers from the Kosmos and Women's Club and the wheelmen who join them for the ride, play supporting roles. They follow her into the fracas, offering high and mighty protestations. The Young Men's Business Association also produces its disciples for the performance, all playing walk-on parts.

In the second act, Emma serves as her advocate, displaying oratory skills rivaling William Jennings Bryan. Many are swayed. Next up, Peter Sawyer. The final character pulls the curtain down before the climax unfolds, leaving cast and audience without an ending.

What about Peter? They broke down barriers of misunderstanding and misjudgment when they ran into each other at the ice cream parlor. They became friends, or so she thought. Would he speak favorably about her mission? Probably not, but she might be victorious in one respect: if he withheld any personal indictments against women cyclists or wearing loose-fitting trousers bunched at the knees. No comments would constitute a de facto vote of support.

Not being in attendance crushed her spirit. Isolated, unable to help herself, she continued to stare into the cosmos.

⚜

Peter watched, hoping to spot Anna, as dozens of people filed into the Read House. It was a judgment day for Anna and a history-making day for Chattanooga. The citizenry would either remember when they stood against the creeping progressivism of the North or when many launched a valiant counterattack against inequality toward women.

⚜

Dressed in all her finery, Bertha Millwood sat near the front, unaccompanied. Again, her husband had disappointed her with a lack of concern for her civic involvements. She twisted around in her seat and marveled at how a grassroots campaign with a few devotees had turned into a community-wide protest. With luck and a near unanimous voice from the crowd, the council would move the legislation forward for a vote. She too had grown tired of the constant back and forth about wheeling and wanted to work on her other projects.

Quite honestly, she did not understand the lure of the wheel. The sooner they put the matter to rest, the quicker she and her fellow philanthropists would advance the business of caring for the downtrodden and needy. A successful effort to maintain the integrity and Southern heritage of Chattanooga would further seal her reputation as a community leader.

Perhaps she would reach out to Anna Gaines and offer to mentor her in the ways of Southern modesty.

Emma Kelly and Rose Byrne sat in Peter's row directly behind Bertha Millwood. He had admired Emma's speech at the first reading and wanted to make her acquaintance. Perhaps later in the evening. As he perused the room, the ballooning crowd shocked him. It seemed Anna had not made it back to the city in time. A bad omen?

The emancipation of women loomed as a burgeoning issue, but only now did he begin to understand the huge role that the bicycle had played in setting women free. Many people across the country were reading about the unfolding theatrics here in their quiet little city. The *Chattanooga Times* had published an article days ago, reprinted from a *New York Times* story that first appeared in late July.

The story proclaimed to the world that seamstress Anna Gaines dared to defy the Chattanooga establishment by cycling in bloomers.

The local fight Anna began weeks ago had turned her into a cause célèbre overnight. Now the attention would be inescapable. Peter wondered who had provided the background of the article to the *New York Times*.

Chapter Thirty-Four

AFTER BRUSHING HER teeth, Anna slipped into her nightgown, wishing she were back home at the community gathering. But Hattie's health came first.

As she opened the covers, Anna noticed the small corner of something stuck in the side pocket of her suitcase. Curious, she retrieved an envelope, evidently placed there by her mother before they left. After pulling out a note from Aunt Harriet, her heart leapt. The perfect prescription to lift her spirits.

She moved the table light closer to her bed and began reading. The correspondence had been written several days ago.

"Dearest Anna . . ."

Anna stopped and pictured them riding the bicycle path to Coney. How wonderful it would be if her auntie lay by her side at that moment, laughing and sharing what she had learned about life. Mere paper and words would have to come alive. She continued to read, the inked sentences jumping from the page, and Harriet's voice whispering across the miles from Brooklyn.

As my favorite chair swallowed me into its soft cushions, I began opening a stack of mail. Several unread editions of the *New York Times* also sat in my lap. Exhausted from teaching a two-day seminar at the university, I scribbled out a grocery list on a blank sheet of paper and sipped the last of my tea. When finished, I perused the front of today's *Times*. As I turned to the second page, this bold headline took my breath away:

A Seamstress Challenges Status Quo in Chattanooga. Battle over Women Cyclists, Bloomers, and Southern Culture. The City Debates Ordinance to Regulate Use of the Wheel.

Giddy, I dropped the paper to my lap and laughed out loud. The young, innocent, somewhat introverted woman who visited me six weeks ago had taken to cycling the streets of Chattanooga, wearing improper clothing no less, and turning the heads of the social haut monde. The feminist Francis Willard, a cyclist herself, would be so proud of you, as am I. By this account, you're smitten by the wheel, entangled in a love affair with a contraption that caused you to begin abandoning your fears. The young woman described in the article—self-confident, defiant, and driven—bears scant resemblance to my niece who quaked in her boots that day in Prospect Park.

Lo and behold, I fished through more mail and found your letter, and I'm imagining the buzz in the city. You're not looking for a fight, but one of monumental proportions has sought you out. Embrace the struggle, Anna. Stay your course as I believe more people will silently support your cause than you suspect.

Take comfort and strength in one of my favorite quotes from colored journalist and women's rights leader, Ida Wells-Barnett: "The way to right wrongs is to turn the light of truth upon them." I am also interested to learn more about these two men in your life, Mr. Biggs and Mr. Sawyer. Humor me as your old auntie offers this advice . . .

Anna read on, enlightened by Aunt Harriet's stories of her first loves and when the real one came along. A long, thoughtful letter, beautifully written. Whether in person or through frequent correspondences, Aunt Harriet always gladdened her heart. Reaching up, she extinguished the lamp and fell fast asleep.

In her dream, the mayor pounded his gavel against the table as the last attendees to the town meeting hurried to their chairs. The room fell quiet.

"Ladies and gentlemen, we have resolved the issue of speeding, or scorching, as the cyclists say. The rules in the ordinance have been passed. The principal reason for this community-wide meeting has also been resolved. Miss Anna Gaines, the sole female cyclist in our city, has chosen not to attend. Therefore, the board has decided that females will not be allowed to cycle within the city limits, and the wearing of bloomers by women is also strictly prohibited."

The crowd turned to side conversations. Bertha Millwood sat in her seat, a smile of victory on her face.

Then Anna awoke with a start.

Chapter Thirty-Five

BY PETER'S ROUGH count, more than three hundred people were crowded into the largest meeting room at Chattanooga's Read House. The unprecedented gathering was thirty minutes late in getting started to allow stragglers to get settled. The mayor and all sixteen aldermen representing eight city wards sat behind the tables, facing the citizenry. He still hadn't seen Anna. The mayor's gavel called the meeting to order.

"Good evening, ladies and gentlemen. To accommodate the growing community interest in our business for tonight, we chose to meet here in the Read House rather than in our small chambers at City Hall. As you are undoubtedly aware, the historic Crutchfield House once stood on this site. Perhaps history will be made again in this place tonight. As we did in our proceedings last month, we will allow several people to speak. So we can avoid being here all night, we will insist on a high level of audience decorum. In other words, we will empty the room if you all become too unruly and go into closed session. We will proceed with some general housekeeping items on our agenda and after that take up the proposed cycling ordinance."

Several quiet side conversations began as the officials voted to approve the minutes of their July meeting and discussed many city road and transit improvements scheduled through the remainder of the year. The chair of the committee planning the Labor Day festivities provided an update, and Peter gave a report on the bicycle races to follow the parade and community picnic. More than two hundred riders from three different states were expected to participate in the amateur contest.

After Peter's report, he stretched his neck to study the room. No sign of Anna or her family. Something seemed wrong. He stopped himself from assuming the worst and focused on the people there who might support women's rights. Whatever prevented Anna from attending would come to light soon enough.

When it came to Emma Kelly, his intuition told him this woman could be trusted to care for Anna's best interests even though he had not spent any time with her. He wondered what she thought of him representing an association whose members spoke of Anna in such condescending ways. As Anna's friend, Emma would undoubtedly speak in her absence, and if not, he intended to carry the banner. No doubt which side Bertha Millwood would take. As far as others in the packed room, he suspected most shared the same sentiment—no women cyclists.

He wondered if Anna still held Grover in high esteem. The troubled, secretive man waged some kind of battle inside his mind and spirit. Something Peter sensed more than witnessed, he still couldn't put his finger on it. Grover had expressed strong feelings for Anna but refused to stand in her defense on this issue. Why?

Emma and Rose sat in his row, three seats down. He leaned forward and to his right. Looking toward the two women, he acknowledged them with a tilt of his head. Emma returned the gesture and turned her attention to the proceedings.

The mayor brought the focus back to the long-awaited main purpose of the meeting. "Ladies and gentlemen, thank you for your patience. We will now proceed with the second reading of the biking ordinance." The mayor read aloud the language about scorching and stopped. He studied the crowd. A murmur rippled across the room. "Now the section about women cyclists and inappropriate dress in public."

The crowd hushed as the matter cut to the heart of why most people had shown up. The future of women being free to cycle within the city limits, let alone wear bloomers when doing so, rested with the decision of this legislative body.

As he had planned, Peter rose and spoke to this point.

"Mr. Mayor and distinguished aldermen, thank you for the opportunity to speak again on behalf of the Chattanooga Cycle Club and all enthusiasts of the wheel. As you might guess, people who ride the bicycle for physical exercise, efficient transportation, and pure enjoyment of one's surroundings do not abide by most restrictions on its use. When government sets bans and restrictions, there will be no limit to what might be imposed next. That goes for the matter of female cyclists."

A voice came from the audience. "No reason to worry about women on wheels after tonight." Several people shouted their verbal agreement, prompting the mayor to intervene.

"Order please—there will be order."

All eyes fixed on Emma as she rose, and not a sound escaped anyone's lips. She gazed down first at Mrs. Byrne. Peter overheard the old woman say, "Give 'em what-for." Emma commanded the room, as he took his seat.

"Oh, my friends, this you can count on: Women will cycle in this community, if not today, then tomorrow, as they have begun to do in most cities throughout the country. The march into a new century is already underway."

Every eye beheld her. Peter basked in her speaking style, tinged with a pleasant Irish brogue.

"Everywhere we look, whatever we read, in ads, books, even in our own newspapers, there are references to the new woman that so many of you deride. Impose a ban now, and I predict the attention of emancipation groups will become focused on our city. National leaders like Susan B. Anthony and Francis Willard will make Chattanooga a target in their march toward suffrage and women's rights."

The crowd's momentary silence gave way to a hum of discourse. The mayor asked, "Are you finished, Miss—I'm sorry. Your name, for the record."

"Kelly—Emma Kelly. Almost done, Mr. Mayor. A remarkable, courageous young woman named Anna Gaines lives in our midst. This woman is a hero, fighting for the simple right of everyone to enjoy God's creation outdoors on a wheel. Every woman in this room should thank her. Instead, she bears the brunt of cruel taunts and crude jokes. The so-called proper people of our city demean and brand her as an immoral exhibitionist. Nothing could be farther from the truth."

Rose stood. "All of you should be ashamed of how you've treated Anna. Such a loving young woman." With hundreds of eyes hurling daggers at her, she sat down.

A crude comment rang out, directed at Emma, who remained on her feet. "What else would you call her? And you have joined her. Both of you will be forced to walk or take a trolley after tonight."

The voice came from a man, but Peter could not tell which one. Incensed, he jumped up at the cheap comment, but Miss Kelly intervened before he could get out a word. He sat down, reveling in her defense of Anna.

"This man proves my point," Emma said. "By the way, she's not here because she and her father are saving the life of a deathly ill Chattanooga woman at a hospital in Atlanta. That's what your so-called immoral exhibitionist is doing tonight. I'm finished, Mr. Mayor—for now. I thank you for letting me speak."

When she sat, Peter sprang to his feet. "Allow me to add something to those compelling words." A chorus of boos and hisses followed. The mayor held his hand up, and the opposition simmered down.

"I echo Miss Kelly's comments about Miss Gaines. She's an inspiration. And on issues of policy, let me say this: There's precedent for cities that overreach in the regulation of cycling like limiting access to certain public corridors."

One of the aldermen responded. "Yes, Mr. Sawyer, we are aware of these instances."

Before sitting, Peter noticed several Cycle Club members clustered nearby. The sneers and jeers were not unexpected, and according to a friend, a majority of members had secretly voted for him to be ousted after tonight. He would beat them at their own game. On the ride over, he had decided to offer his resignation as head of the club.

Emma's approving glance pleased him.

The mayor continued. "Very well, Mr. Sawyer. Next up, I believe, is Mrs. Millwood. The floor is yours, Madam."

This circus was the brainchild of an influential, troubled woman who singled out Anna Gaines, but Peter found himself inexplicably soaked by waves of sadness for her. Would Mrs. Millwood pursue this crusade were she not tormented by the loss of her daughter? She represented the misguided thinking of many people resistant to inevitable change. Change almost always cuts two ways—a double-edged sword with some good and some bad. But relaxing the strict standards for women's clothing hardly qualified as a disintegration of social mores.

※

"Mr. Mayor and Board of Aldermen, my fellow citizens, we must squelch this kind of behavior with an iron fist," Bertha said. "As I've long predicted, we are faced with bold endeavors to confuse our natural differences, donning men's clothing to engage in male-dominated sports. With respect to Miss Kelly's impassioned call to thank our resident woman cyclist and to name her a hero, our men should firmly resist the transformation of their women—such as described recently in the *Times*—from beauty to brawn."

The room exploded in response with many men jumping to their feet. Some women in the audience stood and shouted in solidarity with the men; others remained in their seats, unmoved. She wondered if perhaps those ladies were sympathetic, even supportive of Anna's stand.

Frustrated by the outbreak, Mayor Ochs worked hard to reel in the crowd. Emboldened, Bertha spoke over the shouting and called the bicycle a device of the demon of darkness. Further, she proclaimed that women who wore a man's outfit insulted God. The mayor regained control of the crowd.

Bertha opened her Bible and read.

Bertha held the audience in the palm of her hand. The mayor intervened after several glorious passages.

"This is not a gathering to debate the commandments of the Holy Bible. This is a civic forum for the purpose of gaining public input and sentiment toward ordinances that may or may not be enacted. May I assume you are finished, Mrs. Millwood?"

She smiled at the mayor, and then at the crowd, and launched into a final statement, which concluded with a sweeping truth, at least in her mind. "Men are the stronger sex, and that is that." She sat to the thunderous applause of the men in the room.

For some reason, Edward wandered into her thoughts at that moment.

‹◆›

The tide drifted in support of the ordinance, and Peter feared that women cyclists would continue to struggle for social justice—at least for the foreseeable future. Out of nowhere, Emma stood and shouted out.

"Okay, you all believe that women are the weaker sex and should not be cycling like men! Let's put that idea to the test. I propose we stage a race—Anna Gaines against anyone the Cycle Club chooses to oppose her. In fact, the race would be the perfect final event for our Labor Day meet. Afterwards, the community can evaluate again whether women should engage in sporting activities like cycling."

The crowd went wild with men shouting out names and the aldermen and mayor on their feet trying to restore order.

The mayor pounded the gavel against the table, and with several loud strikes, the uproar turned into a mere disturbance. "Well, this is highly unorthodox. Women cycling is one issue, but I'm certain ladies should not be racing on the wheel. People on both sides of the argument are at least agreed on that point."

Grover took his turn on the floor. "The Cycle Club accepts this challenge. And I propose that our own leader, Peter Sawyer, ride against Miss Gaines."

"No, I can't . . ." Before he could disqualify himself on some grounds, the rest of the bicycle riders in the room jumped up and bellowed their approval.

He had never envisioned being dragged front and center into the fray in direct opposition to Anna. On the one hand, if he accepted, he would be forced to compete against the woman he held in the highest regard. If he declined, he would be shunned and branded a coward. Either choice put him between the hammer and the anvil.

The mayor intervened as the room fell quiet. "Regardless of how we rule, this body reserves the authority to make the final decision on the ordinance. Mr. Sawyer, do you accept your part in this interesting bit of theater?"

All heads turned toward him. Boxed in a corner, he stood to lose any chance at the relationship he longed for with Anna. Would she be open to his affections in the aftermath of all this craziness?

He stood speechless, tongue-tied, a foreign experience for him. Answers swirled through his brain, but none landed long enough to be translated into a reply. An eternity passed with each click of the second hand on the grandfather clock next to the council table. Ten eternities passed, and then another ten, until time simply caught up with him.

The mayor proclaimed, "Hearing no objections, at the will of the people, we will proceed with a race, to be held as the last match of our Labor Day races. This meeting is hereby adjourned."

Before Peter knew what had hit him, the matter was closed.

Chapter Thirty-Six

THE NEXT MORNING, as news of the meeting circulated around Chattanooga, Anna received a telegram sent originally to the hospital and forwarded to Bradley's house. She sat by her father's side in the parlor, correspondence in hand. It came from Emma, probably about the meeting. She ticked off the possibilities in her mind as she prepared to read the contents, but only one decision would prevail. Either female cycling would be allowed in the city or it wouldn't.

When she finished reading, she dropped the short communication in her lap. Shaken, she looked up, a single teardrop falling from the corner of her eye. What did Emma do?

"What's wrong? You're all flushed," Papa said.

He drew her into a father's safe embrace, saying nothing more, allowing her the space to emotionally absorb whatever news she had received. After several moments, she lifted her head from his shoulder and peered at the photograph of Bradley and his wife, Millie, which sat on the table across from them. Taken much earlier in their marriage, they must have faced a lifetime of ups and downs together, of building a family and working hard to secure a strong financial future. At that moment, she doubted whether she would ever find that kind of happiness with the man of her dreams.

"Oh, Papa, I've been so foolish, worshipping the wrong things. Bowing down to a cause, making a good thing into a bad one to prove a point. Now I stand to become a spectacle and to lose a potential friendship that I care about."

In one month, in front of hundreds, even thousands of people, she would race a new friend who might have become something more. Now she would never know. The seed of a relationship between them had been washed away, never to take root.

She laid her head back on Papa's shoulder, dismayed and angry with herself.

Later that afternoon, Grover disembarked from his train at the Atlanta depot and took a trolley most of the way to the home of Clyde and Patsy Biggs, his parents. He walked the remaining distance in a sprinkling rain. A slight trace of guilt made a dash toward his blocked heart and then receded. What on God's green earth was he thinking? He stopped, decided to turn around, take a hotel room in town, and catch the first train to Chattanooga in the morning. But a man from the neighborhood waved to him from the opposite side of the street . . . a friend of his father. Now he was committed, for word of his appearance would get back to his parents. He walked up to the front door, knocked, and was met by a shocked Patsy, her husband by her side. She shuttered, almost fainted, but Clyde guided her to the living room sofa.

"Wait here until I get some water for your mother, and make sure she can withstand this." Unnerved, Grover hovered anxiously at the door, waiting as instructed.

Standing there, he thought about that day, most of it etched in his memory. Could it ever be erased? The anniversary of the worst hours of his life had prompted him to buy the train ticket on Monday, the day before his well-deserved triumph at the Read House. Rather than bask in the glory of yesterday's meeting, he made his way to the station. A serious lapse of judgment, but a decision he was powerless to resist. Some mysterious force drew him forth to Atlanta, as arbitrary as a wintertime hurricane.

Long ago, the bright early-August day had started at mid-morning with a trolley ride to Grant Park and a picnic at Abana Lake. For some reason, he and his brother Harold, three years older, had quarreled, but why he couldn't recall. He just remembered being mad. The heat had boiled like water on the stovetop, and the oppressive humidity danced a waltz with the sun's powerful rays. Despite the shade of the trees beyond the lakeshore, the spot where his parents had planted the blankets and food, he wandered down to the water, jumping in and out to cool down, and walking farther away. As promised, he stayed within eyesight of his family. At first, anyway.

Later, when he spotted his brother walking in his direction, he hid in the trees. Lunch had been readied, and Harold was sent to fetch him. After yelling his name several times and attempting to sight him down and across the lake, Harold dove into the water, surfaced, and swam down several times, evidently afraid that Grover had drowned. On his last try, Grover walked over to the shore, waiting for his brother to surface, but he never did. After park authorities retrieved Harold's body, the official cause of death was listed as drowning.

But his parents had blamed him as the cause of his brother's death. Numbness had engulfed his soul every day since.

The door opened wide again. "Hello . . . Father." His voice cracked. "How is she?"

"Come in, Grover."

Then came something he never expected, a trembling hug from an otherwise distant father. The heat and humidity inside matched the blistering weather from that fateful day. As he turned the corner into the living room, his mother sat upright, swishing her hand fan in front of her face, tears streaming from swollen, bloodshot eyes.

"Mother . . .?"

He approached hesitantly, but she rose and embraced him, kissing his cheek. The show of affection from both of them made him uncomfortable and seemed insincere. Why did he come?

The aftermath of Harold's death had been difficult for his folks, when it came to raising him. They withdrew. While he acknowledged his part, he also assigned the blame for his emotional disengagement to them. As he grew into adolescence, he rebelled against them for laying Harold's death squarely on his shoulders. How much could a young man endure without help and support? Alcohol binges and disorderly conduct achieved his hateful purposes and became a regular occurrence. Along the way, he refused to attend school or show up for work at his father's lumberyard. Soon he began hanging out with hoodlums, always drunk and numb.

The Biggs name carried weight in Atlanta because of Father's successful enterprise and both his parents' civic involvements. He tried to destroy their reputation in the community but to no avail. The process made him feel even more distant from them. And empty. Local officials tolerated much of Grover's disregard for public order, for his parents' sake, until the vandalism became serious. When the police had reached their limit and said they would haul him before the magistrate the next time he stepped out of line, he decided to disappear.

Two years had passed with only one letter between them. Until today, Wednesday, August 7. The mental compartment where he tucked his parents away had been pried open by his own doing, and their release might destroy them. The thought should have disturbed him, but he continued on.

The conversation went smoothly at first.

The questions they asked about his whereabouts and well-being were expected. He told them about his life in Chattanooga, leaving out certain parts, and how he had almost completed the business mission his father had sent him on. The blank look on his parents' faces struck him as odd.

"What mission are you talking about, Son?" Clyde asked.

"You know . . . our talk about getting a new start somewhere. Find a community where we can expand the lumber business. Where growth points toward a need for new construction. Does this ring a bell, Father?"

His parents looked at each other. "No, Son. You left because of all the trouble in town. And we've been terribly worried about you."

What was he talking about? "So now you're worried after blaming me for Harold's death for all those years. Admit it . . . you never loved me like you did him."

"Dear Grover, you're mixed up," his mother said.

"I don't think so. Yes, I admit . . . I lashed out to hurt you. But I couldn't handle your condemnation. So when Father said go and find us a new opportunity, of course I jumped at the chance."

His father rose and stooped by his side, peering into his eyes.

Grover turned away to protect himself from any further abusive behavior and their attempt to rewrite history.

"And I take responsibility for my part, son. Many hurtful things were said between us, but I never spoke the simple words you needed, so I'll say them now. I love you and always have. I'm sorry."

Now the truth wiggled its way into the discussion. Grover pushed down the temptation to cry like he had done so many nights in his old bedroom. "All I got from you . . . self-righteous anger. And blame without help."

Somewhere in his muddled thoughts, swirling like a merry-go-round, he heard, *Heaven help you, boy.*

"For some reason, you've blanked the truth from your mind," his father said. "In the beginning, you experienced a healthy recovery, or so we thought. The burden and trauma from your brother's death took enough of a toll on you. Never would we have saddled you with additional guilt . . . you felt enough on your own. Later, when you began vandalizing the neighbors and I faced the humiliation of settling the damages, I became distant, of no use to anyone, leastwise you. Forgive me, Grover."

The heavy tears and occasional sobs from his mother sent him over the top. He rose and backed away from them, toward the front door. Eager to avoid their delusions, the need to escape overwhelmed him.

"Goodbye," he said, fumbling for the door handle behind his back.

"Son, please stay with . . . "

The rest of his father's plea was cut off when he closed the door.

Children played in their yards as the sun made its usual trek to the other side of the sky. Walking to the trolley, dazed, he wondered, *Did I miss my childhood?*

Just as quickly, he refocused on Anna Gaines who had spurned him. An important task lay ahead. She would rue the day when she crumpled him up like a piece of used paper and threw him into the trash.

Chapter Thirty-Seven

ANNA TOOK THE first train back to Chattanooga on Thursday and decided a walk from Union Station to Rose's house would help to clear her head. The doctors had determined that Hattie suffered from chronic bronchitis, a bad enough ailment in its own right. The prognosis for recovery gave her hope, but Hattie needed many more days of hospital care before being discharged. Afterwards, she would spend a couple of weeks at the farm.

The plan made sense. Papa stayed behind at his cousin's house to monitor Hattie's treatments, visit friends, and call on some important contacts. One of his oldest companions held an executive position with Atlanta-based Coca-Cola, and he always dangled a perpetual job offer in front of her papa's nose. Should he ever decide to trade in his plow for a business suit, the door would be open. Toward the end of the month, he would return to Atlanta to check on Hattie's progress and, with any luck, bring her back to the farm.

One bag in hand, Anna walked at a moderate pace, eager to get home. Two young women walking in the opposite direction whispered to each other as they passed. A voice called back to her, so she stopped. They took a few steps toward her.

"Aren't you the one who's riding the bicycle around town?"

Braced for a verbal attack, Anna met them head on with penetrating eyes and an aggressive tone. "Yes, I am she, and I'm in no mood for trouble. Who is asking?" How rude and unfair. She wanted to kick herself for such a sulky retort.

"Please forgive us," one woman said. "We meant nothing improper."

Guilty and convicted. "No. The inappropriate remarks came from me, not you. My apologies."

"No problem. My name is Caroline, and this is Josephine."

Josephine stepped forward. "My folks wanted a boy after four girls, so they picked the name Joseph. Soon as I came along, they named me Josephine and ended up calling me Jo." They wore practical cotton summer dresses, their hair coiffed beneath fashionable straw hats trimmed with colorful ribbon. Delightful women at first blush.

"Well, my father's name is Joseph, and like yours, the name is time-honored. Such an unexpected pleasure to meet you. Please forgive the abrasive comment. No excuses, but my life somehow became complicated a while back."

"Yes, we've been reading," Josephine said. "The newspapers in the last few days published many stories about you. Even papers in other cities."

"How . . .? I've been helping a sick friend in Atlanta. What are you talking about?"

"Well, first the articles in the *Times* about the meeting on Tuesday night and the Great Chattanooga Bicycle Race."

Someone had named the sideshow already. She asked anyway. "What's that?"

The woman looked at Anna with a puzzled face. "It's what people are calling the contest between the sexes. By the way, we're not the only young people who support you. The story is getting coverage in papers like the *New York Times* and the *Los Angeles Herald*."

"Oh, no." That much she didn't know. Shock set in. The complications in her life doubled.

The women told Anna how their parents opposed her stand on cycling and talked about the issue every night at the dinner table. "Let men be men and women be women," an oft-repeated phrase became the opposition's rallying cry. Jo's mother served in the Women's Club with the likes of Bertha Millwood and her crew.

"Mother is infected with the vitriol these ladies of culture spew at their meetings and teas," Caroline said. "And Father . . .? He's on another planet."

After a few minutes, the women wished her luck and continued on. The chance meeting filled Anna with both assurance and dread. Something new occurred to her. Some coming-of-age girls now considered her a role model, a woman willing to march through a wilderness—alone if need be—for a righteous cause. A leader like Annie Londonderry and Francis Willard. For a young girl who had shied away from the attentions of others for so long, such a label filled her with pride and a sense of accomplishment. But the expectations of leadership also scared her to the core. Would she shrink under the responsibility? The idea of intense local and national scrutiny made her knees buckle and caused her head to swim. A part of her wanted to be inconspicuous, to lead a quiet, normal life. Events had spiraled out of control, taking her in wrong directions. Or right ones. She still didn't know.

A swarm of unknowns had been loosed from Pandora's Box, and Anna would never be able to shoo them back into their chamber.

⚜

She walked through the front door to the surprise of Rose Byrne.

"Welcome home."

A hug from the kind landlord-turned-adopted second mother covered her with the safety blanket she needed for the moment. In a way, the boarding house had become her new home—a safe harbor where she took refuge from the fiery taunts hurled from every corner, each puncturing her armor a little more. Her knights, Rose and Emma, cast a protective barrier at the front door that blocked tribulation from overtaking the house.

"So, I'm not going to fill your head with all the craziness taking place since you left—at least not now," Rose said. "Pretty sure you've gathered enough information along the way. Please tell me about Hattie's condition."

A quick update was all she could manage. Dinner would be served at the normal hour. She promised to give her landlord a complete rundown on the events in Atlanta later. For now, she needed to connect with Emma. The walk up the stairs became a hike over the slopes of Irish Hill. Had the beneficial effects of all her recent physical conditioning evaporated overnight? Each step to the landing pushed the limits of her energy.

At the top, she stopped, right when Emma stepped outside her door. Eerie timing. Several moments of silence passed before they fell into each other's arms.

"The way I messed things up at the community meeting, I figured you would never speak to me again," Emma said.

Anna shook her head. "That would never happen, dear."

"How sorry I am for this horrible quandary. Now you must race Peter in front of all those people."

"Shh. Let's go into your room. Nosey ears may be listening." Anna chuckled at her play on words.

With the door closed, Emma broke the news concerning the house. "The only ones living in Rose Byrne's boarding house now are the proprietress herself and the two of us. The other so-called ladies moved out yesterday without warning. Unfair and unkind to Rose, but no surprise."

"Nastiness is in vogue these days." Her brand of nasty had raised its ugly head on the walk home when she confronted the two young women for no good reason.

In her absence, a battle of wills in the community had taken a sudden unexpected turn and had become a personal contest between her and Peter. Passions flew in every direction, ricocheting off walls and ceilings, pitting neighbor against neighbor. How did Peter respond to this public hue and cry? What about the real work of municipal government like continuing to pave or macadamize some of the less traveled roads? Or keeping the economy on a sustainable path as the city continued to recover from the devastating depression.

Many more of the old oil-burning lamps needed to be replaced by manufactured gas streetlights. Telephone companies marched forward with plans to install phones in every structure. And the citizenry waited for the installation of more electric infrastructure to meet burgeoning demands for power.

The list grew while they argued about bicycle riding. Such childish games. What about the rulebook these parents used to clobber their kids with? Chapter 1—play nice. She asked a simple question.

"What happened, Emma?"

Blow by blow, Emma painted a vivid picture, the back and forth of compelling arguments, the unruliness of the crowd at times. "Of course, I stood and represented your interests—quite well, in my opinion—and Peter surprisingly made an impassioned plea on your behalf."

This revelation about his gallant defense both pleased and confounded her. His proclamations must have erected barriers between his fellow wheelmen and been a real head-scratcher for others who did their shopping at the Sawyer grocery. People expected the Sawyers to be steeped in Southern culture. Why did he allow himself to be pushed into a corner with no retreat?

She began to pace the floor. "Go on, Emma."

"The proceedings went haywire, out of control, with all the talk about women being unable to keep up with men. I lost my composure, and my head, and issued the challenge. Not to Peter. I proposed a race against any male cyclist, and Grover suggested Peter would be the perfect opponent. The room came unglued with people shouting their agreement. Peter looked shocked and saddened."

Anna's decision to take up cycling got worse with each passing day. Did Peter buckle under the impossible circumstances? She wanted to believe this. "What happened next?"

"The mayor recommended against the idea. When Peter failed to speak out, the council sanctioned the race. Everything happened fast, and all of sudden, the mayor adjourned the meeting. I'm so sorry, Anna."

These two men had previously possessed her affections. One—Grover Biggs—remained single-minded in his support of keeping bicycle riding a man's sport. She had discovered him to be dishonorable. And the other—Peter Sawyer—was caught in his own dilemma of divided loyalties. But she still harbored some affection toward him. In the end, would he seek to own her heart?

"Seems like things can't get much worse," she said.

Emma became more uncomfortable.

"Well . . . maybe. Do we count the fact that you are no longer employed?"

❧❖❦

As they descended the stairway, Anna didn't know which concerned her more—the loss of another job or all this crazy talk about a racing match between the sexes. Dubbed The Great Chattanooga Bicycle Race by the *New York Times*, the event would break a well-accepted cycling rule in cities where women rode in droves: Females should not race on the wheel, a caution she readily agreed with. She suspected the talk around the city about this lack of convention and other issues had already reached a fevered pitch and would intensify as September 2 approached.

Rose greeted them and drew their attention to the latest articles on cycling in the local newspaper. "Why don't you ladies head out to the front porch, and I'll bring some tea. I must read you parts of this piece in our *Times*, reprinted from the *New York World*." She chuckled. "It will lift your spirits."

Sitting on the porch waiting for Rose, they allowed the stillness of the night to speak its promise of peace to them. Anna broke the quiet. "What saddens me is . . ."

Emma gave her a moment. "Go on."

Anna hesitated, afraid to face her uncertain feelings about the men in her life. "Just that Grover is out of the picture, and Peter lost interest in our friendship a while back. Not sure why. And now this."

Emma changed the subject. "The news about Hattie?"

"Through the first few days at the hospital, she made steady progress. She should be home by the end of the month or sooner. Whatever will she do to sustain her family with Raymond still missing? He's probably never coming back. I worry for her and the children."

Rose interrupted, her hands filled with a tray of tea and homemade sweet cakes. The Monday edition of the *Chattanooga Times* sat to the side. After Rose passed their cups, she raised hers in a toast. "To my young friends, who give me purpose and, frankly speaking, a lot of fun and adventure with their shenanigans."

They all took a sip, and Anna bit into a cake. She forced herself to put on a happier face. "And here's to our Irish Rose, who should open a dessert shop on Market Street."

Rose set her cup down and picked up the newspaper. "Now, Anna, I saved this for you—the forty-one don'ts for female cyclists. May as well put a positive note on all this babble about bicycles."

Placing her spectacles on the tip of her nose, Rose read down the list and selected one of the dozens of cautions. She forced down a titter. "Don't scream if you meet a cow. If she spots you first, she will run." She peered over the top of the paper to check their reaction.

"Are you kidding?" Anna broke into deep laughter. Emma's response came slower.

"Do they think most women have never been near a cow? A little girl can find her way around a barn and a cow's teat every bit as well as a man." Rose put her hand up to silence the happy outbreak.

"Another grand piece of advice—don't allow dear little Fido to accompany you." The hilarity among them continued. "Here, Anna. Pick one."

Perusing the list, she read several more, trying to keep a straight face. She failed each time. Don't chew gum. Exercise your jaws in private. Don't try to ride in your brother's clothes to see how you feel. Don't wear tight garters. Don't discuss bloomers with every man you're friendly with. Don't let your golden hair be hanging down your neck. The list went on with ridiculous sayings.

The last one gave her pause so she chose not to read the line aloud. Don't race. Leave that to the scorchers.

She began to accept a simple reality. A bicycle racer is what she needed to become.

We are famed the world over for the refinement, the gentleness, the beauty, the womanliness of our women. When they engage in sports that are designed and intended for strong, athletic men, they lose their lovable qualities. It is not pretty or an inspiring sight to see a crowd of women togged out in picturesque costumes, rushing madly over dusty roads, with eyes sunken, cheeks flushed, hair loose, and lips and tongues dry and parched. Let our wives, our sisters, and sweethearts ride their wheels for the pleasure in them, but leave racing for husbands, brothers, and beaux. With the advent of the women's race will begin the decline of the bicycle as an exercise and pastime for women. Let us have no more of it.

—Cycling Life, Sept. 6, 1894
(On occasion of the first women's
bicycle race in the U.S., held at Louisville)

Chapter Thirty-Eight

AT THE END of a busy week, Peter prepared to close the grocery and head home. Many days had passed since the fiasco when Grover volunteered his name as the male cyclist in the race of the sexes. The night when club members had howled their approval of the match, scuttling any chance of a friendship between him and Anna. The night when shock had robbed his ability to respond.

What would he say to her? Good luck, and may the best cyclist win? To be honest, he didn't care about winning. At this point, he just wanted to climb out of the quicksand that threatened to sink him and his sincere desire to court her. As he placed his key in the lock, a lad rolled up behind him on a bicycle and called out.

"Are you Mr. Sawyer?" He turned to face the messenger.

"Yes. Can I help you?"

The boy handed him an envelope with the words written on the outside—For Peter Sawyer's Eyes Only—and ran off. The parcel bore Detective Leland's handwriting. They last spoke several days ago. Anxious for word, he withdrew a short letter, dated the day before, August 15.

Off to Birmingham to pursue an active lead on Raymond Washington. I think we've found him, alive but confined in a notorious county prison work program against his will. May be working in some kind of coal mine under deplorable conditions. If Raymond is there, we'll find him. Will be in touch soon. Look for a telegram from me.

It was a good omen. The detective had proved his value once again. He stuffed the communication into a jacket pocket and retrieved his wheel from the side of the building. As he rode through the streets careful to avoid pedestrians and other vehicles, his commitment to find Raymond Washington grew stronger no matter where the search might lead.

The principal motive for reuniting Raymond with Hattie and their children remained the same: a desire to help a downtrodden family. But the bonus of earning Anna's affections would also please him. Upon reaching the house, he parked his vehicle and entered to greet his folks. After a hug, his mother took his jacket and invited him to sit while she finished preparing dinner.

"Are you hungry, Peter?"

"Starved."

"A few more minutes." She headed back to the kitchen.

He swelled with pride and respect as he watched her leave. Father could afford several servants but employed only one to care for the animals, make deliveries, and manicure the grounds. A college-educated woman, his mother worked full-time as a nurse until she met his father, when she opted to stay home and embrace her domestic role. Over the years, she had volunteered medical assistance to those without resources and handled details related to the Sawyer businesses.

Father came into the room and took the seat beside him. "Smooth day at the grocery, Peter?"

His mind had wandered, so he looked over to his father. "Say again?"

"The store?"

"Yes, everything went well today. We took in a lot of fresh fruits and vegetables from the farms out on the ridge and beyond," Peter said. "Good-looking produce. Plenty of shoppers too—folks stocking up for the weekend."

"Fine, son. Good news."

He changed the subject. "Say, Father . . . are you aware of some kind of state or county prison system in Alabama where they force the incarcerated men to work in mines?"

"Is this related to the Washington case?"

"Yes, sir." The frown on his father's face concerned him.

"There's a practice some Southern states use and Alabama perfected. It's called convict leasing. State and county prisoners, most of them colored, are leased to a company to mine coal while they do their time. The inmate serves out his sentence, the government entities make money, and the company gains cheap labor. The men are housed onsite in makeshift prisons."

In this time of Jim Crow laws and increased segregation, such a system would be ripe for abuse. "What companies are we talking about, Father?"

"Two or three. One of the biggest—Tennessee Coal, Iron, and Railroad Company—is headquartered here in Chattanooga."

The puzzle pieces started falling into place. Raymond Washington left his family to find work. After jobs became scarce in Atlanta, he moved on to Birmingham where something took place that forced him to come before a judge. But one piece didn't square up; the consistent testimony about Raymond's character. By all accounts, the man did not have a criminal bone in his body. What offense did he commit that landed him in a forced labor camp for two years? And how much more sentence time did he owe?

His mother's voice relieved him of this mental exercise.

"Dinner."

❧❖❧

Anna tore open the envelope. A letter from . . .? Scanning to the bottom . . . from Hattie. Back at the top line, she read slowly, wanting to digest each word.

August 10

Dear Anna,

Since you left, been real sick, child, but doctors treating me good here. Doctor Bradley is writing these words as I speak them from my bed. Hard to sleep. Had a dream about Raymond the other night. He vanished from our house, and I searched every room for him, calling out his name. "Ray, honey, where are you?" Went outside into the dark night and heard a familiar voice.

"Who's here?" he asked. His voice sounded deep, different, so I stepped ahead until I found a man on the ground.

Said to him, "Ray, right here, honey. Lawdy, you look awful." The man tried to speak again, but the only thing come out of his mouth is puffs of black, powdery dust. When I woke, a nurse is holdin' a cloth to my lips, covered with blood. I was burning up. Doctor Bradley is watchin' out for pneumonia. Don't fear for me, Anna. Care for my babies. Thank God for you and your papa. Love to you, Hattie

Chapter Thirty-Nine

THE TELEGRAM CAME mid-morning on August 19. Peter Sawyer took the communication back to his office, anxious to read its contents. His eyes went first to the bottom: from Seymour Leland.

> Located RW. In poor health at Coalburg prison mine, as suspected. Injured in recent explosion. Must develop plan for release. Call in favors from government friends as discussed. Medical attention needed. Urge you join me to intervene with authorities. Keep me apprised.

Peter laid the note on his desk, folded his arms, and mulled this latest development. Pleased that his efforts had yielded some early dividends, his conversation with Mrs. Gaines two days before came to mind. She had stopped by the grocery to shop for sundries, but he thought some other reason had prompted the visit. Sure enough, after she paid the bill, they talked at length—about the race and a lot about Anna.

He had not seen or spoken with her in weeks, and he feared the worst. But Mrs. Gaines shared the fond feelings Anna held for him. She also told him the complete story about Hattie, and how her husband, Joseph, had remained at Atlanta's Grady Hospital during her recovery. Anna also had been in Georgia. No wonder he kept missing her at the boarding house, and why she didn't attend the community meeting. Surely Mrs. Byrne knew of these details. Why did she not share them?

As he read Seymour's telegram again, an idea popped into his head. What if Raymond and Hattie crossed paths at the same infirmary? If they secured his freedom, perhaps arrangements could be made for the couple to convalesce together. He pictured a joyous reunion. A bold new strategy began to emerge. Excited, he closed the store and rode to his father's office in one of the first city buildings to be provided telephone service.

Together, they placed a call to Grady Hospital and connected with Mr. Gaines. Courtesy of Alexander Graham Bell, the sound of his voice became instantaneously audible despite the miles separating them. What would they think of next—horseless carriages? Anna's father conferred with Dr. Lynch who said they would find a bed for Raymond when the time came.

As a favor, Peter asked if Mr. Gaines might not mention these plans to his daughter when they next spoke. A request easily granted. After placing additional calls to important friends in high places, Chester Sawyer rose another notch on his son's admiration scale.

On the way home, he fired off a dispatch to Seymour:

Made the arrangements. Will provide details when I arrive tomorrow afternoon at train depot. Let's secure Mr. Washington's release. Good work, detective.

One last stop at Frederick's house. He briefed the apprentice who assured Peter he could handle the grocery on his own. To assist, Peter would arrange for a certain trustworthy laborer who earned his living doing odd jobs for businesses around town, like the grocery, to help

Frederick. The man understood the operation and had dropped by just two days ago looking for work.

The mission filled Peter with equal parts excitement and nervous anticipation. He accepted the horrible odds against prison authorities liberating Raymond from his long nightmare, but nothing would be gained unless he tried. Perhaps Seymour would discover some hidden mitigating circumstances—something damaging enough to compel the county to reevaluate Raymond's case.

The likelihood Anna would ever allow him to call might be equally as dismal. Again, he must try.

❧❖❧

Grover sat erect, anxious to complete his business here as Mortimer Foxx sidled past and sat in the leather chair behind his desk. He disdained the small, balding accountant who spoke with a lisp. For several months he had met with Foxx, reporting on the latest unwitting marks he convinced to invest in the energy scam. Foxx thought he still held the upper hand in their little arrangement, but that was about to change.

The big-eared weasel craned his short neck to peek outside the office. Unsatisfied, he rose. "Better shut the door."

Grover checked his timepiece. "Time is growing short." Once again, he made room for the accountant to pass. The cramped space restricted easy movement.

"Nosey secretary outside and eavesdroppers sitting around her," Foxx said. "We don't want any busybodies catching wind of our lucrative arrangement."

"Lucrative for you. May we proceed?"

The independent practitioner and his accountancy handled the books for the Sawyer wholesale lumber operation—Grover's employer located at the southwest end of Chattanooga on the bank of the Tennessee

River. The thought of being associated with Peter Sawyer in any business rankled him. The accountant's stranglehold brought him to the edge of a darker anger even though he had collected some extra cash along the way.

"Something to drink?" The accountant flashed his irritating smirk. "No need to abandon cordialities even within strained relationships."

"No. I have some issues to discuss." The accountant stalled, on purpose he was sure. Grover couldn't wait to turn the tables on the irritating twit.

"Please excuse me one more minute then. A refreshment sounds good to me right about now. Encouragement to help me get through the rest of the day." The proprietor of Foxx's Accountancy turned to the table behind his desk. Pulling the top from the flask containing his brandy, he poured. As he sat, he took a sip, savoring the drink and the upper hand, or so he thought.

Grover watched him, recalling that frightening first encounter.

The empty room at Sawyer's yard had been easy enough to break into, but he became edgy and tense once inside. As he had rifled through the file cabinet, he jumped at the sound of another voice. He turned to face a short and stout middle-aged man. "What are you doing here, sir? This is someone's private place of business."

"I . . . I . . . work here. I'm new," Grover said.

With trembling hands, Grover had dropped the documents from the storage cabinet, scattering them across the floor. His eyes darted between the accountant and the papers. "My name is Grover Biggs. I hired in about a month ago."

Grover stooped to pick up the mess, but the balding man beat him to the ground. "I'll get these," the man said.

Scanning each page, the man deduced that he was attempting to steal proprietary customer information along with a market analysis. The papers would help Grover to report back to his father on the state of the Chattanooga economy and the prospects for a new competitor in that region. The stranger identified himself as the independent accountant hired to oversee the lumberyard's business receipts and profit-loss records. He sat Grover down for a chat, explained the Keely Motor Company stock offering, and enlisted him on the spot as his Chattanooga-Hamilton County lead generator.

"Here's the deal. I sweep your petty larceny under the carpet. You bring me some potential investors. We take care of buying their shares, providing new information on the energy contraption—whatever. Make the services up. We'll offer them all for a low, one-time advance of five hundred dollars. The investor, of course, pays the cash to me."

Grover began to perspire. "So . . . this little incident will remain a secret between us?"

"Got my word. The stock finder's fee from Keely will add more sweetening to the mix. And I might float a bonus to you every once in a while if you cooperate."

Cooperate he did over the next several months. And here he sat, watching Foxx soothe his insides. Still satisfying his own needs, the accountant brought a burning match to a long cigar and clumsily puffed away.

Grover had had to sit through one too many of Foxx's sob stories about the difficult times that had beset the accounting agency during the three-year depression, about how his practice continued to shrink, and how he had devised several ways to make up the shortfall. A necessary evil, he bemoaned. "How else will I satisfy my wife's proclivity for shopping and incessant desire to dine out?"

The blackmail scheme forced Grover into dangerous elicit activities he would rather avoid. Dishonesty had also become necessary for him to survive, but he preferred his own methods. Not to mention, picking his people to work with.

After one last brandy, the man asked, "So what can I do for you today, Mr. Biggs?"

"I want out—now," Grover said, with a new commanding tone. "If things go well, I will be leaving Chattanooga the first week of September with my bride-to-be. I fulfilled my end of the bargain and expect you to do the same."

"Well, Mr. Biggs, I'm afraid your services are still required. Perhaps you can continue wherever you and your lady decide to settle. Would hate to inform the local police about your indiscretions."

Grover stood, and for the first time, he eyeballed Foxx with confidence. The accountant flinched.

"You are not the only one holding on to a little secret, Mr. Foxx. Been busy keeping my eye on you since the first day. I know you're up to something low-down with Sawyer's lumber business. That much I'm sure of, although I haven't quite figured out what. Daily trips to the bank, multiple deposits—more than normal on an accountant's salary."

Foxx stammered. "I . . . I . . . I . . ."

"Tell me, Mr. Foxx. What other scams you been working besides the stock deal?"

The accountant broke into a sweat. "Allow me to remind you . . ."

"No matter. Sure enough, investigators will find something unexpected if they conduct an inquiry, won't they?"

"The truth is . . . I . . ." He sat speechless.

"That drink would be perfect right about now, Mr. Foxx."

Chapter Forty

Coalburg Coal Mines
North of Birmingham, Alabama
Wednesday, August 21

AFTER ARRIVING LATE in the day and getting a good night's rest in a fine hotel arranged by the detective, Peter prepared for the encounter with the Coalburg employees.

On the slow buggy ride to the prison, Seymour shared some of the details his team had gathered the day before about the mine explosion and Raymond's overall condition. The prison agreed to provide Peter and Seymour access to Raymond for a limited time. The physician where Raymond recuperated told Seymour that he had sustained a concussion and some lacerations on his scalp.

Perhaps more disturbing, he had also developed a bad case of dysentery, a killer disease if left untreated. Seymour had uncovered a published assessment of conditions at the facility, which stated that the flux ran rampant among the prisoners, most of them Negroes. Many of the incarcerated men made their final prison break in a pine box.

Raymond had another six months before his term expired. The possibility of him surviving the infection grew more remote with each passing day. The doctor reported that his symptoms would continue to increase in severity, insisting the staff had done everything in their power to make him comfortable.

Seymour warned that continued incarceration translated to Raymond's death sentence. The prison drew its drinking water for inmates from a putrid five-mile creek running beside the buildings. The day before, Seymour had walked a long stretch of the water. "A cesspool and virtual breeding ground for the organisms infecting his intestines. And let's not forget the worm-infested food."

"Why, Mr. Leland, I didn't realize you were such a scientist."

"I read. Remember, investigation is my business, and this work is a science."

As they traveled on, he witnessed the impacts of the mining operation on the local environment. Seymour shared what he learned from the people in Birmingham. The rows of coke ovens by the river, made of refractory brick and blocks, belched out flames and issued dense clouds of smoke. The skies turned dull, and the gases destroyed the surrounding vegetation. The Sloss Iron and Steel Company turned the coal into ingots to be burned as fuel or as a reducing agent in blast furnaces used for smelting the ore.

The business benefited from the cheap labor, paying about nine dollars a month for each offender leased from Jefferson County. "Government also turns a profit by avoiding the normal costs of criminal detention," Seymour said. "The losers are men like Raymond Washington who are robbed of the most precious thing they possess—their liberty."

Through his pursuit of the case, the private detective discovered that Raymond's punishment for a crime he never committed was twenty days of time through the county convict leasing program. "But this system also requires the convict, in this case Raymond, to make payments to the sheriff, clerk, and those who gave witness against him. So Raymond, with no money in hand, had another nineteen months of imprisonment to work off, at a rate of around thirty cents a day. And—"

"Hold on, Seymour. Fraudulent testimony?"

The detective pulled on the buggy's reins.

"Yes. Like I said, these people took away Raymond's freedom on charges that have no basis in fact."

The details of Seymour's inquiry uncovered a troubling truth about the local courts. The investigator, pleased with his team's conclusions, highlighted the analysis as they approached their destination. Shocked, Peter mumbled to himself.

Death from pestilence and accidents took a huge toll on the prison population. Still they came—new victims of the convict leasing system to fill in the empty spaces. If Raymond somehow paid his debt to society without another continuation, and if he avoided being crushed by falling boulders or suffocated by noxious gases in the mine, he would be released. But first, he would have to survive the dysentery, and that seemed unlikely.

The magistrates had already attached another three months to his original sentence based on additional accusations. All false.

The equation left one too many *ifs* for Peter. They had to free Raymond.

⚜

Raymond muttered in his sleep. "Been thinking, Hawkins . . . need more time."

The man twisted on his decrepit mattress, sleep-talking in a dialogue only he understood. Peter hovered over him while Seymour lectured the attending doctor and a prison official about the deplorable conditions. The man's head was wrapped in bandages to protect the wounds he incurred two days ago in the horrific mine explosion. Peter shook his head, trying to put himself in Raymond Washington's shoes . . . unable to work so his family could eat and live in decent quarters. He lay there, helpless in a decrepit hospital bed, his insides crawling with microscopic bugs eating away until there would be nothing left of his emaciated body to sustain life.

The accident had claimed ten lives. The thick wall of debris had trapped the others, all presumed dead. A few lucky souls, like Raymond, worked in spots closer to the entrance, allowing rescuers to reach them.

The bedridden man spoke again. "Are you proud of me, Mama? Important alderman . . ."

The words stopped as his eyes began to open. He looked at Peter, appearing confused by his presence. He glanced at the other three men, one dressed in a morning suit who angrily poked his finger on the chest of another well-dressed man. The doctor listened to their heated argument.

The convalescent turned his attention back to Peter. "Should I know you? What's happening here?"

"No, we've never formally met, but I'm from Chattanooga, and we're here to help you and Hattie and your kids. I'm Peter Sawyer." Upon the reference to his family, the man sat up too quickly and moaned.

"Easy, Mr. Washington. Let's ease you back down and take the pressure off your head," Peter said.

Raymond fought back his emotions. "The owner of the grocery in town? My Hattie shops at your store. Have you seen them . . . her or my children? Are they well?"

The man became agitated. "Don't worry," Peter said. "All are fine. But we need to get you out of here."

When Seymour had noticed Raymond waking up, he left the others to join Peter at the bedside. After introducing himself, he assured Raymond that enough evidence existed against the county and prison owners to press charges. Raymond would leave this place and be transported to a hospital where he would receive proper medical assistance and soon be reunited with his family.

The man no longer held back. Moisture collected in the corners of his eyes. Peter choked back his own emotions. The doctor and prison official rejoined the group, objecting to what they called empty promises of hope.

Seymour threatened to contact the Alabama governor to gain Raymond's release.

Peter made the threat real. "Perhaps the higher-ups at Sloss, or Mr. Sloss himself, would prefer to deal with the governors of Tennessee or Georgia? And perhaps a couple of senators? Several officials have already offered to support our efforts to free this man. Proof of a vile miscarriage of justice is sitting on their desks, and we're ready to contact the newspapers."

The official turned to the private detective. "May I say, Mr. Seymour, that—"

"The name is Seymour Leland. Mr. Leland to you." The investigator stepped forward to within two feet of the man and blew a heavy stream of pipe smoke into his face.

"Mr. Leland. This criminal . . . sorry, his name again?" The man coughed.

"Washington," Peter said. "Mr. Raymond Washington, a former alderman of Chattanooga, distinguished and respected."

Peter gazed down at Raymond with admiration and tipped his bowler hat as he bowed. Not in such a gracious mood, Seymour took the opportunity to land a disparaging blow. "So sorry, sir. Afraid your name escapes me."

"As I already said, Thomas Palmer, the—"

"Third. Ah, yes."

The official became exasperated. "Please, I'm trying to tell you that this lawbreaker received a fair hearing. Found guilty, with several witnesses testifying against him, and duly sentenced by a Jefferson County judge."

Seymour had a trick up his sleeve about the phony process. "Shall we begin with the positive identification I requested yesterday?"

The doctor had appealed the request, calling it unorthodox and not healthy for the patient. The deep cuts required stitches, and chances for infection remained high. Peter denied the doctor's protests. Unwrapping the head bandage would reveal evidence of the man's identification. A new dressing would be applied when they finished. The doctor left the decision to his patient.

Raymond gave his quick approval. "Yes, sir, you all can examine my head. Not sure what you're looking to find, but go on."

Eager to finish, Peter turned to the doctor. "Please proceed."

Careful not to bump or twist Raymond's head, the doctor unwrapped the gauze, one rotation at a time until Seymour viewed part of the identifying mark. The final turn of the bandage revealed the full scar on Raymond's forehead—the reminder of a brutal institution etched forever on his body and in his mind.

"This is indeed Raymond Washington, and you best tell your superiors to reopen this case," the detective said. "The charge against him—gambling, I believe."

Palmer confirmed. "A solid prosecution."

"At my behest, one of the finest law firms in the country did some preliminary checking," Seymour said. "The court's prosecution can only be deemed a joke, a sham in our opinion. No specific charges are recorded at the county. Perhaps you find this fact as unorthodox as I do."

The prison official appeared stupefied. Raymond tried to stifle a laugh. Peter, too, enjoyed watching his private detective at work.

Unnerved, Palmer took exception with the allegations against the county courts. "Let me assure you the proper procedures—"

"Listen, you can tell your bosses at Sloss that we will expect two years of lost wages and the equivalent of another year for pain and suffering inflicted upon this man. All expenses into the future will be handled for Mr. Washington until he achieves a total recovery in the finest institution of his choosing. Of course, we will pursue these and all legal fees should we be forced to go to trial."

Seymour paused while the Coalburg men stood speechless. "The matter is closed—for now. Am I making myself clear, sir?"

"Perfectly. This will take some time to sort out."

Peter jumped in. "Well, don't take too long, Mr. Palmer. We will be waiting in town. Excuse us for a moment while we confer with Mr. Washington."

The two prison men stepped away. Curious, Peter asked Raymond if he remembered anything about his dream, the reference to someone named Hawkins and working on something.

"Hawkins may be dead by now, what with the disaster and all. The man wanted to know whether I'd join the prison break that day, but I put him off until the last moment. When we marched down into the mineshaft, I told Hawkins to count me in. Suppose to be five of us, but not long after, the mine blew."

Peter bid goodbye to Raymond but promised they would continue to work on gaining his release. As they began walking away, Peter turned back to address Thomas Palmer. "One last thing. This man is to remain hospitalized for now. He will receive critical treatment for any and all ailments, starting with his dysentery."

"But . . ."

"We'll be checking all hospital records when we return, which will be soon. Good day, sir." Peter bowed and pulled the front of his hat. In the end, he behaved as a refined gentleman.

On Friday the twenty-third, they transferred Raymond from the prison to the train station in Birmingham. Peter told him they had secured a bed at Grady Hospital in Atlanta where he would convalesce until he recovered from his illness. Afterwards, he would return home to Chattanooga. One fine detail Peter failed to include: Hattie also convalesced at Grady, and the two would be reunited sooner than he expected. Raymond listened but responded only by nodding his head.

The train's interior boasted rich leather seating and elaborate wall hangings. The sideboards, rugs, and paneling added to the railcar's homey atmosphere. From his seat, Peter viewed wilderness and desolation out of both sides of the car once they left the city, but the inside furnishings revealed a marked contrast. The passengers found creature comforts and some luxuries abundant to the eye and available.

Seymour withdrew a cigar and matches from his vest and joined four straw-hatted men smoking on the vestibule platform at the front of the car. Peter and Raymond locked eyes. He tried to imagine how astonished the man must be. One minute he's rotting away in a prison with little prospect of leaving alive. The next he's wearing a new suit of clothes and riding in a car with strangers who pledged he and his family would soon be together.

Peter prodded Raymond into talking about his reversal of fortune. "Are you baffled by all this?"

Now settled into the train ride, Raymond broke his silence. "Yes, Mr. Sawyer."

"You must call me Peter."

"Only if you call me Raymond. Since the other day, been wondering if this is true—that I'm not going back to that disease-infested pit."

"Not only will you never go back to Coalburg, I pledge to work against the unjust system of convict leasing."

"Why? Why you all doing this for me?"

The question slipped away unanswered. Raymond would find out soon enough.

Chapter Forty-One

Atlanta, Georgia
Friday, August 23

THE AMBULANCE CARRYING Raymond stopped in front of Grady Hospital as did the buggy with Peter and his private detective.

In the end, the phone calls from the Tennessee Governor's office helped secure Raymond Washington's freedom. One call to Colonel James Withers Sloss, the founder of Sloss Iron and Steel Company, which owned and operated the Coalburg mine, did the trick.

The Sloss operation, now run by investors in Richmond, Virginia, received a scathing report earlier in the year from the Jefferson County Health Officer in Alabama, detailing the abhorrent conditions and high death rates at Coalburg. The damning assessment produced negative publicity for the entire Alabama convict leasing system, and Sloss and his backers decided a gesture of goodwill might work in the program's favor. The owners accepted all terms negotiated by Seymour to avoid further scrutiny.

Joseph Gaines and Dr. Bradley Lynch emerged from the medical building with a stretcher as the two men exited the vehicle sent to collect them from the train depot.

"Happy to be with you, Mr. Gaines." Peter tipped his hat out of respect. "Please meet my associate, Mr. Seymour Leland, a businessman and resident of Atlanta."

"Yes, Mr. Sawyer. Believe we made acquaintances along the way once or twice. Mr. Leland, a pleasure. And this is Dr. Bradley Lynch, my cousin. Now let's dispense with formalities between us. The good doctor here is aware of your agency in Atlanta and says you're one of the best in the business. Judging by how fast you found Mr. Washington, I understand why your work is held in such high esteem."

The investigator beamed at the compliment. "Thank you, Joseph. But several people played a key part in making this happen, starting with Peter here. A fine young man with a charitable heart. Of course, the phone call from his father to Governor Turney moved the situation along."

Peter passed the accolades to someone else. "In my estimation, sir, your daughter deserves much of the acclaim. Because Anna came to the aid of a sick lady, a happy ending to this sad story appears at hand. I'm honored and privileged to help."

As the driver prepared Raymond for transfer to the facility, the three men moved closer to the stretcher. Joseph whispered, "Does he suspect anything?"

"No," Peter said. "And what of Mrs. Washington?"

"Suspects nothing. The wonderful people working here are beside themselves waiting for the reunion. We wouldn't spoil this moment for the world."

The unsuspecting lovers would find themselves face to face after two years of separation—two years of hardship and uncertainty—two years that almost killed both of them. They loaded Raymond onto the stretcher and began carrying him toward the entry. At the door, Bradley stopped for a moment and stooped down to speak with his patient.

"How are you feeling?"

"Oh, my head's healing up. But doctor, I still got a mighty thunderstorm in my gut."

"Detective Leland wired us about your injuries in the mining disaster. I'm sure you lost some personal acquaintances, maybe friends. A lot of good men died. Horrible tragedy, and we're so glad you're free now."

The doctor began asking questions about Raymond's intestinal disorder. He explained how his hospital maintained supplies of a small bush found on the rocky hills of Southwest Texas and Northern Mexico. The wild shrub showed great potential in curing severe diarrhea.

"The medicine is called chaparro amargosa, nicknamed bitter bush." Every section of the thorny plant—the roots, branches, foliage, and fruit—was boiled to create a fluid extract the color of weak tea. Patients took the substance orally and rectally for several days until their symptoms subsided.

"Done had my fill of bitterness," Raymond said.

"Yes, the medicine will leave an unpleasant taste in your mouth. Nothing a good chunk of bread can't take away. With some luck, depending on your official physical examination, this bitterness should lead to your release in a week or two. You'll continue your remedy at home for a while."

Raymond's disbelief turned into a hopeful optimism. He became tearful again. "Home. Going home to be with my family. To hold my Hattie again. My babies. Oh, Mr. Sawyer, can't believe this. The dingy prison almost killed me."

Peter stooped down to look Raymond square in the eyes and firmly grasped his arm. "That's a pledge you can believe."

They stopped in the reception area. Bradley pulled Joseph and Peter aside for a brief conversation, after which they returned to the others.

The doctor and Peter would go upstairs to take care of a few details while Seymour and Joseph helped the new patient check in.

"I'm sure you're tired from traveling, Raymond," the doctor said. "Tonight, rest is what you need most."

⥇◈⥆

On their way to the second floor, the two men reviewed Hattie's case. With treatment, today she bore little resemblance to the weary, emaciated woman who entered the hospital in early August. The chest inflammation and her coughing had been controlled, and she had regained an appetite along with some additional weight. Without a relapse between now and the end of the month, the Washingtons might be allowed to leave together to rejoin their children.

She sat up on the bed, her face beaming with the radiance of a full moon. "May I say, Hattie, you are a lovely sight to behold," the doctor said.

As Peter stepped into full view, his presence lit her face. "Why, Mr. Sawyer, what you doin' here?"

"Come to check up on you, Hattie. And you're looking fine."

He made up a story. A business opportunity had required his presence in Atlanta, and his friend Anna Gaines had asked him to check on her condition. He would be leaving in the morning and would relay to Anna the doctor's good reports on her condition and his own assessment of how she looked.

"And may I compliment you on the lovely dress," Peter said.

"Why, thank you. Doctor done told me . . . now Hattie, you g'won and wear that new dress the nurses gave you. And come to think of it, do your hair, too."

"And it too looks lovely," Bradley said.

The birthday present surprised her because she had mentioned the date—August 24, tomorrow—in passing weeks ago. She chattered away about how she should be getting ready for bed, not dressing up for a night on the town and about how God had saved her and used one of his angels, Dr. Bradley, to do His heavenly work. The doctor and Joseph Gaines had visited often and made certain she received diligent care.

"I hope God been taking as much time in His schedule keeping watch on my Raymond—wherever my man be at this moment," she said. "Been feeling better. Cough gone. Miss my little ones real bad."

"Joseph tells me they're doing fine at the farm," the doctor said. "Handling their share of the chores, eating like tomorrow will never come. Eager, I might add, to be reunited with their mama. Come sit on the side of the bed for a moment while I take a listen."

He put his stethoscope to her back. First, she breathed normally as he moved the chest piece around the corners of each lung. "Okay, now breathe—"

"Deeply."

"Sounds like you been through this drill," Peter said.

Inhaling, she coughed a couple of times but recovered and pulled in several more deep breaths. The doctor shifted his instrument to her chest, and they repeated the process. He removed the earpiece. Peter's excitement about the reunion threatened to spill forth like a limerick crying out to be read.

"Well—how's everything sound inside, Dr. Bradley? Been much easier for me to breathe."

"Much improved. The bronchitis is retreating more each day. Now I want you to remember—this illness can come back, but don't panic. We'll be able to put you back on your feet before the sickness progresses too far. So how about if the three of us go for a short walk before bedtime? A little exercise will do us all some good."

They started out, Hattie strolling sure-footed beside the doctor. When they reached the stairs, she placed her arms inside his and Peter's to protect against falling. At the bottom floor, she stopped to catch her breath. As the three strolled, Hattie detected more people milling about than normal for this hour.

When they turned a corner, Peter studied her face, awaiting her initial response. Hattie gaped at the man who now stood in the middle of a small gathering. "What . . .?"

One side of Raymond's face was turned away from them as he spoke with an attendant. She tried to wipe the apparition from her eyes, but he didn't disappear. Peter couldn't think of a time he enjoyed a scene more. As she pulled him and Bradley a few feet closer, one nurse raised a hand to her mouth in anticipation of the pending revelation.

The attendant blocking a full view of Raymond's face moved to his right. The men in the group around him turned to face Hattie so Raymond did the same. His eyes met Hattie's, and neither of them comprehended the obvious. Raymond scrunched his forehead and nose and raised one eyebrow. He was immobilized by incertitude.

"Baby, you here?" Confusion turned to surprise. His eyes widened as he moved forward. Peter and the doctor released her.

"Raymond?"

She began to weep rivers. Hesitant, she lifted one hand to touch his face, to confirm flesh and blood stood before her not some familiar-looking phantom. With one finger, she traced the line of his scar and brushed along his mouth. "Still got the small bump from the split lip. Didn't heal so well. Serve you right for fighting. Must mean you be real."

"Got the black mole on the back o' my neck too, crazy woman. I'm your husband, and God, how I've longed for you."

"Lawdy, you looking skinnier than a half-starved prairie chicken," Hattie said. "Need to put some meat on them bones. Can I trust these old eyes?"

Hattie's shock turned to quiet joy and gratitude. She turned to Peter and Dr. Lynch and nodded her head, a tacit acknowledgment of their part in this reunion. As she faced Raymond again, they considered each other for a moment longer until Hattie fell into his embrace. They stood locked together for several minutes, the tears on their faces intermingling. No one around him or her moved an inch, held speechless by the powerful moment.

"Oh, dear love, how can I ever make you realize how I missed you and our babies," Raymond said.

She kissed his mouth. "Be all right. Tomorrow be my best birthday ever, praise God."

❧❖❧

The man sat down at his desk late Friday night with pen in hand. He addressed the envelope first: To Miss Anna Gaines, care of the Byrne boarding house.

August 23

In case you want the truth about Peter Sawyer, he is planning some scheme to either embarrass you or disqualify you on race day to guarantee he is victorious. He has nothing but disdain for you and all you did to destroy the peace of our community. Don't be fooled. Withdraw and participate in the Labor Day festivities like everyone else. From the stands. Take this advice from someone who cares.

He reviewed what he wrote. A stranger, perhaps a young lad he would hire for a dime, would place the letter inside the screen door on the front porch of Rose Byrne's house. The first person to walk out of or into the house would deliver the warning to the addressee.

Finished with his work, he pulled the advance payment for his services from his shirt pocket. The three dollars would come in handy this evening when he and his drinking mates would be hitting the local bars and drifting through the streets, making mischief as most of Chattanooga slept. These small jobs over the last few weeks had provided the perfect chance to pick up some extra pay.

Harassment and intimidation: the kind of work he performed well.

Chapter Forty-Two

Chickamauga Valley
Friday afternoon, August 30

CHATTANOOGA PLUS A holiday weekend equaled small town America awash in celebration. The expectations for Monday's observance hit the crescendo of a full-scale symphony orchestra. Anna simply wanted to survive the experience and go back to a normal life. But would anything ever be normal again?

She rose early, dressed for another workout with Oscar, and sat at the kitchen table nursing her initial cup of coffee. With yesterday's paper before her, she read the detailed lead-up to race day.

The Labor Day Association and its committees had completed all the arrangements. Multiple activities were scheduled throughout the day—a barbecue, field sports at East Lake Park, a grand procession of marchers, a splendid display of floats, and the wheelmen races. Events for the kids and adults included a blindfold wheelbarrow race and a three-legged competition. The watermelon contest would be open to twelve boys. With hands tied behind their backs, the first boy to devour one quarter of a watermelon would receive one dollar. The second place prize would be fifty cents, and the third, one of Mrs. Rawlins's famous homemade apple pies. The Chickamauga Rifle Club planned their regular weekly meet at a range south of the lake.

The cavalcade would kick off the celebrations at nine-thirty in the morning, and the bicycle contests at the driving park would be the stirring finale from two-thirty until five o'clock. Dancing until midnight would round out the day's exciting activities.

The Cycle Club envisioned this as the first annual Labor Day races. The local citizenry embraced the idea as sports like baseball had become a favorite form of entertainment among men and women over time. Her brothers would babble on about Strang Nicklin, son of the former mayor and one of Chattanooga's favored athletes. Many enthusiasts came out to watch amateur baseball because of him.

As the Labor Day races approached, the final match—the Great Chattanooga Bicycle Race—caught the most fancy and would draw additional citizens to the track. She stopped reading. There it was again, the bane of her existence. The race between the sexes. Even if she won, she was certain little would change in the city concerning female cycling. At least for now.

Pursuing a woman's right to ride a wheel remained important, but fell a notch on her list of priorities. She was determined to never again quit on a personal challenge like she had done many times before for so many years. Anna had changed, grown. She now understood Hattie's point all those weeks ago. Find her source of strength and compassion and she would recognize her true value as a human being. The elusive truth now smacked her in the face: She was a child of heaven, wonderfully made despite her physical infirmity and graced with a fount of strength to withstand any crucible of character.

And if women cyclists were granted their rights, that would be great too.

She lamented that along the way, neighbors had become pitted against each other. She hated the sneaky acts of maliciousness like the destruction of Choo Choo's front wheel and the vicious attack on Oscar. And whatever unpleasantness Peter Sawyer might be planning for race day. His duplicity numbed her. The mystery letter delivered to Rose's house must be true, given that Peter had avoided her for days.

They stood by their wheels on the starting line for their practice race. Anna appeared trance-like, so Oscar called her out. "Hey cousin. Come back—you're miles away."

No, I'm right here about to give you a trouncing.

Oscar waited for Anna's one-word signal, ready to quick-mount his bicycle and challenge her on a one-mile practice course. The mid-morning session, following several over the last two weeks, proved her growing skill as a racer. The teacher now found keeping up with the student to be difficult. Earlier, Oscar had put her through some grueling drills: sprints, scaling hills, and racing on a five-mile track through the woods and open fields.

Out of nowhere, Anna shouted. "Go!"

She got the initial jump and pulled one bike length ahead for most of the first quarter-mile. Oscar took the lead halfway through the course, which included a few twists and turns and a long straightaway. They rode neck and neck to the finish line, which Anna crossed first by the measure of her front tire. Slowing to a stop, they both dismounted. Oscar lifted his head and puffed his chest out.

"This is the first time my protégé has beaten me in a race," he said, proudly.

"Miles away, cousin?" Anna asked.

"Evidently not."

Before the race began, her thoughts had been fixated on Peter. But beating Oscar on a short course became her complete focus. She reveled in the accomplishment and gave her cousin a quick hug. "You're a great instructor, and I'd be lost without you, Oscar."

"Wow, what a finish—you squeaked right by me. And I gave you no advantage. No doubt—you're ready." After a series of five short sprints, they concluded the workout and headed toward the farm. On the leisurely ride back, Anna didn't say much. Oscar allowed her to retreat.

The open spaces captured her attention as usual. But reservations about Peter put her in a solemn mood. Just as she had begun to understand him, he dropped out of sight and may have hatched some plan to disadvantage her on race day. The rivalry seemed pointless, and the recent revelation didn't make sense. The test of her adult life approached, and Anna would rather be in Atlanta seeing Hattie through her illness.

Another unexpected parcel had arrived at the post office two mornings prior, and Anna arranged for its delivery to the farm. The package still sat on the hutch in the kitchen when they left for the workout. Now curious about the contents, she made a mental note to open the parcel as soon as she got home.

When she came through the back door, she found Mama sitting at the table, ashen-faced and crying. Her brothers, aunt and uncle, and cousins surrounded her mother.

"What's wrong?" Nobody answered. "Someone speak to me . . . please."

Mama gathered herself, wiped her eyes, and adopted a stoic posture. "A horrible wreck near Macon. The train meant to carry Papa back to us. No word on his condition, but reports indicated some deaths and many injuries."

She handed Anna the telegram from Bradley Lynch. The engine and three cars filled with the Macon Knights of Pythias and their friends left the track at 10 a.m. and ran down an eight-foot embankment at Pope's Ferry. The accident occurred about twelve miles from Macon.

The news sent her into immediate shock. The room began to spin. A weakness in her knees caused her to teeter. Afraid she might faint, Oscar led her over to a chair. She sat and wept, face down into her arms. The family gave her space with their solemnity, allowing her to come to grips with this devastating news. In an instant, her head popped up, as she transitioned from acceptance to denial.

"But Mama, this must be a mistake. It can't be. Macon? He's been in Atlanta this whole time, and he said in his telegram the other day he expected to return with Hattie in time for Labor Day."

Sarah stood and went to her daughter's side. "We need to be strong for each other. One of the boys is going to drive me to the depot, and I will catch a train to Atlanta. Cousin Bradley will meet me at the terminal, and we'll go on together to Macon. I will be in touch as soon as we learn something."

With an incredulous gasp, she challenged the plan. "No, Mama. I will travel with you. Please don't ask me to stay behind. Not knowing will be unbearable."

"Listen to me, dear," Mama said, gently placing both her hands on the sides of Anna's head. "You cannot change whatever happened, and we must hold out hope, dear God, that he may be fine. One thing's certain: He would want you to race on Monday and to stand tall no matter what happens."

Another wave of silent tears fell. Anna's heart broke. "Oh, Mama."

Her mother tenderly lifted her chin. "Your papa is so proud of you. So am I."

The words of approval gave her strength. As she regained her composure, Anna's purpose for crossing the finish line took on a whole new focus. She centered herself and told Mama to tell her father she would cycle on Labor Day—just for him.

"I need a favor. Can someone drop by the boarding house and tell Emma about Papa and the train wreck? Tell my friend I need her now."

⁂

Bertha tidied up the house as she did every Friday. Not a full cleaning. The housekeeper did the menial work on Mondays and whenever they entertained during the week. She couldn't recall the last time they had invited guests to the house. A social event might bring Edward and her together in a common activity. Anything to stimulate conversation between them might help.

For today, afternoon tea with her friends would fill the void. She glanced at the grandfather clock. With plenty of spare time, she decided to visit the grocery on the way to her social appointment. She might try to disabuse Mr. Sawyer of his fanciful opinions about female bicycle riders.

The trolley ride featured the familiar sights and sounds of another pleasant day. Expansion throughout the valley brought its host of challenges to overcome, some concerning infrastructure and quality of life. Like the continued paving of the streets. She took stock of the positive role groups like the Kosmos played in solving the people issues of the day. After stepping off the trolley and walking a short distance to the grocery, she spied Miss Kelly exiting the premises in a hurry. Bertha slipped into a nearby shop to avoid a chance encounter and waited until she viewed the woman rushing past.

"May I assist you?" The attendant began promoting his sale items only to be interrupted.

"Not at all," Bertha said. "Nothing here interests me. Thank you." The retailer's perplexed expression didn't concern her as she exited the store and walked toward the grocery. Out in front, she peered through the glass window. The floor appeared unattended. Hesitant, she checked again, this time capturing the attention of a policeman walking along the street. "Oh, afternoon officer. Just making sure this establishment is open."

He said nothing but acknowledged her by tipping his hat as he passed. She entered the building and approached the counter. Still nobody present, and the back door appeared halfway open. An envelope near the cash register piqued her curiosity. The writing on the front—For Peter Sawyer's Eyes Only—further intrigued her. Miss Kelly must have encountered an empty store as well and dropped off the message in her haste to travel to another destination.

No longer able to contain herself, she opened the unsealed envelope and read the short message. Miss Gaines asked her friend to notify Mr. Sawyer: something about her father's involvement in a train accident. Such a shame about Joseph Gaines. People lived a fleeting life, his and her daughter's more so than others.

She replaced the letter in its original position by the coffee grinder. After taking another quick glance in all directions, she tucked the correspondence into her handbag and left the store. Peter Sawyer would never read its contents.

⌖

The Chattanooga Cycle Club's Labor Day Committee met one last time on Saturday, out at the Driving Club track where the races would be held. Several amateur racers ran drills, becoming intimate with the course in preparation for the coming contests. Once gathered, the group of four sat in the stands for ten minutes watching the activity before them.

Peter called the men to order. Despite his intentions to part company with the club, he had stayed on. After the races, he would step down.

"Gentlemen, I'm sure we would all like to proceed with the rest of our day, so let's begin. How about a report on the lineup of races and prizes. After that, we'll move on to the wheelmen's parade."

Each man reviewed the list of events and entries starting with the One-Mile Novice race. The first-prize winner would take home a mandolin. Next up would be the Half-Mile Open, the One-Mile Boys' competition, the One-Mile Open, and the Five-Mile Handicap, among several others. The last one-mile race, sure to keep folks from leaving early and the highlight of the day's festivities, would start at around five o'clock if everything went according to schedule. The contest would last around three minutes. Chattanooga's first female cyclist would challenge the Cycle Club president: him.

As Peter began to wrap up the meeting, W. F. Reed spoke up. "One final matter, Peter."

He frowned, certain the committee had circumvented him again on some detail concerning the one challenge he wished to be scratched from the program.

"Yes, Mr. Reed. What issue did you all decide behind my back?" A cynical comment, but one not without cause.

"Since the ordinance about appropriate female riding clothes is still outstanding at the City Council, we believe Miss Gaines should not be allowed to wear bloomers for this event. Also, many of our younger citizens will be in attendance, and such a costume would not be acceptable."

Peter turned livid but lowered his emotional temperature before responding. "How do you expect her to race? A shortened skirt would be too unwieldy for her to cycle, let alone a cumbersome dress."

"The difficulty will be her concern. She shouldn't be racing in the first place."

First, the club sanctions a crazy idea for a race, and at the final hour imposes a condition making Anna's participation almost impossible. He would not stand for this. As he began to register his disapproval, another committee member, L. B. Hostetler, stood.

"For the record, this afternoon we sent an official correspondence to the Gaines farm notifying Miss Gaines of our decision."

The deed had been done and would not be undone. "I will disavow any involvement in this vote," Peter said.

"Such a position will be difficult. We signed the letter from Peter Sawyer, president of the Chattanooga Cycle Club."

⚜

In the early evening, before darkness settled on the Chickamauga Valley, someone knocked on the front door of the Gaines farm. Anna heard the knock through her open bedroom door and simply rolled over on her bed, lost in a maze of conflicting thoughts. About her papa, the race, and Peter Sawyer. No one answered, so the visitor tried again. She rose and stood at the bannister, staring down.

As Emma climbed the first two stairs to deliver water to Anna in her bedroom, there was a third knock. Emma set the water down on the family room table and called out from behind the door. "Who is knocking this late?"

"Are you Miss Anna Gaines?" Anna made her way from the upstairs hallway to the middle landing. She stopped to listen in.

"No. Can I help you?" Emma asked.

"Madam, I was hired to deliver this to Miss Gaines."

Opening the door, Emma stood opposite a young boy and his wheel. He carried a personal communication in his hand.

"Yes . . .?"

"Is she home?"

"Yes, but she's unavailable. May I ask what this is about?"

The boy squirmed. "If you please, Madame. My instructions are to make sure I hand this—"

"Over to Miss Gaines. Under the circumstances, you must rely on me to make the final delivery. Or you can return the item, if you choose."

He hesitated but handed over the note and then left. Anna returned to her room, depressed and afraid to view any correspondence in her state of mind. Tomorrow would come soon enough. The contents of this message would wait, so she called down from her door.

"Emma, leave the envelope downstairs and come up. I need your strength to support me through this night. I'm so discouraged."

So far, no telegram had come from her mother.

⌖

On Sunday morning, the day before the national holiday, most people professing faith like Anna and her family gathered at one of the many places of worship.

A culture of hard work and entrepreneurship over the years had created an economic base strong enough to survive the decade's leaner years. Now many Chattanoogans considered Labor Day 1895 to be a pivotal juncture in time, one that would propel the city, indeed the country, toward future prosperity. Hope and optimism abounded as the people welcomed the new century on the horizon.

The Gaines family and Emma attended church services in the Chickamauga Valley where the pastor delivered a timely sermon about the value of toiling and the importance of Sabbath rest. As she attempted to clear her mind, the picture of her father's mangled and crushed body, lying in some deep ditch, resurfaced many times.

The reverend completed his message, and Anna emerged through the sanctuary doors, praying for Mama and Papa.

Later, unable to sit still and wait, Anna harnessed Winnie to the buggy and left the farm to visit the Chickamauga telegraph office. The sign in the window read, *Closed for the holiday. Will reopen Tuesday.* No chance that any messages would be transmitted over the next two days. Mama must have made a similar discovery that most establishments in Macon and Atlanta, including the telegraph offices, were also closed.

That night, Anna paced her room, frantic.

Chapter Forty-Three

LABOR DAY BEGAN to dawn, promising to be warm and sunny. Although they didn't expect any rain, Bertha recognized the fickleness of their local weather. How the unexpected often showed up.

She sat in her rocking chair on the porch and welcomed the first radiance of sunrise casting soft hues of red and orange against the sky above the eastern ridges. She had enjoyed the solitude since four in the morning when she yielded to sporadic sleep and came outside in her robe to think. The quiet would soon be lost to the sights and sounds of their Oak Street neighborhood, awakening to greet the long-awaited day.

The barking dogs, crowing roosters, song sparrows, and woodpeckers blended into a cacophony of voices marking every new morning. Evidence of life abounded, but Bertha's acute sense of righteous purpose had faded, and she struggled to comprehend why. She sipped the last of her tea and shut her eyes.

A shadow of her dead daughter flashed before her, agitated and speaking in some otherworldly language Bertha did not understand. The vision frightened her. The familiar voice of her girl pleaded with her: "Not like this, Mother." Somehow she understood those words.

Then Bertha sprang upright in her chair, as a single tear collected between her nose and upper lip. Such eerie nightmares haunted her with increasing regularity.

Anna stirred in her bed. Pulling her covers back, she swung her feet to the side and sat on the edge of her mattress. Still half asleep, she yawned and inched toward the window only to step on the boot she had cast to the floor the night before. She twisted her left ankle and almost dropped to the floor.

The sprain seemed mild, so she sank all her weight onto her feet and walked to the window where she discovered why the room remained so dark. A blanket had been thrown over the window treatment, filtering out the first light of day. The prolonged darkness had helped her to sleep longer. The cover came down easily, and she drew open the curtain.

Morning still had not broken, but now she distinguished the faint outlines of the furniture in her room—enough to ignite the lantern by her bed.

A quick glance at the timepiece revealed a quarter past six. She picked up the lamp, and as she walked the hallway to the stairs, her ankle started to throb. Perfect—just what she needed on race day. She descended the steps, careful not to make any noise lest she wake up the whole house. On her way to the kitchen where she planned to fire up some water to make tea, she detected something on the fireplace mantel. The envelope from last night. She had forgotten. She scooped up the correspondence and sauntered toward the stove. The water she put up soon came to a boil.

The first sip of tea burned her tongue. She hated when that happened. So far, two mishaps marked the start of her day. Waiting for her scalding drink to cool, she tore open the envelope and withdrew a typed letter addressed to her, dated September 1—the day before. The words shattered her heart. When she reached the bottom, she gasped. Signed by Peter Sawyer. Dropping the message to the table, she wondered, *What else could possibly go wrong?*

No bloomers allowed in the race today. She might as well withdraw. Racing in a full-length garment would be impractical, even dangerous. The ensemble she sometimes wore for casual rides wouldn't work. Defeated, the obvious struck home—Peter and his dastardly club had gone to extraordinary lengths to force her withdrawal. How underhanded.

Another light illumined the kitchen behind her. "Good morning. You're up early," Emma said.

"Welcome to another disappointing day, Emma." The greeting set a negative tone, but she couldn't help herself.

Walking around her, Emma placed the lamp she carried on the counter near the sink. The opened letter caught her eye. "Delivered by the lad late yesterday."

Anna passed the dispatch without saying a word. The short message took Emma only a moment to read. She extended her hand to Anna's, hoping to comfort her. "Unbelievable."

"I'm spent, Emma. I can't do this today."

A minute of silence skipped by before Anna realized the parcel from the post office still sat on the side of the kitchen hutch with several items stacked on top. Curious, she brought the package to the table. The writing belonged to her aunt. Why hadn't she observed this before? Eager to view the contents, Anna ripped apart the paper and opened the box. Inside she found a note.

Dearest Anna—

As you continue to enjoy riding your wheel, I'm certain you will appreciate yet another clothing option. My friend Ida Rew, a successful dressmaker, is now seeking a patent for her Athletic Suit for Ladies. I passed on your measurements and asked her to prepare an outfit for you. An amazing design, I think you'll agree. Meets the physical demands of riding, but also satisfies the urgent calls for feminine modesty. She made me one as well. Next time you visit, we can cycle in matching clothes. Write to me . . . and outrace Peter Sawyer.

Almost like she had anticipated this latest dilemma, Harriet sent the new cycling attire in the nick of time. A stroke of luck. She handed the note to Emma and lifted the costume from the box. As Emma read, she glanced at the tag attached to the item: *A safe, reliable, and easy lady's suit, graceful in outline, hygienic in construction, light in weight, and of handsome and modest appearance. Pedal safely.*

Below the words, Anna read the name I. M. Rew. She laid each piece out on the table. Emma looked up after reading Harriet's note. "This aunt of yours in New York is really an angel sitting on your shoulder."

The consternation Anna had experienced moments ago turned to amazement. A possible solution to an unsolvable problem had appeared out of thin air. The practicality of the pants combined with the cover of a skirt excited her. Technically speaking, these were not bloomers. "I must try this on. Now!"

"What about all the men in this house?"

Unconcerned, Anna began to disrobe right in the kitchen, but she became entangled as she tried to pull the garment over her head. "Help."

"Wait." With a little maneuvering, Emma straightened the gown and lifted it off her body.

"Emma, dear. Do me another favor. Retrieve my riding boots while I dress."

Anna began suiting up. First the trousers, which attached to the bodice and were supported by shoulder straps rather than hanging from the waist. Next, she put the skirt on over the pants, and it fell to her ankles. Emma returned with the boots.

"Can you figure out what this inside material is for?" Before Emma answered, the reason for the strips became apparent. When attached to the trousers, they kept the skirt from blowing upwards, thus preventing an embarrassing circumstance. The garment also would not swing back and become ensnared in the bicycle chain.

"Pure genius," Emma said. "The cyclist can pedal freely, and the individual who finds bloomers improper is now satisfied. In theory, anyway." Emma tried to couch her cynicism.

With boots on, Anna stood and turned before Emma. The clothing might be practical, but without at least a hint of style, she might pass. "Well . . . what do you think?"

"Smart looking, I must admit."

The race would go on. She found Peter's outright attempt to disqualify her to be unforgivable. The biggest challenge of her young life still lay ahead. Hours from now, she would push herself to climb onto her bicycle and chase the wind—for her papa, if no other reason.

But could she tackle this impossible task with no word about whether her papa lived or had died in the train wreck? She closed her eyes and turned to the only place left—prayer. When she finished, Anna looked to her friend.

"What do you say we begin rustling up some food? A hungry crew is about to rise."

Chapter Forty-Four

THE ENTIRE GAINES clan, minus Joseph and Sarah, gathered on the east side of Market Street, north of Ninth. Thousands of excited citizens lined the streets, eager to view the procession. Dressed in her unique, never-before-seen Ida Rew creation, Anna attracted more than a few second looks as she mixed with the multitude. Emma and Rose stood by her side.

Several minutes past the official start time of nine-thirty, Anna heard music and soon after spotted the first marchers—the parade's Grand Marshal, the advance guard, the platoon of police, and Sheriff F. S. Hyde and his deputies. Behind them marched a twenty-five-man brass band, led by a spiffy drum major with his baton. First, he faced the players and marched backwards to conduct, and at the perfect time, he pivoted forward with enthusiasm and flair. The ensemble, replete with musicians dressed in wool jackets, Prince Albert style, and stovepipe hats, created a rousing sound, blowing on bugles, trumpets, trombones, clarinets, cornets, and tubas. Two drummers set a solid beat. Confetti began to rain down from rooftops and second-story windows. Anna's heart welled with satisfaction, tempered with occasional bouts of sorrow.

"I love a rousing parade," she declared to Emma.

Hundreds of wheelmen cycled by, all in formation, waving. At the front rode Peter Sawyer, looking solemn and somewhat uncomfortable with all the attention. Had he ignored the letter Emma left for him at the grocery? All she wanted was some sign, a way to know he cared. She fought back her sadness and anger. Grover Biggs also took a spot toward the front, in his element, soaking up the crowd's applause. The actions of both men in recent days left her baffled.

The lineup paraded north all the way up Market, and at the end of the street, circled around to the other side and came back in a southward direction. At the corner of Market and Ninth again, the cavalcade turned and headed east. As the people strode down the boulevard away from the parade route, the din of the crowd grew faint. People dispersed, many to board trolley cars for the ride to the East Lake picnic grounds. Anna and Emma would stop at the boarding house to collect their bicycles and meet everyone at the lake.

The car pulled to their stop, and they exited for the short walk to the house. Emma looped her arm into Anna's as they strolled. "How are you?"

"Surprisingly well. Been thinking of Papa, wishing he was here. Like me, he loves parades."

In a few hours, this whole bicycle mess would be over. News about her papa might be forthcoming.

⤞◈⤝

Peter sat with his family at the picnic grounds, eating his favorite meal—fried chicken and mashed potatoes. Labor Day should have been a joyous occasion, but he labored inside. Anna must hate him by now, and he took the responsibility. But truth be told, since the raucous community meeting, the birthplace of the so-called great race about to transpire, he had not figured out how to be around her, to tell her of his deep affections.

As he admired Anna from afar, eating with her family, he tried to summon the courage to address her. Wise in matters of love, his mother might have some appropriate words for him, so he turned toward her and found her already looking his way. Had she caught him staring at Anna?

"The time is perfect, Peter. Go to her before this circus begins. Ease your troubled heart."

He took another bite of chicken. "Hmm, Mother . . . delicious, as usual." He would rather not respond but swallowed as he considered her advice. "And tell her what?"

"Start with how you regret that so much time has passed since you last visited. Tell her why. The right sentiments will follow."

She turned to her husband and chattered on about the parade. Peter finished his chicken breast and potatoes, rehearsing in his mind the first things he would say if he made the move. The words, disjointed fragments, fell far short of what he wanted to convey and left him alone, defenseless. He had no clue how to proceed.

All around him, families gathered on blankets spread over the scraggly grass; wicker baskets and knapsacks were emptied and set aside, their contents now at the center of each family's attention. The midday sun bearing down did not dampen the laughter as multiple generations enjoyed home-cooked food and thirst-quenching drinks. He took a swig of his mother's lemonade. Older children and young men with their fathers and friends skipped flat stones along the surface of the lake, challenging each other on whose rocks would skip the most times before sinking. Some girls and boys waded ankle high into the water.

Everyone basked in this day away from work. But he did not celebrate.

✥

The Gaines family put on a joyful face, but the unknown weighed upon them. The absence of Anna's mama and papa became the focus of the mealtime prayer and much of their conversation.

To keep from dwelling on what they couldn't control, Emma, Rose, and Anna carried on about working ladies and whether career and family responsibilities could be balanced so neither suffered. About the new women who continued to emerge across America, daring to lay claim on the twentieth century, pushing against the limits of male domination, and attempting to seize control of all aspects of their lives—personal, social, and economic.

Each addressed the question: Am I a new woman? About to make a profound point, Anna shifted her eyes to the left and stopped mid-sentence. A distraction swept away her brilliant idea, never to be recorded for posterity.

Emma turned her head in the same direction.

"Anna . . .?" Silence. "What are you looking at?"

"Over to the left, coming toward us." He wore a sporty vest with an insignia. The vest complemented a white shirt, long shorts extending to his knees, and shoes without socks. A perfect riding ensemble. Anna trembled. Did she shake from fear or excitement?

Emma spotted him, darting in and out of spaces, careful not to trample on the small plots of land separated by so many blankets. "Uh-oh. Stay calm now."

Intent on keeping him from entering their temporary sanctuary, Anna stood and moved forward several feet. Whatever he came to say would be too little too late, and the damage between them would never be undone. But the strong resolve to send him on his way melted as it always did. Moments later, they came to within three feet of each other, waiting for someone to speak. His cheeks crimsoned.

Someone had better start talking. She lobbed the first salvo.

"Well, Peter . . .? Can I do something for you?" No response for several seconds.

He cleared his throat. "I . . . um . . . came to. . ."

"Say you're sorry for not inquiring after my father? Concede you are avoiding me like the plague after plotting this stupid challenge? Admit you hired those thugs who beat up Oscar and attacked Emma and me? Go right ahead, Mr. Sawyer. I am listening."

Neither fear nor excitement at seeing him caused her to shake. Rather, her pent-up anger fueled her vitriol. What had gotten into her?

"What are you talking about?" Peter said.

"Yes, you must be experiencing remorse and want to confess. Perhaps you're thinking twice about whatever deed you intend to perpetrate against me during the race. Surprise, Mr. Sawyer—I've been warned."

Emboldened, she took two steps closer to him. His jaw dropped as she unleashed her merciless anger on him. She fought to keep her rawest emotions from spilling out, to refrain from saying something else she would later regret, but she failed. Peter endured her slings and arrows like a gentleman, not lashing back, which began to temper her indignation.

"I'm confused," he said. "I came to apologize for not making contact since the community meeting. For some time, I was away, and when I returned, I tried to leave a letter at the boarding house. Nobody answered the door. On the third attempt, I left it with Mrs. Byrne, who informed me you were out of town. Did you not receive it?"

No, she hadn't, but she gave him his due, doubtful about the veracity of his story.

"Wait a minute, Anna. What happened to your father?"

As if he didn't know. He had received the news from Emma's letter. Now he brazenly lied to her face. "Papa might well be dead in a Macon, Georgia, morgue from a horrible train derailment. But you already know that, don't you?"

309

"Dear God. I am unaware of this tragedy. I would have been the first to pay my respects and offer my services in any way to be helpful. Please allow me to console you and your family now. Believe I'm speaking the truth—please."

Her resistance melted like ice in the sunlight. Something inside wanted to presume him innocent until she caught herself. The letter bore witness to her contentions. "Are you asking me to accept a lie—that you never read the correspondence that Emma dropped right on the counter at the grocery?"

"Indeed, I am not lying. I never received nor cast eyes on any such dispatch. If I did, trust that my response would have been swift. For some reason, the note never reached my hands."

Might he be telling the truth? "Emma delivered word to the grocery on her way out to the farm. Pay closer attention to who comes in and out of your market, sir. Are you claiming someone stole the message? And if so, for what purpose?"

He looked desperate. "Sometimes when I'm alone, I leave to check our stock in the back. The floor may be unsupervised for a few moments, but I trust my customers. I can't imagine anyone undertaking a deception like this—stealing a piece of mail addressed to me. But I'm left with no other conclusion."

Again, she became less resolute. Her guard began to slip as Emma had mentioned that the back door was left partially open that day.

"I prefer to end this disagreement as I find the subject unfathomable," she said. "We will do our parts to satisfy the curiosities of the crowd at the track and go our separate ways."

She turned and took her place on the blanket, with her back to him. The curt, biting words she had spoken to him, perhaps unfairly, made her sad.

By two-thirty, the stands on McCallie Avenue overflowed, as several thousand turned out to enjoy the first annual meet of the Chattanooga Cycle Club. People crowded together on both sides of the tiered structure and up against the railing around the track to view the action close-up. The mayor, who had been selected to serve as the designate referee, had not arrived at the track. A few others assigned to act as timers and judges were also absent. Officials delayed the races until the vacancies could be filled.

After some time, with all systems ready, the six entrants in the One Mile Novice category took their positions on the pristine track. Seeing all the racers in formation, Will Stone withdrew from his satchel an oversized pistol he had imported from Turkey for the occasion. He raised the gun high. A shot rang out and the race began.

The crowd roared its approval, cheering on the cyclists as they reached the white ribbon at the finish line. The timer huddled with the judges, and they made the decision to stage the event again because the best time went over the three-minute limit. On the next run, the first place winner made the mile in two minutes and thirty-four seconds.

Anna watched all the events from the stands, seated with her friends and family. At close to five o'clock, after the last official contest, the crowd became restless, chanting for the long-awaited race to start.

Emma squeezed Anna's hand. "Faith, Anna. Ride well."

Unlocking hands, she gazed at Emma for a final dose of courage and descended the stairs leading to the track.

As Anna reached the gate, she glanced back at the crowd. Many shouted unkind taunts, but some cried out words of encouragement. The stress mounted. She took several deep breaths hoping to coax her heart into a more normal rhythm. Retrieving her wheel from the area where entrants stored their bicycles, she walked to the starting line and joined Peter Sawyer and Martin French who stood in for the mayor.

Everyone rose, and a hush descended. Peter tried to make visual contact with her, but she averted her eyes to Martin.

Keep your mind in the game. The first advice Oscar had given her during their lessons.

Martin stepped forward with instructions. "Time for you two. This is a one-mile heat. One time around is a half-mile, so you can do the math. I will count one—two. The gunfire will be the third count, your signal to skedaddle. Someone will stretch the white ribbon across the railings once you both pass the halfway mark. Best of luck to you."

He moved to the side.

They stood about ten feet apart. A curious sensation overwhelmed her. Did the world stop to behold a grotesque, transformed woman ride the bicycle, her once ballerina-like body now riddled with bumps and bulges? Was she the Greek-goddess the *Times* article talked about weeks ago, turned into something unsightly?

Peter peered at her with admiration.

Had Annie Londonderry experienced these feelings when she journeyed across the country and around the globe and received her own jibes and sneers? Did Annie believe people judged her unfairly or viewed her through some skewed lens as being repulsive?

Both riders stood in position, at the ready. She glanced over at Peter, who said, "Anna, when this is over, I . . ."

"One—two." A gunshot rang out, and she jumped aboard Choo Choo, pushing all thoughts of Peter from her mind. The crowd bellowed as Peter burst into the lead like a wild-eyed horse.

Chapter Forty-Five

THE OBSERVERS SHOUTED their encouragements as Peter made the first turn and went into the backstretch, away from the main crowd, with a commanding lead.

Anna paced herself, playing Oscar's advice in her head: *Pull on the bar with a rowing motion.* Doing so counteracted the force of her legs and transferred energy to the pedals rather than into unnecessary motion. She limited the movement in her upper back. As she found her cadence and began to settle into the ride, she pulled to within three bicycle lengths of Peter.

From the rear, she admired his posture—head up, elbows in and bent, and his arms in line with his body. He cycled with ease, but she rode with heart. Pumping harder, she gained on him as they raced back in front of the stands. The enthusiastic crowd applauded and shouted for their favorite rider to take the day. At the half-mile point her breathing became labored, so she practiced the exercises Oscar had taught her. She increased the force of her breaths instead of the frequency.

So far, no surprises. Did Peter plan to fix this race, or had he changed his mind? Maybe the warning she received . . . *stop*. She willed herself to concentrate on the race.

As they turned into the distant stretch again, she pictured Papa's face encouraging her forward. His spirit comforted her, but a picture of him unconscious in a hospital bed almost caused her legs to stop pumping. She banished the vision and replaced it with Hattie's inscrutable countenance and then let the warm companionship of Emma and Rose wash all over her, compelling her to push harder. She took the lead for a brief moment, but Peter managed again to move ahead.

She pulled to within half a bicycle length as they entered the final turn. Several hundred people standing behind the railing appeared fuzzy, a single mass of humanity with no definition. Indiscernible shouts blended into a shrill noise, and the frenzy gripping the people contorted their faces into the most bizarre poses. Her eyes played tricks as her legs pumped the pedals harder than ever before.

Pulling into the final stretch, she drew upon every ounce of energy she held in reserve. Her left calf began to cramp, but she ignored the discomfort, convincing the muscle to relax. Now in a dead heat, the racers fought to capture the lead. The audience went wild. As Anna pulled ahead, about thirty yards from the white ribbon, her bicycle became unstable, the front wheel sliding side to side.

"What is happening?" she whispered to herself. The handle bar turned to the right, and she went down hard, inches away from Peter's bike as he sped through the finish line.

The crowd rose and sounded a collective gasp.

Papa stood over Anna, calling out her name. "Come on, honey. Open your eyes." The familiar voice pulled her out of unconsciousness and into the half-dream one experiences before waking up.

She responded, "Okay, Papa," like at the farm when he woke her for breakfast. When her eyes opened and she realized she wasn't in bed, his face threw her into a state of confusion. Even more disorienting, she lay on her back in the dirt somewhere. How did she end up here? The obvious hit her—the face she least expected.

"Papa! Am I dreaming? Are you here?" She sat up, as Joseph Gaines took one knee and brushed his hand through her hair. A familiar touch. The same caress forever locked away in her memories, the comforting stroke that warded off the monsters of the night so long ago. Another man stood beside him. Peter maintained a respectful distance from the circle.

"Yes, Anna. I'm here with Mama and some others you will be happy to greet."

She wrapped her arms around him and wouldn't let go. In a delayed reaction, she pulled away to look at his face. A white dressing covered part of Joseph's forehead, protecting the scrapes and cuts sustained in the derailment. Anna gently traced her finger around the edges of the bandage. "Papa, is this your injury from the train crash? Are you hurt bad?"

"Many others suffered more serious wounds."

"But how . . .?"

"By God's grace, Anna, I survived. Plenty of time to tell the whole story when we are all back at the farm. The doctor here is going to examine you now. Make sure you didn't knock yourself silly or break any bones. Sir . . ."

The physician stepped forward. He checked her pupils to rule out concussion and ran his hand across her feet and arms for any obvious broken bones. "How do you feel? Any dizziness or nausea?"

"No. Nothing."

"What is today's date?"

She hesitated, but only for a moment. "September the second. Labor Day, right? No way to forget this day."

"Good," the doctor said. "Now where are you?"

"The track. The bicycle race with Mr. Sawyer." She glanced at him. "I think I'm fine. Really. Got the wind knocked out of me, that's all."

"Young lady, I want you to rise to your feet, but slowly. Your father will help you. Think you can do that?"

"Sure I can, Doctor." As she did, thousands of people clapped and cheered for her.

Papa pointed to the stands. "Look, sweetheart. Most of the people here respect you, and they love an underdog. You rode like a winner with heart and grace. Mama and I are so proud of you."

She hugged him tight. After a few minutes, Peter started to approach her, but she turned away lest he woo and weaken her. The designated referee, Martin French, and the man judging the race, finished probing her bicycle and came over.

"Well, it appears your tumble happened because of a flat tire," Martin said. "We also found a rut in the track that you may have dipped into. Might have been created during the earlier races. Fixed the track already. Near as we can tell, a pinhole in the tire caused the leak."

Anna didn't understand. How did she pick up a pinhole, and why didn't the tire flatten earlier? She had checked both wheels when they left Rose's boarding house for the racing track and again after the picnic. The tires were inflated.

Martin glanced at her father. "Miss, I don't much like the idea of female cycling, truth be told. But you're one brave lady, and well . . . I suppose you got the same right as me or anyone else to ride a wheel."

She nodded and whispered, "Thank you."

"My point is this: Someone pricked your wheel using a small instrument like a pin. Something sharp that would cause the air to be slowly released."

Papa tied this information together. "So someone must have pricked Anna's tire right before she grabbed her wheel for the race. And the uneven track helped to bring her down. Right?"

Martin swatted his neck. "Damned mosquitos. Been a plague on this town all summer." All eyes were fixed on him, waiting for a response. "What y'all looking at?"

Papa tried again. "The act must have been done just before the event."

"Yeah. Suppose you're right enough," Martin said. "Hard to believe anyone would act in such a dishonorable way. The young man over yonder is using his kit to patch up your tire. Should be good as new in a few minutes."

She welcomed the courtesy. "Much appreciated."

"The least we can do is put your wheel back in good working order. No winner can be declared in this race. Where do we go from here? The audience is waiting to find out."

Her outrage took deeper roots. The perpetrator stood in their midst. Some kind soul had tipped Peter's hand by writing the letter of warning, but she hadn't known when or how he would strike. With the cruel deed exposed, she abandoned all restraint.

"So why, Peter? Why did you poke a hole in my tire?"

All eyes now turned to Peter, who stumbled backwards, his eyes darting between each person in the huddle. "Do you believe me capable of perpetrating such a loathsome act? And for what reason—just to win a trumped-up race?"

For the first time, she detected a seething uncharacteristic of Peter Sawyer. The fire in his eyes took her aback. Yet he said little in his defense.

Joseph shook his head. "No, Anna. This is not possible. Peter is a good man, and I'm certain his motives toward you are honorable."

"All respect, Papa, I love you, but you are wrong. I have proof."

⚜

Being the target of Anna's odium stung him to the core. The weight of the universe collapsed upon him, stars tumbling all around. Worlds collided and chaos reigned, and he stood in the middle. The order in his life—honesty, honor, and love—withered like blades of grass. Anger blinded him. He walked away, marshaling his self-control to keep from lashing out.

He must dismiss his indignation. The truth would become obvious to her in a few moments when she learned the lengths to which he had gone to orchestrate the reunions.

As the wound to his pride faded, he questioned whether he had misjudged her character. The possibilities for a deeper relationship, the courtship he had imagined, turned to sand and blew away in the winds of these accusations. Was it naive to think he might pick up the scattered pieces with Anna after this race? Maybe she and Grover Biggs deserved each other.

She needled him further, her words stopping him in his tracks. "Speechless, Mr. Sawyer? Surely an indication of your guilt."

Peter took a deep breath before speaking. "First, Anna, I am offended by the charge I somehow punctured your tire. It is such an absurdity and proof of how little you know me. Misfortune struck your family so I took action." He looked over to her father. "Mr. Gaines, sir, welcome home. I am heartened to find you in good health."

"Much appreciated, Peter."

A look of understanding passed between them. A bond of mutual respect, forged by their involvement in bringing the Washingtons together again. He turned back to her.

"Finally, Anna, I'm relieved you too are standing here, unhurt," Peter said. "Now . . . I challenge you to another race, to occur here and now. This time five miles, if you're recovered enough from the fall to proceed."

A random hunch told him that a conclusion to this spectacle might be the medicine to heal their estrangement. With not a moment's hesitation, she accepted. "You're on, Mr. Sawyer."

Her father stepped forward. "Listen to me. It's not possible . . ."

"Trust me," she said. "Like you said, we'll sort all this out later. Please go back to the stands with Mama and know my world is brightened by your presence." He hugged his daughter and left the field.

The crowd, still on their feet, murmuring about what would transpire next, turned quiet when a man stepped forward and began talking into a megaphone.

"This contest must be counted out because one rider's tire went flat." The news caused an outcry in the stands. The announcer lifted his hands to regain their attention. "Please, if you will. Both riders have agreed to a rematch to be held now. A five-mile race."

The spectators roared their approval, chanting, *"The Great Chattanooga Bicycle Race!"* over and over again.

Chapter Forty-Six

AT THE STARTING line, Peter offered to make this a staggered start, with him placed twenty yards behind. Anna declined. In the end, she would win or lose on an equal footing with her male opponent.

The referee, Martin French, reminded both racers that five miles equaled ten times around the track. Another countdown and gunshot would begin the race. When they reached the starting point after eight full laps, Martin would signal with a red flag that a single mile—two final revolutions—remained.

"The white ribbon will be visible as you approach the home stretch. Are we clear?" Both of them nodded.

The designated timer handed them glasses of water. Anna swallowed the drink slowly. Out of the corner of her eye, she caught Peter gazing at her. He made no attempt to avert his eyes. Instead, he wished her well. "Ride safe."

The flames of anger she had detected earlier in Peter burned away to embers. These eyes reflected something softer—maybe sorrow? Perhaps disappointment. What drove his emotions at this moment? In the heat of a verbal battle, she'd incriminated him, sullied his reputation. Now he responds with what—a gentleness of spirit? From the beginning he had acted dishonestly toward her. How could she be such a poor judge of character?

She concentrated on her riding strategy. A five-mile course played into her strengths. Oscar had ridden at her side as she sped through forested paths and across long meadows and flat roads in the Chickamauga Valley, her stamina increasing and her completion times lessening with each training session. Her cousin had proclaimed her a natural long-distance rider and expanded her last couple of practice runs to ten miles.

The countdown centered her attention. "One, two . . . " The shot from Will Stone's pistol signaled the last count, and off they went. This race would be about patience and endurance—knowing how to read her more experienced opponent and how to counter his moves. Monitor breathing, cadence, and pedal stroke through the entire course. Wait him out to make the first move.

Both riders took short lines into the first turn, and Peter broke free on the straightaway, taking a commanding lead. The audience's excitement escalated, turning into a thunderous response as people rose to their feet. Smaller ones caught the action on the shoulders of their fathers, and others craned their necks between the heads in front of them. The disadvantage lasted for two full revolutions around the track—one mile with no letup. In a calculated decision, Anna held back.

He's taunting me. Let him tire, but don't allow him to take any greater lead. Patience. Feign weakness.

Well into the third mile, Peter settled into a consistent, strong pedal stroke, less of a sprint. Matching his speed, she maintained her position—about twenty-five yards behind. The intense response to Peter's initial burst of energy quieted to a murmur as they passed before the stands, headed into the fourth mile. At that juncture, she detected a shift in his strategy.

Finally, he's weakening, or at least resting. This is my chance. Push hard on each pedal at the top of each revolution.

On the straightaway, she dug into her reserves. Her stroke quickened, increasing her speed, and her rhythm remained steady as a heartbeat. To the delight of the audience, she pulled to within ten yards of Peter going into the back turn. Her counter to his plan was simple: Maintain this distance, and save the best for the final half-mile.

They passed in front of the stands again as Martin French waved the red flag. The last mile—two more times around the track. The heat and humidity and her need for water took their toll. Into the first turn, she suffered cramping in her right calf and her neck, forcing her to vary her attack until—luckily—the cramp passed on its own. She shrugged her shoulders up and down to ease the spasms developing in her upper back. By the time she reached the back turn, Peter had made up the ten yards he lost earlier.

The people, standing throughout the contest, responded with increased excitement as the racers entered into the last half mile. Peter held a comfortable lead. To pass him now seemed inconceivable, and Peter appeared to be the hands-down winner. They cycled through the turn and into the backstretch. As she calculated he would, Peter eased up.

He's reserving energy for a final blast to the finish line. Go now, when he's overconfident. Ignore the pain.

The race, which had transcended the initial furor over female cycling and the erosion of morals and appropriate dress to become the most anticipated sporting event in the city's recent memory, came down to the last one-eighth mile. Down to the final yards. She dug deeper, tapping into a superhuman fount of determination, when something unforeseen happened. Peter's left foot slipped from the pedal, throwing his balance and rhythm off. What were the chances? Had he done this purposefully? A collective moan came from the stands.

He recovered as quickly as possible, but not before Anna took the lead by two bicycle lengths. With the finish line ahead and victory within her grasp, the tides of fortune poured Anna's way. For some inexplicable reason, she glanced to the right, over beyond the railing, past the ribbon. What she viewed made her skip a breath and threw her own concentration off.

Locked in a full embrace, Grover kissed some woman she did not recognize.

As she processed this revelation—that she meant nothing to him, and he had used her all along—Peter pulled to within inches of her lead. The two front wheels crossed the finish line in a hair-splitting finale. The contestants and spectators began asking the same question. Who won?

People in the stands argued both ways as the judge, referee, and other officials conferred at the side of the track. Meanwhile, Peter and Anna slowed their wheels and dismounted, dropping their bikes to the ground and hunching over to catch their breath. Other observers brought them water and light sustenance to replenish their energy.

He came to her as she stood. "Quite a race, Anna. You proved to be a formidable competitor."

Caught off guard, she worked hard to summon up some modicum of graciousness. "And . . . you are a skilled cyclist."

The crowd and the racers waited in silence for an eternity. Martin French emerged from the circle of judges with megaphone in hand and walked toward the stands to make an announcement.

"Thanks for your patience. As you witnessed, this competition came down to a close finish. A clear difference in the positions of the riders could not be detected as they passed the ribbon. Because the judges are unable to call a winner, we must rule this race to be a tie."

People flooded onto the track from the stands, chattering about the decision. Supporters surrounded each rider. One bystander shouted out. "The final time?"

Martin French lifted the megaphone to his mouth. "Yes . . . the time. Almost forgot. Thirteen minutes and thirty-five seconds. Impressive finish for a five-mile race. Remember folks, other Labor Day celebrations are continuing into the evening. The dance goes until midnight, featuring the boot-stomping sounds of Hank Holloway and his Barnyard Fiddlers. Bring your sweethearts and kick up your heels."

The adulation caught her unprepared, but she held her head high and made direct eye contact with each person who congratulated her. Some of the girls called her a shining example of womanhood, saying she had expanded their horizons and given them a different idea about what they might do with their lives. As the crowd thinned, her mama and papa, Emma and Rose, and the rest of the family walked up. When they reached her, they separated. Two adults and three children emerged from behind.

The unexpected encircled her.

⌖

"Hattie . . .? Sweet Jesus, you're so . . . healthy." They embraced, and Anna held the hug for several moments.

When Anna and her papa had rushed Hattie to the farm, the woman could no longer walk under her own strength. Delirium had robbed her of the ability to care for and protect her children, but just weeks later here she stood, inches away. A drawn, pallid, seamed face had been replaced with rosier cheeks that now took a fuller shape, making her appear years younger. The late-day sunbeams bounced from her eyes, reminding Anna of the glinting waters of East Lake on a bright summer day.

"If not for you and your papa, I'm thinking I be dead by now. Only God knows where my babies would be."

325

The children stepped up, and each one hugged and thanked the young woman who had made such a difference in their lives. "Oh, you're all so welcome. Forever friends, right?"

They responded in unison. "Right."

Anna noted the quiet stranger at their side. "Who might this gentleman be?"

"This be my man, Raymond."

She stuttered, unable to respond. "Raymond Washington . . .? Your husband who went missing two years ago? How is this possible?"

A chatterer by nature and one of the things Anna loved about her, Hattie recounted the story, describing how he had regained his strength at Grady Hospital after a reunion and how she doted on him. How they spent hours together in the common areas of the facility and retreated to their separate wards when the doctors and nurses insisted. Raymond still mourned Hattie's declining health and the privation inflicted on his loved ones. She cried as Raymond told Anna's family the stories of extreme cruelty and inhumanity—beatings meted out to crush his pride and grueling work conditions that almost broke his body.

Anna imagined the loss of two years, the crucibles they each endured apart, and how such a separation would destroy lesser marriages.

"Got lots to rebuild, but with Ray and my children together under one roof again, the future's lookin' bright to me," Hattie said.

Raymond moved forward, drops rolling down his face as he tried to blink away his emotions. "It's my family you saved—you and your papa, and Doctor Bradley. And I will be forever beholden to Peter Sawyer."

The comment stung her. "Peter? I . . . I don't understand." Seymour entered the circle.

"My name is Detective Seymour Leland from Atlanta. Fortunate to be in the employ of the Sawyers for several weeks now, and I can verify Mr. Washington's testimony. The story is long and interesting, one I'm sure you will learn more about. For now, suffice to say, Peter must take credit for uncovering this gentleman's whereabouts."

"Peter? But . . ."

"And his father, who pulled strings at the highest levels of state government to secure Mr. Washington's release from a horrible Birmingham prison. They held him captive for two years on false charges."

"Why? Why would Peter do this?"

Her papa answered. "Because of his strong sense of justice and compassion and because of his feelings for you—his desire to bring you happiness. Anna, I tried to tell you."

"But . . . but . . . the letter I received. What about the person who damaged my bike and arranged for the gang attack on us out in the valley? I thought—"

"The culprit was Peter? No, my love," her papa said. "Detective Leland investigated all these incidents at Peter's direction and has identified the culprits."

She glanced over to where Peter stood, but he had left.

Chapter Forty-Seven

BY THE SATURDAY after Labor Day, life had returned to normal in Chattanooga. As she left the boarding house, Anna took stock of all that had transpired.

Opinions still varied over who won the race, and Anna's detractors maintained their stubborn insistence that women should not gallivant about town on a wheel. The bloomer outfit remained a point of derision toward her. Had anything of substance been achieved by all the hoopla? The question troubled her.

The Washington family stayed on at the farm where Hattie and Raymond continued to make progress toward full recoveries. In one week, Raymond would begin training for his new position as manager of the Sawyer grocery, replacing Peter, who would transition to other family business interests. The two employees, Raymond and Frederick, would make an effective team with Peter's guidance. The money settlement from the State of Alabama, combined with the generous compensation package offered by his new employers, allowed Raymond and Hattie to begin searching for a modest home to rent.

They concentrated on Hill City across the Walnut Street Bridge on the North Shore of the Tennessee River.

Pressure from someone in Chattanooga led the staff at Loveman's to rehire both Anna and Emma and fire their former supervisor, Hawkeye Helms. The source remained a mystery.

The mysterious disappearance of Grover Biggs the day after the race distracted her for a while. Nothing more remained between them, but she had invested emotional energy in the man. Deep down, beneath the anger and hurt over being deceived, she still cared for him. However, the other man in her life took most of her attention. A day of accountability loomed ahead, and this would be that day. She owed Peter a huge apology.

The bright noonday sun shined down as she contemplated life in the city without the protection of a good straw hat. She went from Ninth Street to Market, heading north.

Many younger women on the streets wore plainer, simpler, and more practical dresses, and some opted for walking skirts like hers that fell to the ankles. Blouses in various shades—white, pastels, deep colors, and stripes, depending on the skirt—brightened the new stylish ensembles of the season. The new woman, the feminist ideal that had emerged across the country, seemed to have taken a foothold in Chattanooga over the summer. She popped up in great numbers on the streets. Had this been going on all around Anna, and she failed to notice? Her eyes were opened in the aftermath of the great race.

What she saw next stunned her. A young woman, no more than eighteen, rolled by sitting astride a new Columbia safety bicycle with a drop frame.

The woman's outfit appeared current and smart: a daisy skirt trimmed at the bottom about three inches. A stylish, navy blue and white striped blouse with a rolled collar and a loose cravat, and a simple straw hat much like the one Anna sported. Beneath the hat, her black hair lay wavy and unbound. Quite the departure in hairstyle, even for Anna, although the woman's daring display inspired her. She wore walking shoes with gaiters.

Someone other than Anna and Emma now had the temerity to turn convention on its heels, to cycle on the streets with grace. Had Anna's example given the woman permission to enjoy the utility of a wheel? After she recovered from the shock, Anna reached her hand up in the air, hoping to catch the young woman's attention. A quick talk would answer so many questions, but the cyclist had passed too far beyond, and Anna decided it would be futile to call out.

Maybe she had moved the emancipation of women forward in her own small way in this place. The possibility astonished her.

She pictured herself cycling side by side with Annie Londonderry, waving to young girls and women who shouted out their appreciation for the trailblazers. Imagination gave way to the reality of the moment, knocking her off her high horse. Anna continued toward her date with destiny and the reckoning she dreaded.

The intersection of West Eighth and Broad is where she stopped. Standing on the corner, she gazed at the grocery in the middle of the block on Eighth as people marched in empty-handed and exited with bags and containers full of food and sundries. Would he be too busy to talk? Like a statue, she remained in one spot for several minutes while the pedestrian traffic all around her increased. People darted in and out on their way to lunch dates and business appointments and doing the simple things people do in smaller cities like window shopping and visiting with friends.

Fear or embarrassment or pride—or a combination of all three—tethered her in place, unable to move forward.

A handsome young man emerged from the grocery dressed in a relaxed waistcoat and brown houndstooth pants, wearing a straw boater hat trimmed with a black and red grosgrain ribbon folded into a bow. Before she recognized the well-dressed gentleman, he began to walk in her direction. When their eyes met, she regretted the decision to seek him out. Faced with the prospect that he might spite and shun her, and with good reason, she wanted to turn and run and not look back. But she held her ground. Peter walked in a hurried manner, perhaps on his way to a meeting of some sort.

He stopped to greet her. "Miss Gaines. Fancy running into you." The formal greeting was not lost on her as she had taken to calling him by his surname before the race.

Mortified, she attempted to cobble together a coherent explanation for why she appeared to be loitering on the corner. "Yes . . . well . . . good morning." Usually a quick thinker, her mind went blank. "Umm . . . I missed my connection with Emma somehow. We planned to rendezvous here for a shopping excursion. Maybe she passed by the grocery?"

"If she did, I am unaware." He lingered a few moments through the awkward silence. "Well, I'm afraid I must be on my way." He tipped his hat and bid her a good afternoon.

Halfway into the street, he turned back toward her, his intent uncertain. He pulled a timepiece from his coat and squinted at the face. This would be her last chance. He turned again to resume his walk and casting out all caution, she called out to him. "Mr. Sawyer . . . please wait." She ran out to meet him. "Actually, I'm not out to shop with Emma. May we talk?"

In a sudden move, he grabbed her shoulders and jerked her to the left. "Mr. Sawyer, what the . . ."

Three cyclists whizzed past them.

"Scorchers. There ought to be a law." When the obvious irony sank in, they laughed. "A conversation would indeed be good but not here in the middle of this busy street. A lunch counter would be more suitable, and safe. And not until we dispense with the formalities. Deal?"

Safe enough. "Yes, Peter, it's a deal. A lunch counter will work." With his arms clasped behind his body, his wide and easy grin gave her hope that more days together would come.

❧❖❧

Later that afternoon, Peter reflected on their time, thankful they had begun to clear the air of misunderstandings. The day brought new possibilities between them. Tomorrow they would attend church together at First Presbyterian and ride their wheels to the farm for a family dinner.

He whistled "Dixie" while he and Frederick tidied the displays, picked over by the legion of shoppers preparing for their own Sunday dinners. The door opened, and Detective Seymour Leland entered. Smoke billowed up from his pipe as he approached Peter. "Oh, heavens. I forgot to extinguish my pipe. Give me one minute while—"

"Stop, detective. You'll stay inside, and you will enjoy your pipe." The private detective extended his hand to shake, but Peter embraced him with a quick hug instead, an uncharacteristic display of affection for him. Both men cleared their throats. "Hold on. Been saving something in the office for you."

When he returned to the floor, Peter held an envelope in one hand and a bag in the other. The show of generosity caught the detective off guard. "For me?"

"Go ahead. Open them."

"But I brought no parting gifts." The detective tore into the envelope, and his eyes opened wide when he viewed the contents. "A check, with a rather large number. For what? You already paid the balance on your account."

Peter's fondness for Seymour had increased by leaps and bounds, and he viewed him with great respect and admiration. "A bonus for a job well done. Thank you, sir. I will be forever grateful. Now open the bag."

Peeking inside, Seymour beamed with pleasure. He pulled out a pouch filled with pipe tobacco. "From you, my non-smoking friend, this is quite a gift. Thank you."

"Your favorite—Sir Walter Raleigh Yale Mixture. Right, Seymour? Please say I got the right brand."

"Perfect, Peter. So kind of you."

The detective shared the final chapter on the Grover Biggs-Mortimer Foxx scams. Officials at the Sawyer lumberyard had long suspected their accounting agency of skimming from their revenues, and on Labor Day, when everyone enjoyed the day off, Seymour worked with them, combing the books. After finding the smoking gun, Seymour consulted the bank manager where the yard kept its finances. The evidence pointed to Foxx himself, with a private, inflated account indicating a significant source of income. The dates the lumber revenues disappeared matched the dates when Foxx's deposits were made. When the police questioned him, he admitted his guilt and implicated Grover Biggs as a co-conspirator.

When they picked Grover up, he spilled the truth about everything—his theft of proprietary information, the Keely Company stock ring that preyed on elderly widows with money—even his involvement in the priest scandal back in Atlanta. He told them he had nothing to do with skimming the Sawyer accounts, that Foxx had threatened to turn him in for stealing files if he breathed a word or stopped finding stock leads.

"How did things resolve?" Peter asked.

"The way they should—Foxx charged with fraud, embezzlement, and a host of other minor infractions of the law. He won't see the light of day for some time. Discredited in his profession, he will never practice accounting again. At least, not in a reputable firm."

"And Grover?" The compassionate side of Peter hoped something might be done for this troubled man, but justice must also be served.

Seymour sighed. "This man's been through the mill." Peter smiled, but Seymour seemed oblivious to the pun. "A tough go of things. His father arrived in town yesterday and is working with authorities on next steps. Your father decided against pressing charges for lifting the marketing file. Thing is, what he took dated back to the early 1890s anyway."

"Pretty much outdated and useless information," Peter said.

"Exactly, and Grover's father said he never planned to expand in Chattanooga. Grover will answer for his scams back home, but given the man's psychological problems, I suspect they'll work to get him help rather than throw the book at him."

They sidled up to the front door, knowing they would part ways for now, that Seymour would finalize his other business dealings in Tennessee and head home to Atlanta.

"I'll miss you, Seymour." A tapestry of time, place, and people had brought them together to accomplish a grand purpose. Happenstance? Maybe. A new friendship had been woven into the fabric of their lives, and for that he gave thanks to the master weaver.

"Don't get all sappy on me, Peter Sawyer. Come down to Georgia and visit an old man." With that, he turned and began to walk away. "Oh . . . almost forgot to tell you. My men picked up the McMannis brothers, the hoodlums behind all the nasty business leading up to race day. Nabbed 'em over in Nashville. Did as you requested concerning the person who hired them."

After conferring with his father, Peter had instructed Seymour to save Bertha Millwood the public humiliation of being taken to jail. An appropriate punishment would be worked out later in private conferences with a judge, something that would not tarnish her position in the community or her good works. The McMannis boys were warned—at the first sight of them in Chattanooga again, they would be incarcerated and charged.

Peter tipped his straw boater hat at Seymour.

The difficult conversation meeting inside the Millwood residence heated up as Edward stoked the fire.

"Do you understand? Only the grace of the Sawyer family saved you from being hauled off to jail. Your involvement in these despicable acts sickens me, Bertha."

Edward had been silent for a long time, but now he spoke forcefully, and something inside filled her with a sense of being cared for, a longing that at last was being filled. She acknowledged that her employment of petty thieves to achieve her selfish purposes had reached beyond the pale.

"Dearest Edward, I . . ."

"You embarrassed me before a prominent family and a friendly business associate. How can I ever look him in the eyes again? Disgraceful."

The veneer hiding Bertha Millwood's inner pain cracked, allowing her deepest wounds free rein to surface. She wept, her dead daughter's face rolling through her mind. Constance would have been equally disgraced by her foolish actions. For two years, in the midst of her grief, she had condemned her daughter for such foolhardy behavior with a man she didn't even know. And now, she had to face her own reprehensible choices.

Had Constance left because of her? If so, she could never forgive herself, but maybe grace from Edward would help.

"My heart grieves over the way I acted, Edward. Truly it does. The life seeped out of me when our Constance died, little by little, day by day. Why did she disobey me? I tried to lead her, to restore her to a proper Southern lady, but she would not listen. I guess I tried again with Anna Gaines . . . you know, a second chance at being a mother. Like our daughter, she had a mind of her own."

Edward took her hand as he spoke. "The thing is, Anna Gaines is not our child. We must build a new life . . . find our way back to a new normal. Let's let Anna live her own life and make her way forward."

"Oh, Edward, can you ever forgive me? I only wanted to do the right thing, but I lost my way. I must have been a terrible mother. I must . . ."

She wept again for several minutes. He moved closer to her on the couch and handed her a kerchief from his coat pocket. Weary, she laid her head on his shoulder. Hesitant at first, he put his arm around her and brought her face to his chest, their first physical touch in over a year. Heaven laid its hands on her, and for the first time in a long time, she experienced comfort.

"Bertha, I owe you an apology. Truth is, I haven't been much of a husband, closing myself off, hiding from my own pain. I'm sorry, too."

They shared with each other long into the night. She swore that her wrongdoings would be made right.

Chapter Forty-Eight

Chickamauga Valley
Dedication Ceremonies
Chickamauga-Chattanooga National Military Park
September 19

THE BLOODY CHICKAMAUGA and Chattanooga battles in 1863 claimed the lives of more than thirty-five thousand soldiers. Peter gained a visual perception of this enormous number as a passerby mentioned that attendance at this first dedication exceeded forty thousand people. The anticipation of these ceremonies swelled in the weeks prior to the official opening of the nation's first military park, which included lands along Missionary Ridge and Orchard Knob, Lookout Mountain's Point Park, and Signal Point on Signal Mountain.

The time arrived, and much of the Chickamauga-Chattanooga valley came to celebrate. Peter loved a good celebration, especially one with historical significance. But after lengthy orations of two United States Senators and renowned former combatants, including General James Longstreet, Anna and Peter chose to cycle the acres of open fields, rivers, streams, and forests within their reach. Peter asked permission of Joseph Gaines, and off they went with the promise of reuniting with the family back at the farm for dinner.

The land stood little changed, save some underbrush and felled trees, since the valley campaign. Thousands milled about the same areas, reviewing the first beautiful monuments and markers dedicated to the men and units that battled on this ground. They cycled for miles, in and out of paths Anna used to train for the race, which now seemed a lifetime ago, and ended up in an open meadow near Lafayette Road.

Anna stopped, stepped off her wheel, and planted herself on the ground. Peter followed suit. They sat facing each other, but her gaze turned to the nearby trees where migrating vireos, thrushes, and hawks landed for a brief respite before journeying farther southward.

He found her more attractive than before—soft features, light skin, bright blue eyes that were penetrating and alive, and hair that perfectly framed her face. The real attraction went beyond her physical beauty. Over the course of the summer, he had watched a somewhat awkward, fearful, but likable young woman transform into this person of deep courage and heart. At the same time, she possessed an innocence, what some called naiveté—a lack of life experience. Above all else, she had a humbleness about her, the character quality he most admired.

Peter broke her concentration. "These open meadows are a refuge for me. Is this particular place special to you in some way?"

She didn't address the question. "Sorry. Just thinking about people and places. The passage of time and the impact one family—even one person—might stamp on succeeding generations. Take my grandfather, Abraham Gaines."

Peter expressed interest. "Tell me about Abe. I love family history."

Before continuing, she pointed to the road, distracted by several groups of cyclists traveling in both directions. "Look, Peter. What a wonderful contraption. A second emancipator, freeing people from the restrictions of their circumstances."

Although the community had exempted women from cycling, he believed in what the first great emancipator called the "better angels of our nature." Right and fairness would be vindicated in the end. He lifted his hand as if clinking glasses.

"I say—long live the bicycle." She raised her imaginary glass, and they tilted them together in a toast.

"Anyway, this patch of land is a big part of my family's story."

"Ah, yes. Abe."

"As we grew up, Papa would bring the boys and me here to Poe's Field on the anniversary of the battle. As we sat like we are today, he would regale us with the events of September 19, 1863, at four-thirty in the afternoon. Right on this spot. The Tennessee Twentieth Regiment Infantry, Bate's Brigade, fought valiantly in this field and was almost annihilated. Thirty percent wiped out in an hour of fighting."

"This is where Abraham comes in." He hung on every word, enchanted by her charms.

"Yep. Granddad tried to rescue an injured comrade and took the brunt of a fusillade that almost cut him in half. Abraham and his wife, Angelica, were raising three children at the time, my father being the oldest. After the war, Angelica brought the kids to Chickamauga to be close to where her husband fell."

"Now, that's a brave woman. Some of that rubbed off on you."

"A pioneer woman. Grandma amassed enough cash through a large inheritance to buy a farmhouse on a plot of land, and after purchasing additional land—well, the rest is history, as they say. Papa took things over and made the farm a growing enterprise."

He digested the story. "So, this place holds meaning for your father and for you."

She nodded, a glint of pride in her eyes. "When I think of my kinfolk, I'm proud of their legacy of Christian generosity. Commitment to family and neighbors. I can't help but wonder—will anyone examine my life and think I changed anything?"

She made a difference in his life. How did he feel about her? Smitten, for sure. Falling in love? Perhaps. Having never been in love, he didn't know. One thing was beyond question: He loved being in her presence. Every day they were apart, he wondered where she might be at any given moment. He learned something new about her each hour they spent together. The Sawyer and Gaines families shared many of the same values. His mother and father approved of the potential match.

He would do this right. Later, after they all gathered for the evening meal, he would ask Mr. Gaines for a couple of minutes of his time alone, so he might pose the burning question about courtship.

They both stared up into a hazy sky that had started to turn bluer. After a while, he lay down, closed his eyes, and in the silence practiced the right words he would say to Mr. Gaines. Anna's expression of incredulity woke him as he began to nod off.

"Oh, Peter . . . look."

Near the timberline rode a group of five cyclists, all women.

Two of them wore bloomers.

⌖

"Come on, let's go." Anna brought Choo Choo to a standing position.

"Where?" Peter asked.

Already pedaling ahead, she looked back. "To catch up with the family. Back to Snodgras Hill before they head home so we can cycle alongside. Together."

They had ridden for about a quarter mile on the main road when their eyes met. The carriage headed toward Chattanooga slowed to a stop in front of them. Anna also rolled to a standstill and planted both feet on the ground without dismounting. A quick look at Peter helped her to rise to the occasion.

"Mrs. Millwood. Perfect day for a drive." The woman shifted in her seat.

"A good excuse to get out too . . . with the celebration and all," Bertha said.

They stared at each other for a moment, and Anna put her right foot back on the pedal. That simple movement reminded her of the trepidation she experienced before mounting the wheel at Prospect Park in Brooklyn.

"Well . . . enjoy the rest . . ." She ran out of words.

"The whole thing about cycling was . . ." Bertha said.

"What? Nothing personal?" Anna asked. "Sure seemed like it to me."

"I hope you learned from the experience."

Edward cast a stern look at his wife.

Bertha's shoulders slumped. "That is to say . . . I mean . . . I certainly did."

"A lot," Anna said. "I learned it's not a sin for a woman to ride a bicycle. The City Council evidently agrees with me. For the so-called weaker sex to branch out, attend a university, and pursue a career is not unnatural."

Bertha stiffened in her seat. "Time will tell whether your analysis is right or woefully wrong."

"Time may also see you, Mrs. Millwood, casting your vote for our governmental leaders."

"Perhaps. Anything is possible. But for now . . . well . . . I do owe you an apology. I'm not proud of how I conducted myself these past couple of months."

Anna noticed Edward's affectionate smile.

"Apology accepted, Mrs. Millwood. I hope you both enjoy your ride back to our wonderful city. Good day."

Anna pushed her foot on the pedal and launched like Aunt Harriet taught her so many weeks ago. Peter doffed his straw hat and grinned as off they rode. She sat high in her saddle.

Respectful, but bold. That felt good.

The End

Acknowledgments

FIRST, A TIP of the bowler hat to my wife of forty-four years, Karen. A voracious reader and a longtime book club member. Without her understanding and patience during many long days of research and writing, I could never engage my passion for telling stories like this one.

And thank you, Mary Helms, for extending your hand of friendship and hospitality when we traveled to Chattanooga to do field research. Head of the History and Genealogy Department of the Chattanooga Public Library, Mary gave me an amazing peek into the life of this wonderful city circa 1895. She is a consummate pro and a beautiful soul, a hidden gem on the third floor. Go pay her and the library a visit.

Quite randomly, Karen found Keith Wilkinson, now a good friend and owner of Adventures with Keith. I retained Keith's services for a full day to drive us through the local battlefields of the War Between the States, and to a dozen Chattanooga locations that played a role in the book. Keith is top notch, a great tour guide. He knows his stuff.

And to the fine people at Redemption Press—Athena, Hannah, and all the rest that I had the pleasure to work with…Thank You!

Order Information

REDEMPTION
PRESS

To order additional copies of this book, please visit
www.redemption-press.com.
Also available on Amazon.com and BarnesandNoble.com
Or by calling toll free 1-844-2REDEEM.

CPSIA information can be obtained
at www.ICGtesting.com
Printed in the USA
LVOW08s1152230517
535499LV00004B/570/P